WHAT THEN MUST WE DO?

And the multitudes asked him, saying, What then must we do?
And he answered and said unto them, He that hath two coats,
let him impart to him that hath none; and he that hath food,
let him do likewise.

(LUKE III 10, 11)

Lay not up for yourselves treasures upon earth, where moth and
rust doth corrupt, and where thieves break through and steal:
but lay up for yourselves treasures in heaven, where neither moth
nor rust doth corrupt, and where thieves do not break through
nor steal: for where your treasure is, there will your heart be also.
❡ The light of the body is the eye: if therefore thine eye be single,
thy whole body shall be full of light. But if thine eye be evil, thy
whole body shall be full of darkness. If therefore the light that
is in thee be darkness, how great is that darkness! ❡ No man can
serve two masters: for either he will hate the one, and love the
other; or else he will hold to the one, and despise the other. Ye
cannot serve God and mammon. ❡ Therefore I say unto you,
Take no thought for your life, what ye shall eat, or what ye shall
drink; nor yet for your body, what ye shall put on. Is not the life
more than meat, and the body than raiment? . . .Therefore take
no thought, saying, What shall we eat? or, What shall we drink?
or, Wherewithal shall we be clothed? (For after all these things
do the Gentiles seek;) for your heavenly Father knoweth that ye
have need of all these things. But seek ye first the kingdom of God,
and his righteousness; & all these things shall be added unto you.

(MATTHEW VI 19–25, 31–3)

It is easier for a camel to go through the eye of a needle,
than for a rich man to enter into the kingdom of God.

(MATTHEW XIX 24; MARK X 25; LUKE XVIII 25)

Leo Tolstoy photographed with Maxim Gorky in 1900

WHAT THEN MUST WE DO?

LEO TOLSTOY

Translated by
Aylmer Maude

Introduced by
Ronald Sampson

GREEN
BOOKS

What Then Must We Do? was first published in 1886
This translation first published in 1925 (revised in 1935)
by Oxford University Press

Reissued in 1991 by
Green Books
Ford House, Hartland
Bideford, Devon EX39 6EE

Typographic design and photosetting
in 10 on 12.5 pt Mergenthaler Sabon
by Five Seasons Press, Hereford

Cover design by Linda Wade

Printed by Biddles Ltd
Guildford, Surrey

Printed on recycled paper

British Library Cataloguing in Publication Data
Tolstoi, L. N. (Lev Nikolaevich) *1828–1910*
What Then Must We Do?:
1. Soviet Union. Social life. History
I. Title
947

ISBN 1 870098 33 1

SUMMARY OF CONTENTS

SUMMARY OF CONTENTS *(continued)*

PUBLISHER'S NOTE

The footnotes to Tolstoy's text are those made by the translator, Aylmer Maude, for the revised (1935) edition.

In order to avoid confusion, all references in the text and footnotes to the value of Russian currency at the time of publication in 1935 have been removed. The approximate current (1990) equivalent of the 1886 ruble is £4 and the equivalent of the kopek around 4p.

INTRODUCTION

A MID-LIFE CRISIS around the age of fifty is by no means uncommon; but rarely can it have had such dramatic consequences as in the case of Tolstoy. 'My question', he wrote in *A Confession*, which first circulated in Russia in 1882, '—that which at the age of fifty brought me to the verge of suicide—was the simplest of questions . . . "Why should I live . . . is there any meaning in my life that the inevitable death awaiting me does not destroy?"'

Born in 1828, he had in his twenties begun to write for publication, with immediate success: a remarkably perceptive account of childhood, tales of life-like naturalism set in the Caucasus, scenes of warfare described with unprecedented realism drawn from the carnage of the Crimean War, as he had himself experienced it. His third decade saw the completion in six years of his Homeric epic, *War and Peace*; and in the eighteen seventies there followed the immortal domestic tragedy, *Anna Karenina*. After such exertions it is perhaps not surprising to find Tolstoy in near-suicidal state of mind, but his despair was in fact the fruit of a religious conflict which had long been raging within him, and which could no longer be contained. Out of that despair emerged his monumental *The Four Gospels Harmonized and Translated* (1881–1882); his work on this book played an important part in the development of his belief that the teaching of Jesus is absolutely opposed to violence of any kind.

Such was the spiritual background from which in 1882 Tolstoy found himself confronting the shocking and (for him) novel experience of the life of city dwellers in some of Moscow's worst slums. Deeply affected by this confrontation, on the third of February he sat down to write an article on the subject only to find to his shame that he had no solution to offer. Four years later (1886) he published the great book which so profoundly disturbed the conscience of the Western world, *What Then Must We Do?* People outside as well as inside Russia acknowledged the tremendous power of his account of his own suffering as a result of his helplessness to help child prostitutes, old, emaciated and dying washing women, or to change the conditions of the destitute living in the squalor of disease, overcrowding, drunkenness, and promiscuity. But while people's hearts were touched and consciences pricked, the most widespread response to Tolstoy's social and economic theorizing was to reject it outright as unrealistic and inadequate, even absurd, reactionary and ethically unsound. Nevertheless, the first fifteen chapters of the book were immediately suppressed by the Russian Censorship. Those were the chapters in which the suffering of the poor was contrasted with the hypocrisy of the fabulously wealthy, who lived their idle lives often within a matter of yards of those dying of deprivation, exhaustion and emaciation from harsh and excessive labour.

Filled with shame at the way he and his class lived cheek by jowl with people in extreme poverty—some 50,000 in Moscow alone—Tolstoy was unable to find any relief for his anguish at his own inability to help. The sheer weight of numbers of the poor, the fact that they stood in need not of charity but of facilities with which to help themselves, alike drove him to address directly the question as to what is the cause of poverty. Why is it, he asks, that whereas all basic wealth—without which we would all rapidly die—results from the toil of peasants in the village, the greater part of it is transported to the towns and cities for consumption? Flour, corn, pulses, flax, hemp, wool, horses, cattle, pigs, poultry, butter, eggs—all this passes out of the hands of the producers into those of the landowners, the dealers, officials and middlemen and ends up in the hands of the wealthy. This is the process whereby the two classes of the rich and the poor are created in Russia, and indeed everywhere else. But it does not explain why it is that some people are deprived of the sources of wealth, land and implements of production, while others are in possession of them.

Tolstoy considers the question historically: through endless generations, how have people been kept in servitude by others? The historical developments have necessarily been pragmatic, based on ingenuity, convenience and experience. Beginning with personal or chattel slavery, the conquered, instead of being put to the sword and slain, were put to work and kept in servitude. Later, a more efficient and convenient method was developed, whereby the tribe would be left to work the land but tribute would be demanded by their new 'owners'. Alternatively, tribute was extorted periodically in convenient measures such as skins or gold. In the Middle Ages chattel slavery was replaced by feudalism, a hierarchy of command and allegiance, where the serfs or villeins discharge their 'obligations' by direct labour. In recent times all these methods have, under the intensification of centralized governmental power, given way to the enslavement of men through the means of money, mainly in the form of taxation.

Modern man has invented sophisticated means, exemplified in a great variety of taxes, of dividing the land between the rich owners who enjoy and consume a large proportion of the wealth, and the poor who labour to produce it, and consume more often than not a bare subsistence. Tolstoy quotes the peasant saying: 'A rouble hits harder than an oak cudgel.' Tersely, he describes the regimen at the stocking factory, whose daily whistles marking the divisions of the working day he himself hears from his own bedroom. At 5 a.m. a youngster stands to, with only a tea break at 8 a.m., until noon. At 1 p.m. work is resumed, with a thirty-minute break at 4 p.m., until 8 p.m. A working day, that is, of over thirteen hours every day of the week. For the rural enslavement, let the reader turn to the picture drawn in Chapter 25 of the race of the labourers at harvest time, working to the utmost limits of their strength, old men and women, young children too, all alike driven to exhaustion to harvest the precious grain or hay on which they all well know depends their ability to survive the coming winter—while up at the manor house the guests are arriving for their evening pleasures, having driven in a carriage harnessed to four well-fed horses for ten miles at a cost of ten roubles. Upstairs they have just finished eating, and will soon eat again until midnight or even cock-crow, their fare being fillet steaks and sturgeon, each person attended by two servants. Since the world began men have struggled to wring from nature that which is necessary for their common needs. By what right is it that while the lot of the majority is one of ceaseless toil, a few are exempt from their share of this necessary task? Who are these few, and by what logic are they accorded their certificates of exemption?

Once the argument was that those emancipated from the common lot of unremitting toil were a special breed, people of purple blood. When people eventually grew sceptical, a new theory appeared that the exempt were God's appointees to watch over the people's welfare. But the coming of Christianity dealt an effective blow to the credence hitherto placed in such superstitions, as the consciousness of human equality and solidarity continued to develop. 'Science' was then called in aid to buttress the threatened justifications of the privileges of the few. Malthus, now totally discredited, is given short and ironic shrift by Tolstoy for his 'law' that poverty results not from the greed and egotism of the rich but from the propensity of the poor to produce too many children, thereby reducing the amount of food available to each person. All theories motivated by self-interest are perverted thereby; accordingly they have their brief day and perish. In Tolstoy's own youth the fashionable philosophy was that which represented the State and those who administered it as the highest expression of the spiritual. Currently a biologically-based sociology is enthroned, assembled out of bricks manufactured by Adam Smith, Comte and Darwin. Humanity is an organism subject to all the laws of evolution, a principal law being the division of labour among the different parts of the organism. Under this evolutionary law some people, the vast majority, do the heavy oppressive manual and muscular work, while others do the directive brain work, which automatically carries with it exemption from heavy labour. Tolstoy insists that he is not rejecting the principle of specialization of labour which has always existed and always will. But valid specialization of labour depends on its being just, fair, rationally defensible, and above all on the product of the labour being useful to people, necessary for them to survive but also for them to live in harmony with one another.

How is it possible, Tolstoy says, for people endowed with reason and conscience to be deceived by argument so manifestly irrational and directed by the self-interest of the privileged few? It is a sleight of hand performed by means no different from the old methods. For the findings of reason and conscience within are substituted external findings: those of revelation in the case of religion, those of the philosophy of the spirit in the case of Hegel, and currently, in the case of experimental science, the discoveries of external facts by observation and measurement. And thus through adjudication by observation, we are dragooned by the facts of what allegedly constitutes reality, and in the process lose sight of that saving consciousness of the vital distinction between good and evil, as understood by countless generations of our forebears. Our faith in reason is deliberately undermined, while in its place we are insistently invited to place all our faith in enquiries to amass and accumulate detailed facts, whose infallible authority derives from their selection within a framework of positivist metaphysic and an unproven hypothesis of biological evolution.

Since Tolstoy's death in 1910 the only significant change in the picture has been in dimension and scale. It no longer requires any effort to ensure that the rich, who are immensely richer, do not have their pleasures marred by having to witness the distress, the malnutrition and the dying of the poor, who starve and die prematurely as they have always done, but instead of being in the neighbouring village or at the other end of town, are as a rule in a different country, or in a more remote part of the planet. The concealment of the sufferings of the poor occurs spontaneously by such geo-demographic factors as the North/South divide and the separation of the 'advanced' industrial nations from the 'backward' or 'underdeveloped' Third World. Nor have the theories of justification been significantly modified: positive evolutionism in the West, and, until 1989, Marxist-Leninism in Russia and Eastern Europe—the seeds of which were amply evident to Tolstoy, although they had not yet borne fruit in revolution. And while capitalism and its theorists do not pretend to a cure of poverty, the one element in Marxist theory that might have portended the elimination of poverty, namely the withering away of the State, predictably resulted in practice in the enormous growth in power of the State.

Whereas Tolstoy, in addressing the causes of poverty, concentrated his attention on consumption and sought the remedy in attempting to restrict consumption, Marx looked to production and sought his remedy in expansion of production. It was obvious that it would be Marx, not Tolstoy, who would achieve popularity and gain massive support from the ranks of the poor. But the race does not always go to the swiftest, nor do those who appeal to the most powerful and durable appetite necessarily carry the day in the struggle to conquer the most ancient and persistent human vices and weaknesses. The struggle to master the world-wide evil of poverty, almost always self-inflicted by humanity on its weaker brethren, is, alas, still in its infancy.

Throughout the nineteenth century workers endured pitifully small wages, barely adequate for subsistence, and hours of work which represented the utmost limits to which they could be driven. Where competition between rival firms or owners of capital became particularly ferocious, for instance when one was striving to oust a commercial rival, the combination of sweated labour conditions and starvation wages sometimes resulted in the actual death of the workers. (Witness the case, documented by Marx, of Mary Anne Walkley, milliner, twenty years of age, in June 1863. 'Death from simple overwork' was the headline. Average hours of work were sixteen and a half hours; during the season workers often laboured thirty hours without a break.) Under these circumstances the workers' struggle concentrated naturally on the demand for higher wages and a shorter working day. Marx, by his concept of 'surplus value', brilliantly and lucidly demonstrated that these humanly intolerable conditions were not the product of accidental circumstance but the result of the characteristic working of an economic system under which the means of production were owned not by the workers but by a tiny class of privileged people who appropriated the worker's surplus, that is, the amount that he could and did produce over and above the necessities for his own maintenance.

Why should not a remedy be found simply by enacting legislation to ensure better working conditions and by increasing the power of the workers to claim their fair share? The problem is that to the extent that unrestricted market forces are relied upon to determine what and how much should be produced, the psychology which determines the play of those forces determines also the tendency of capital to accumulate, and the greed for indefinite expansion so as to produce and absorb ever more surplus value. Such is the system, moreover, that even the most humane of employers are compelled to bend before the ceaseless pressures, or be submerged or taken over by rivals more ruthless than themselves. Independently of machiavellian business psychology, employers have to reckon on ceaseless revolutions as a result of technological inventions in the methods of production themselves, and consequently the depreciation of the existing but now outmoded capital. And because the only moral law is the Hobbesian war of all against all, all alike are under the necessity of ceaseless striving to improve the product, to expand the scale of production, to keep prices down merely to keep going and not be swallowed up by a rival predator. It will be objected that we have taken no account of labour's most potent weapon —the strike—with which to limit the exploitation of the surplus value created. In many parts of the world that weapon is nullified by the ruthlessness of the owners; elsewhere it is weakened by the liability of the workers themselves to forfeit the strength of solidarity by succumbing to a better deal for their separate group or through unwillingness to endure further hardship. And always there is the grim fact that while an army marches on its belly and the reserves of the workers are limited, the owners normally possess reserves large enough to enable them to hold out indefinitely.

Given this harsh but unalterable logic, the workers' share of the product of their labour is always restricted to less than they can or would wish to consume, whereas capital's share is always larger than capital can consume. The surplus value lost to labour is ever growing larger and therefore when every avenue of domestic investment has been exhausted, fresh outlets must be sought abroad. Eventually, even after trading with each other, all capitalist countries with developed resources still have an unconsumed surplus, which they are obliged to sell to countries which still have undeveloped resources. But resources are finite: the consumption of them in the manufacture of armaments is tolerated by people less and less now that the threat of nuclear warfare hangs over us all.

It is true that the recent events in the USSR and Eastern Europe, with the near total collapse of the centralized command system enforced by terror, have changed for ever the underlying conditions which were seen to explain and even 'justify' the arms race between the Super-Powers and their junior 'partners' and would-be rivals. But there are no grounds for supposing that these changed circumstances, welcome though they are, will abolish, let alone replace the fierce competition to dominate world economic markets. On the contrary, with much more than one sixth of the world's land surface, apparently, now attempting to convert to the capitalist economy of the free market, to the philosophy of endless economic growth, the struggle for domination will inevitably intensify. In such circumstances what hope is there of achieving the necessary permanent reversal of existing economic trends? The need could not be more urgent. As Viktor Astafyev of Ovsyanka in the eastern USSR summed it up in *Moskovski Novosti* (Moscow News) of 13th May 1990:

The arable land of our planet is largely exhausted and saturated with poisonous pesticides, forests are being felled or are perishing from chemicals and industrial waste, many countries are short of drinking water, there are holes in the ozone layer and the sky hangs in tatters polluted by soot.

In these extremely hazardous circumstances, it is tempting to ask: might it not be safer to emulate the Luddites and conclude that the only solution is to break the machines themselves that reduce human beings to even greater passivity, that in fact 'decreate' them as well as producing mountains of goods that are either largely undesirable or, because of the need to artificially support the price paid to the producer, undistributable and hence unconsumable? Nothing is more calculated to unite socialist and capitalist alike than this proposal. What! Destroy the fruits of man's inventive scientific genius, that has produced such a wonderful cornucopia? Such a suggestion can only be born of madness or total despair—it is not even to be discussed.

But within the parameters of the fundamental nature of humankind, what other solution in the long, now rapidly shortening, run is rationally available? Let capitalists and socialists meet round a table and negotiate mutually acceptable economic quotas and mutual trade on fair and equitable terms to both sides and to all competing commercial firms? Where have we heard this before? Would it not be more rational to put an end to the insane and destructive arms race by multilateral negotiated disarmament, or for that matter to agree to decide the issue at stake by a jousting or chess competition rather than by the destruction of millions of lives in modern warfare? Such proposals condemn themselves as absurd and self-contradictory precisely because they negate the original premise that human nature is unchangeably machiavellian, egotistic, power-seeking and competitive.

The root difference between Marx and Tolstoy is that Marx accepts uncritically the role of the machines in creating wealth, and accordingly concentrates his attention on the problem of maximizing consumption to ensure that the worker is no longer deprived of his surplus value in a cake that is for ever growing larger. Tolstoy is criticized for seeing the world through the subjectively narrow vision of the peasant; but if we take a world-wide perspective we must inevitably concede that the primary source of wealth is the land, as Tolstoy contends. And accordingly the primary cause of poverty is not wage-slavery in the factories so much as the expropriation of the peasant from the land in the feudal conditions still obtaining in large areas of the Third World, and indeed in the concentration of land ownership in the hands of the great landlords, as in Britain. And where the peasant does own the land he is normally subject to heavy direct government taxation. Tolstoy reported that 'Nine-tenths of the Russian people hire themselves out when the taxes are being collected and on account of these taxes.'

By its simplicity and sincerity, Tolstoy's common sense refuses to be driven back from its position of personal individual responsibility in the matter of ownership and use of the land, the source of all wealth, a source as vital to all that lives as the sunshine and the rain. In what way is it less unjust to corner the market in land than it would be to do so in the sources of warmth and irrigation? To deny anyone access to these elementary means of life is to deny access to labour itself, and labour is not only the means to life, it is the meaning of life, of health, of creativity, the key to life-giving equality and harmony. 'What then must I do?' he asks himself. 'Where one man is idle, then another man must be poor.' Nothing can alter this law. That the poor are always with us is attributable to the equally unending presence of the rich, who consume but do not labour. So the first thing I can do is to get off the back of the poor labourer or of him who is denied access to labour, do my own share of the common task, which common justice demands, and consume no more than I absolutely need, not for reasons of asceticism (hair shirts are expensive, not cheap) but for reasons of love for my fellow creatures. The rich must be taught that their dissolute example is no longer to be tolerated; the poor have to learn to strengthen themselves so as no longer to succumb to servility, by ceasing to support by their labour the idle and exploitative. For this is the fatal combination out of which poverty is inescapably born.

But Tolstoy is no Luddite—an unjustly maligned group of workers driven to desperation by unemployment—nor is he an opponent of true specialization of labour. Those who concentrate their efforts on increasing productivity at all costs have ceased to regard the individual as a whole person whose primary concern is the total meaning of his life, and have reduced him to the status of an indispensable unit of production. In Tolstoy's vision, essentially spiritual and religious, the meaning of a person's life is to be found in labour, not sweated, exploited labour, but in labour for its own sake as an essential means to a healthy and kindly life. Such a one labours not for the sake of results, but for satisfaction, which will increase as his skills improve, develop and diversify, produced by useful work well done, and this satisfaction will be entirely independent of the implements available to him. If a worker has the use of a steam plough, then by all means let him use it; but others may have only a horse plough, still others only a wooden peasant plough, while their poorest neighbour may have to rely on no more than his spade. All who labour not for the sake of property or wealth will derive equal satisfaction from labour equally useful and equally productive of the necessities of life. This satisfaction will require no supplementation in the shape of ever more sophisticated forms of transport, elaborate housing and furniture and feasting in order to provide a healthy and truly enjoyable life, that will be no longer clouded by the guilt of exploitation. And similarly such labour will rest on true specialization, that which arises from an individual's free and rational choice of means which differ according to circumstance.

In renouncing land ownership, in renouncing money and in not serving the State, in not lying to and deceiving oneself, in not resting on others' labour, in gaining one's bread by the sweat of one's brow, lies the way forward to the only rational solution of poverty with all the suffering to homeless and hungry millions, and in particular to those most defenceless of all victims, the very young and the very old, that poverty unendingly entails. However utopian and unrealistic this way may sound, the harsh fact is that all the other ways that have been tried rest on obvious and intolerable contradictions, are morally indefensible and in a state of manifest crisis and breakdown. Thus we have no genuine alternative; and so however long it may take, the old traditional ways of doing things are doomed to be superseded by people who will look back with incredulity upon forefathers who were capable of living lives so patently devoid of reason and compassion. With each fresh step based on new-found self-discipline will be found a rewarding joy in life that will give ever-renewed strength and confidence in a human nature more elastic, less rigid than that always supposed by the narrow, unimaginative exponents of pessimism and false realism.

R. V. Sampson
September 1990

CHAPTER I

I HAD SPENT MY LIFE in the country, and when in 1881 I came to live in Moscow the sight of town poverty surprised me. I knew country poverty, but town poverty was new and incomprehensible to me. In Moscow one cannot pass a street without meeting beggars, and beggars who are not like those in the country. They do not 'carry a bag and beg in Christ's name', as country beggars say of themselves; they go without a bag and do not beg. When you meet or pass them they generally only try to catch your eye; and according to your look they either ask or do not ask. I know one such beggar from among the gentry. The old man walks slowly, stooping at each step. When he meets you he stoops on one leg and seems to be making you a bow. If you stop he takes off his cockaded cap, bows again, and begs; but if you do not stop he makes as though this were merely his way of walking, and goes on, bowing in the same way on the other leg. He is a typical educated Moscow beggar. At first I did not know why they do not ask plainly. Afterwards I learnt this but still did not understand their position.

Once, passing through the Afanásev side-street, I saw a policeman putting a ragged peasant who was swollen with dropsy, into an open cab. I asked: 'What is this for?' The policeman replied: 'For begging.' 'Is that forbidden?' 'It seems it's forbidden!' replied the policeman.

The man with dropsy was taken away in the cab. I got into another cab and followed them. I wanted to find out whether it was really forbidden to ask alms, and in what way it was repressed. I could not at all understand that it should be possible to forbid a man's asking another man for anything; and also I could not believe that asking alms was forbidden, for Moscow was full of beggars. I entered the police station to which the beggar was taken. There a man who had a sword and a pistol was sitting at a table. I asked: 'What has that peasant been arrested for?' The man with the sword and pistol looked at me sternly and said: 'What business is it of yours?' Feeling however that he ought to explain something to me, he added: 'The authorities order such people to be arrested, so it has to be done.' I went out. The policeman who had brought the beggar in was sitting on a window-sill in the entrance-hall looking dejectedly at a note-book. I asked him: 'Is it true that beggars are forbidden to ask in Christ's name for alms?' The policeman roused himself, looked up at me, and then did not exactly frown but seemed to drowse off again, and sitting on the window-sill said: 'The authorities order it, so that means it's necessary'; and he occupied himself again with his note-book. I went out into the porch to the cabman.

'Well, what's happened? Have they arrested him?' asked the cabman. He, too, was evidently interested in this affair.

'They have,' I replied. The cabman shook his head disapprovingly.

'How is it that it is forbidden, in this Moscow of yours, to ask alms in Christ's name?' I inquired.

'Who knows?' said the cabman.

'How is it?' I said. 'The destitute are Christ's folk, yet they take this man to a police-station.'

'Nowadays that is the law. Begging is not allowed.'

After that I several times saw how the police took beggars to a police-station and afterwards to the Usúpov workhouse. Once, on the Myasnítski street, I met a crowd of these beggars, some thirty of them. In front and behind went policemen. I asked: 'What is it for?' 'For asking alms.'

It turned out that in Moscow, by law, all the beggars (of whom one meets several in every street, and rows of whom stand outside every church when service is on, and who regularly attend every funeral) are forbidden to beg.

But why some are caught and shut up and others not, I was never able to understand. Either there are among them some legal and some illegal beggars, or there are so many that they cannot all be caught, or else as quickly as some are captured others appear.

There are in Moscow beggars of all sorts. There are some who live by it, and there are genuine beggars who have come to Moscow for some reason or other and are really destitute.

Among these latter there are many simple peasants, both men and women, wearing peasant clothes. I often meet them. Some of them have fallen ill here and have come out of hospital and can neither support themselves nor get away from Moscow. Some of them have also taken to drink (as no doubt had the man who was ill with dropsy); some are not ill but have lost their all in a fire, or are old, or are women with children; while some are quite healthy and capable of working. These quite healthy peasants, asking alms, interested me particularly; for since I came to Moscow I had for the sake of exercise formed the habit of going to work at the Sparrow Hills with two peasants who sawed wood there. These two men were just like those I met in the streets. One was Peter, a soldier from Kalúga; the other was Semën, a peasant from Vladímir. They owned nothing but the clothes on their backs and their own hands. With those hands by working very hard they earned 40 to 45 kopeks a day, of which they both put something by: Peter, to buy a sheep-skin coat, and Semën, for the journey back to his village. For this reason was particularly interested in such people when I met them in the streets.

Why do these work and those beg?

On meeting such a peasant I generally asked how he came to be in such a state. I once met a healthy peasant whose beard was beginning to go grey. He begged. I asked who he was and where he was from. He said he had come from Kalúga to find work. At first he had found some work—cutting up old timber for firewood. He and his mate cut up all the wood at one place. Then he looked for another job but found none. His mate left him, and now he had been knocking about for a fortnight having eaten all he possessed, and he had nothing with which to buy either a saw or an axe. I gave him money for a saw and told him where he could come and work. (I had arranged beforehand with Peter and Semën to take on another man and to find him a mate.)

'Well then, be sure and come. There is plenty of work there,' said I.

'I'll come—of course I'll come. Does one like to go begging?' said he. 'I can work.'

He swore he would come, and it seemed to me he was in earnest and meant to.

Next day I joined my acquaintances the peasants and asked if the man had turned up. He had not. And several others deceived me in the same way. I was also cheated by men who said they only needed money to buy a railway ticket home, but whom I met on the street again a week later. Many such I recognized and they recognized me; but sometimes, having forgotten me, they told me the same story again. Some of them turned away on seeing me. So I learned that among this class too there are many cheats; but I was very sorry for these cheats; they were a half-clad, poor, thin, sickly folk: the kind of people who really freeze to death or hang themselves, as we learn from the papers.

CHAPTER II

WHEN I SPOKE TO MOSCOVITES of this destitution in the city I was always told, 'Oh, what you have seen is nothing! Go to Khítrov market and see the dosshouses there. That's where you'll see the real "Golden Company"!'

One jester told me it was no longer a 'Company', but had become a 'Golden Regiment'—there are now so many of them. The jester was right; but he would have been still more so had he said that in Moscow these people are now neither a company nor a regiment but a whole army numbering, I suppose, about 50,000. Old inhabitants when telling me of town poverty always spoke of it with a kind of pleasure—as if proud of knowing about it. I remember also that when I was in London, people there spoke boastfully of London pauperism: 'Just look what it is like here!'

I wanted to see this destitution about which I had been told, and several times I set out towards Khítrov market, but each time I felt uncomfortable and ashamed. 'Why go to look at the sufferings of people I cannot help:' said one voice within me: 'If you live here and see all the allurements of town-life, go and see that also,' said another voice; and so one frosty windy day in December 1881, I went to the heart of the town destitution—Khítrov market. It was a week-day, towards four o'clock. In Solyánka Street I already noticed more and more people wearing strange clothes not made for them, and yet stranger foot-gear; people with a peculiar, unhealthy complexion, and especially with an air, common to them all, of indifference to everything around them. A man went along quite at his ease dressed in most strange, impossible clothes and evidently quite regardless of what he looked like to others. All these people were going in one direction. Without asking the way (which I did not know) I went with them, and came to Khítrov market. There were women of a similar type, in all sorts of capes, cloaks, jackets, boots and goloshes, equally at ease in spite of the hideousness of their garb; old and young they sat trading in goods of some sort, walking about, scolding and swearing. There were few people in the market. It was evidently over, and most of the people were ascending the hill, going through and past the market all in one direction. I followed them. The farther I went the more people of that sort there seemed to be, all going one way. Passing the market and going up the street I overtook two women: one old, the other young. Both wore tattered, drab clothes. They went along talking about some affair.

After each necessary word one or two unnecessary and most indecent words were uttered. Neither of them was drunk, they were preoccupied with something, and the men who met them and those who were behind and in front of them paid no attention to their way of speaking which seemed to me so strange. It was evident that here people always talked like that. To the left were private dosshouses, and some turned into them while others went farther. Ascending the hill we came to a large corner house. Most of those among whom I had been walking stopped there. All along the pavement and on the snow in the street people of the same type stood and sat. To the right of the entrance door were the women, to the left the men. I passed both the women and the men (there were some hundreds of them), and stopped where the line ended. The house outside which they were waiting was the Lyápin Free Night-Lodging-House. The crowd were lodgers awaiting admission. At five p.m. the doors open and people are let in. Nearly all those I had overtaken were on their way here.

I stopped where the line of men ended. Those nearest began to look at me and drew me to them by their glances. The tatters covering their bodies were very various, but the expression in all the eyes directed towards me was just the same. They all seemed to ask: 'Why have you, a man from a different world, stopped near us? Who are you? A self-satisfied rich man who wishes to enjoy our misery to relieve his dullness and to torture us—or are you what does not and cannot exist—a man who pities us?' This question was on every face. They looked, caught my eye, and turned away. I wanted to speak to some one of them, but could not make up my mind to do so for a long time. But while we were yet silent our glances already drew us together. Widely as life had divided us, after our glances had met twice or thrice, we felt that we were akin and we ceased to fear one another. Nearest to me stood a peasant with a swollen face and a red beard, in a torn coat and with worn-out goloshes on his bare feet. There were eight degrees Réaumur* of frost. I met his glance three or four times, and felt so near to him that instead of being ashamed to speak to him I should have been ashamed not to say something. I asked where he came from. He answered readily and began talking, while others drew near. He was from Smolénsk, and had come to seek work, hoping to be able to buy grain and pay his taxes. 'There is no work to be got,' said he. 'The soldiers† have taken all the work. So I am knocking about, and God knows I have not eaten for two days!' He spoke timidly with an attempt at a smile. A seller of hot drinks,‡ an old soldier, was standing near and I called him. He poured out a glass. The peasant took it in his hands and, trying not to lose any of the heat, warmed them with it before drinking. While doing so he told me his adventures (the adventures, or the stories of them told by these men, were almost all alike). He had had a little work but it came to an end; and then his purse with his passport and what money he had had been stolen here in the Night-Lodging-House. Now he could not get away from Moscow. He said that during the day he warmed himself in the drink-shops and ate scraps of bread which were sometimes given to him; but sometimes they drove him out. He got his night's lodging free in Lyápin House. He was now only waiting for a police-search, when he would be put in prison for having no passport, and sent by *étape*** to his native place. 'They say there will be a police search on Thursday,' added he. (Prison and the *étape* were to him like the Promised Land.)

While he was telling me this two or three others among the crowd confirmed his words and said they were in the same plight. A lean youth, pale, long-nosed, with nothing over his shirt (which was torn at the shoulder) and with a peakless cap, pushed his way sidelong to me through the crowd.

He was shivering violently all the time, but tried to smile contemptuously at the peasant's speech, thinking thereby to adapt himself to my tone, and he looked me in the face. I offered him, too, some

---

* Fourteen degrees above zero Fahrenheit.　　† Soldiers were often hired out to work at cheap rates.　　‡ 'Sbíten', made with honey and spices.
** On foot, with others, under escort.

sbíten. On taking the glass he also warmed his hands on it, but he had only begun to speak when he was shoved aside by a big, black, aquiline-nosed fellow in a print shirt and a waistcoat but no cap. The aquiline-nosed man asked for some *sbíten.* Then followed a tall, drunken old man with a pointed beard, in an overcoat tied round the waist with a cord, and wearing bast-shoes. Then came a little fellow with a swollen face and watery eyes, in a brown nankeen pea-jacket, with bare knees showing through the holes in his summer trousers and knocking together from cold. He shivered so that he could not hold the glass but spilled it over himself. The others began to abuse him, but he only smiled pitifully and shivered. Then came a crooked, deformed man in tatters, and with strips of linen tied round his bare feet; then something that looked like an officer, then something that looked like a cleric, then something strange and noseless: all, hungry, cold, importunate and submissive, crowded round me and pressed near the *sbíten* till it was all finished. One man asked for money and I gave him some. Another asked, and a third, and then the crowd besieged me. Disorder and a crush ensued. A porter from the next house shouted to them to get off the pavement in front of his house and they submissively obeyed his command. Organizers appeared among the crowd, who took me under their protection. They wished to extricate me from the crush; but the crowd that had at first stretched along the pavement had now become disorganized and gathered round me. They all looked at me and begged; and each face was more pitiful, more jaded, and more degraded than the last. I gave away all I had with me, which was not much, only some twenty rubles, and following the crowd I entered the Night-Lodging-House. It was an immense building consisting of four departments. On the top stories were the men's lodgings and on the lower stories the women's. First I entered the latter: a large room all filled with bunks like the berths in third-class Russian railway cars. They were arranged in two tiers, above and below. Women old and young—strange, tattered, with no outdoor garments—entered and took possession of their bunks: some below and some above. Some of the older ones crossed themselves and prayed for the founder of this refuge. Others laughed and swore. I went upstairs. There the men were taking their places. Among them I saw one of those to whom I had given money. On seeing him I suddenly felt dreadfully ashamed and hurried away. And feeling as if I had committed a crime, I left the house and went home. There, ascending the carpeted steps to the cloth-carpeted hall and taking off my fur coat, I sat down to a five-course dinner, served by two lackeys in dress clothes with white ties and white gloves.

Thirty years ago in Paris I once saw how, in the presence of thousands of spectators, they cut a man's head off with a guillotine. I knew that the man was a dreadful criminal; I knew all the arguments that have been written in defence of that kind of action, and I knew it was done deliberately and intentionally, but at the moment the head and body separated and fell into the box I gasped, and realized not with my mind nor with my heart but with my whole being, that all the arguments in defence of capital punishment are wicked nonsense, and that however many people may combine to commit murder—the worst of all crimes—and whatever they may call themselves, murder remains murder, and that this crime had been committed before my eyes, and I by my presence and non-intervention had approved and shared in it. In the same way now, at the sight of the hunger, cold, and degradation of thousands of people, I understood not with my mind or my heart but with my whole being, that the existence of tens of thousands of such people in Moscow—while I and thousands of others over-eat ourselves with beef-steaks and sturgeon and cover our horses and floors with cloth or carpets—no matter what all the learned men in the world may say about its necessity—is a crime, not committed once but constantly; and that I with my luxury not merely tolerate it but share in it. For me the difference between these two impressions was only—that there all I could have done would have been to cry out to the murderers who stood around the guillotine arranging the murder, that they were doing wrong, and to have tried by all means to hinder it. Even then I should have known in advance that my action would not prevent the murder. But here I could have given not *sbíten* alone and the trifling sum of money I had with me, but the overcoat I wore and all I had at home. But I had not done it, and I therefore felt and feel and shall not cease to feel that as long as I have any superfluous food and someone else has none, and I have two coats and someone else has none, I share in a constantly repeated crime.

CHAPTER III

THAT SAME EVENING after returning from Lyápin House I told my impressions to a friend. He, a town dweller, began to explain with some satisfaction that it was the most natural thing in a city, and that it was merely my provincialism that caused me to see anything particular in it. Things had always been so and would and must always be so; it is an inevitable condition of civilization. In London it is still worse . . . so there is nothing bad in it and one ought not to be dissatisfied with it. I began to answer my friend; but I did it so warmly and irritably that my wife ran in from an adjoining room to ask what had happened. It seems that, without noticing it, I had cried out with tears in my voice and had waved my arms at my friend, exclaiming: 'One cannot live so; one cannot; one cannot!' They put me to shame for my unnecessary ardour, and told me that I cannot talk quietly about anything but become unpleasantly excited, and in particular they proved to me that the existence of such unfortunate people cannot justify my spoiling the lives of those about me.

I felt that this was quite just, and I was silenced; but in the depth of my heart I felt that I too was right, and I could not feel at ease.

Town life, which had seemed strange and foreign to me before, now became so repulsive that all the pleasures of the luxurious life I formerly enjoyed became a torment to me. And try as I would to find in my soul some justification for our way of living, I could not without irritation behold either my own or any other drawing room, or any clean, elegantly laid table, or a carriage with well-fed coachmen and horses, or the shops, theatres, and assemblies. I could not help seeing beside them the hungry, cold, downtrodden inhabitants of Lyápin House. I could not escape the thought that these two things were connected and the one resulted from the other. I remember that the consciousness of guilt which I experienced from the first moment remained with me, but another feeling was soon added to it, obscuring it.

When I spoke of my impressions of Lyápin House to intimate friends and acquaintances, they all replied as the first one (at whom I shouted) had done, but they also expressed approval of my kind-heartedness and susceptibility and gave me to understand that the sight had acted so strongly on me merely because I—Leo Tolstóy—am a very kind and good man. I willingly believed them. And before I had time to look round there came to me, instead of the feeling of shame and repentance I had first experienced, a feeling of satisfaction at my own beneficence, and a desire to exhibit it.

'Really,' said I to myself, 'the fault probably lies not in my luxury but in the inevitable conditions of life. An alteration in my life cannot cure the evils I have seen. By altering my life I shall only make myself and those near me unhappy, while the destitute will remain as badly off as ever.

'Therefore the task for me is not to change my own life, as I thought at first, but as far as I can to aid in improving the position of those unfortunates who have evoked my sympathy. The fact of the matter is that I am a very good, kind man, and wish to benefit my neighbours.' So I began to devise a plan of philanthropic activity in which I could exhibit my goodness. I should mention, however, that when devising this philanthropic activity I felt all the time in the depth of my soul that it was not the right thing, but, as often happens, reasoning and imagination stifled the voice of conscience. It happened that preparations were being made at that time for the Census. This seemed a good opportunity for starting the charity in which I wished to exhibit my goodness. I knew of many philanthropic organizations and societies in Moscow, but all their activities seemed to me falsely directed and insignificant in comparison with what I aimed at. So I planned the following: to arouse sympathy for town poverty among the rich; to collect money, enrol people willing to help in the affair, and with the Census-takers to visit all the dens of destitution and, besides compiling the Census, get into touch with the unfortunates and investigate their needs, helping them with money and work or by getting them back to their villages, as well as by putting their children to school and the old folk into refuges and almshouses. More than that, I thought that from among those engaged in this work a permanent society could be formed which, dividing the districts of Moscow among its members, would see that poverty and destitution should not be allowed to breed, but would constantly nip them in the bud and perform the duty not so much of curing town poverty as of preventing it. I already imagined that, not to speak of the totally destitute, there would be none left in want in the town, and that I should have accomplished all this; and that we, the rich, could afterwards sit at ease in our drawing-rooms, eat five-course dinners and drive in carriages to theatres and assemblies, untroubled by such sights as I had witnessed at Lyápin House.

Having formed this plan I wrote an article about it, and before sending it for publication I went about among my acquaintances from whom I hoped to receive help. To all whom I saw that day (I specially addressed myself to the rich) I said the same thing—almost exactly what I said in the article. I proposed to take advantage of the Census to become acquainted with the Moscow destitute and to come to their aid with work and money, and to take such action as would abolish destitution in Moscow; and then we, the rich, could with quiet consciences enjoy the good things to which we are accustomed. They all listened to me attentively and seriously, but with all of them without exception the same thing occurred. As soon as they understood what it was about, they became ill at ease and rather shamefaced. It was as though they were ashamed chiefly on my account—that I should talk nonsense, but a kind of nonsense which it was impossible plainly to call nonsense. It was as though some external cause obliged them to be indulgent to this nonsense of mine.

'Ah! yes, of course! It would be a very good idea,' said they. 'Of course one can't help sympathizing with it. Yes, your idea is excellent. I had a similar idea myself, but . . . our people are so indifferent that one mustn't expect much success . . . For my part, however, I shall of course be ready to help.'

They all said something like that. They all agreed, but as it seemed to me not because they were convinced nor from any wish of their own, but from some external cause which prevented their not agreeing. I noticed this also from the fact that not one of those who promised to help with money fixed the sum he or she intended to give; so that I had to fix it by asking, 'Then I may count on you for three hundred, or two hundred, or one hundred, or twenty-five rubles?' and not one of them handed me the money. I mention this because when people give money for what they want, they generally give it promptly. For a box at the theatre to see Sarah Bernhardt they hand over the money at once, to clinch the matter. But here of those who had agreed to give money and had expressed their sympathy not one offered the money at once, but they only tacitly consented to the sums I named. At the last house I went to that day in the evening, I happened to find a large gathering. The hostess of that house has for some years been engaged in philanthropy. Several carriages stood at the entrance and several footmen in expensive liveries were sitting in the hall. In the large drawing-room, round two tables on which stood lamps, sat married and unmarried ladies in expensive clothes with expensive ornaments, dressing little dolls. Several young men were there also, near the ladies. The dolls these ladies were making were to be disposed of at a lottery for the poor.

The sight of this drawing-room and of the people collected in it impressed me very unpleasantly. Not to mention that the fortunes of the people there assembled amounted to some millions of rubles, or that the interest on the cost of their dresses, lace, bronzes, jewellery, carriages, horses, liveries, and footmen, would a hundred times exceed the value of their work, the cost of this one gathering alone: the gloves, clean linen, and conveyances, with the candles, tea, sugar and biscuits provided, must have exceeded a hundred times the value of the things produced. I saw all this and could therefore understand that here at any rate I should find no sympathy for my plan, but I had come to make the proposal, and, difficult as I felt it, I said my say (almost the same as was said in my article).

Of those present, one lady said she was too sensitive to go among the poor herself but she would give money. How much, and when she would send it, she did not say. Another lady and a young man offered their services to go among the poor, but I did not avail myself of their offer. The chief person to whom I addressed myself told me it would not be possible to do much, for lack of means. Means would be lacking because the rich in Moscow were all well known and what could be got out of them had already been got. All the philanthropists had already received rank, medals, and other honours, and for a monetary success it would be essential to secure a fresh grant of honours from the Government, and this—the only thing that is really effective—is very difficult to obtain.

After returning home that day I lay down to sleep not merely with a foreboding that my plan would come to nothing, but with a sense of shame and a consciousness that I had been doing something very nasty and shameful all day. But I did not abandon the attempt. In the first place, it had been started and false shame kept me to it; secondly, the mere fact of being occupied with it enabled me to continue to live in the conditions habitual to me, while its failure would oblige me to abandon these and seek new ways of life—a thing I unconsciously dreaded. So I did not trust my inward voice, and continued what I had begun.

Having given my article* to be printed, I read it, in proof, at the Town Dúma. While reading it I felt so uncomfortable that I hesitated and blushed to tears. I noticed that everybody present was also uncomfortable. On my asking, at the end of the reading, whether the Census organizers accepted my proposal that they should remain at their posts to act as intermediaries between society and the necessitous poor, an awkward silence ensued. Then two members made speeches. These, as it were, corrected the awkwardness of my proposal. Sympathy was expressed with my idea, but the impracticability of my thought (of which every one approved) was pointed out. After that all felt more at ease. But when subsequently, still wishing to carry my point, I asked the organizers separately whether they agreed to investigate the needs of the poor during the Census and to remain at their posts to serve as intermediaries between the poor and the rich, they all again appeared uncomfortable. Their looks seemed to say, 'There now, we smoothed over your folly out of respect for you, but you are again obtruding it!' That was what their looks said. But verbally they consented, and two of them separately, as though by arrangement, remarked in the self-same words, 'We consider ourselves *morally bound* to do it.'

When I said to the students engaged to take the Census, that besides the usual aims of the Census the aim of philanthropy needed also to be kept in view, my communication produced a similar effect on them. I noticed that when we talked about it they were ashamed to look me in the face, as one is ashamed to look a kindly man in the face when he talks nonsense. My article had the same effect on the newspaper editor to whom I gave it, and also on my son, and on my wife, and on the most diverse people. All, for some reason, felt uncomfortable, but all considered it necessary to approve of my idea, and all after expressing approval at once began to express doubts of its success; and all without exception began also to condemn

* 'About the Census in Moscow', 1882.

the indifference and coldness of society and of everybody, except (evidently) themselves.

In the depth of my soul I continued to feel that all this was not the right thing, and that nothing would come of it; but the article was printed and I undertook to take part in the Census. First I had started the affair and now it dragged me along.

CHAPTER IV

AT MY REQUEST they allotted me for the Census the district in the Khamóvniki ward near the Smolénsk market, along Protóchny side-street between Riverside Passage and Nikólski side-street, in which are situated the houses generally called Rzhánov house or Rzhánov fortress. These houses formerly belonged to a merchant named Rzhánov, but now belong to the Zímins. I had long heard of it as a den of most terrible poverty and vice and had therefore asked the organizers to let me take that district.

After receiving instructions from the Town Dúma, I went—a few days before the Census—to inspect my district, and easily found Rzhánov house by the plan they gave me . . . .

I entered the adjoining Nikólski side-street. This ends on the left with a gloomy house which has no exit on that side, and by its appearance I guessed that this was the Rzhánov fortress.

Descending the slope of the Nikólski street I overtook some boys of ten to fourteen years old, in jackets or thin coats, sliding down the slope or going on one skate along the frozen pavement by that house. The boys were ragged and like town boys in general they were alert and impudent. I stopped to look at them. From round the corner appeared a ragged old woman with sallow flabby cheeks. She was going towards the Smolénsk market-place and wheezing like a broken-winded horse at each step she took. On coming up to me she paused, breathing hoarsely. Anywhere else this old woman would have asked me for money, but here she only began talking. 'See,' she said, pointing to the skating boys, 'all they do is to get into mischief. They will be just such Rzhánovites as their fathers.' One of the boys, in an overcoat and a cap that had lost its peak, heard what she said and stopped. 'What are you rowing at us for?' he shouted at the old woman. 'You are a Rzhánov bitch yourself!' 'And do you live here?' I asked the boy. 'Yes, and she lives here. She stole the leg of a boot!' shouted the boy and, putting a foot out in front of him, skated away. The old woman broke out into a stream of abuse interrupted by coughs. Just then an old man all in rags, with quite white hair, came along the middle of the road descending the slope and swinging his hands, in one of which was a string of bread-stuff and cracknell rings. The old man had the appearance of one who had just fortified himself with a glass of vodka. He had evidently heard the old woman's scoldings, and he took her part. 'I'll give it you, little devils, uh!' shouted he at the boys, pretending to make for them; and having reached me, he came onto the pavement. On the Arbát* this old man would strike one by his age, his weakness, and his destitution. Here he was a merry workman returning from his day's work.

I followed the old man. He turned the corner to the left into the Protóchny side-street, and having gone the whole length of the house and its gates he disappeared into a tavern.

Two gates and several doors open onto the Protóchny side-street; there are taverns, gin-shops, some provision shops and others. This is the Rzhánov fortress itself. Everything here is grey, dirty, and stinking—the building, the lodgings, the yard, and the people. Most of those I met here were ragged and half-dressed. Some walked and some ran from one door to another. Two were bargaining about some rag or other. I went round the whole building from the Protóchny side-street and the Riverside passage, and on returning I stopped at one of the gates. I wanted to enter to see what was going on inside, but felt timid about it; what was I to say if asked what I wanted? After some hesitation, however, I entered the gate. As soon as I did so I noticed an abominable stench. The yard was horribly filthy. I turned a corner and at that moment, upstairs to the left, heard the clatter of feet running on the wooden gallery, first along the boards of the balcony and then down the steps of the staircase.† A lean woman in a faded pink dress, with turned-up sleeves and with boots on her stockingless feet, ran out first. Following her came a shock-headed man in a red shirt and very wide trousers that looked like a petticoat, and with goloshes on his feet. At the bottom of

* *One of the main streets of Moscow.* † *The courtyard was enclosed by the house, which had a balcony all round it looking onto the yard.*

the stairs the man seized the woman: 'You won't get away!' said he, laughing. 'Listen to the squint-eyed devil!' began the woman, evidently flattered by his pursuit, but she caught sight of me and shouted angrily: 'What do you want?' As I did not want anybody I grew confused and went away. There was nothing remarkable about all this; but this incident, after what I had seen outside in the street: the scolding old woman, the merry old man, and the sliding boys, suddenly showed me quite a new side of the affair I was engaged on. I had set out to benefit these people by the help of the rich, and here for the first time I realized that all these unfortunates whom I wished to benefit, besides the hours they spend suffering from hunger and cold and waiting for a night's lodging, have also time to devote to something else. There is the rest of the twenty four hours every day, and there is a whole life about which I had never thought. Here for the first time I understood that all these people, besides needing food and shelter, must also pass twenty-four hours each day which they, like the rest of us, have to live. I understood that they must be angry, and dull, and must pluck up courage, and mourn, and make merry. Strange to say, I now for the first time understood clearly that the business I had undertaken could not consist merely in feeding and clothing a thousand people as one feeds and drives under shelter a thousand sheep; but that it must consist in doing them good. And when I understood that each of these thousand people was a human being with a past; and with passions, temptations, and errors, and thoughts and questions, like my own, and was such a man as myself—then the thing I had undertaken suddenly appeared so difficult that I realized my impotence. But it had been started, and I went on with it.

CHAPTER V

ON THE FIRST APPOINTED DAY the student Census-takers began work in the morning, but I, the philanthropist, did not join them till towards noon. I could not get there sooner because I only got up at ten, and then drank coffee and had to smoke to help my digestion. I reached the gates of the Rzhánov house at twelve o'clock. A policeman showed me the tavern on the Riverside passage, to which the Census-takers had said anyone should be shown who asked for them. I went into the tavern. It was very dark, smelly, and dirty. Straight before me was a bar, on the left a small room with tables covered with dirty table-cloths, on the right a large room with columns and similar tables at the window and by the walls. At some of the tables men, tattered or decently dressed, probably workmen or small shopkeepers, and some women, sat having tea. The tavern was very dirty but one saw at once that business was good. The look of the man at the bar was business-like and the waiters were prompt and attentive: I had hardly entered before an attendant was ready to help me off with my overcoat and to take any order I might give. It was evident that habits of prompt and attentive work had been established. I inquired about the Census-takers. 'Ványa!' cried a small man, dressed German-fashion, who was arranging something in a cupboard behind the bar; this was the owner of the tavern, Iván Fedótych, a Kalúga peasant who leased half the lodgings in Zímin's houses, sub-letting them to lodgers. An attendant ran up, a lad of eighteen, thin, hook-nosed, and with a yellow complexion. 'Take the gentleman to the Census-takers; they are in the big building above the well—get along.' The lad laid down his napkin and put on an overcoat over his white shirt and white trousers,* as well as a cap with a large peak, and rapidly moving his white legs he led me through a back door that closed by a counter-weight. In the lobby of a greasy smelly kitchen we met an old woman who was carefully carrying some very malodorous tripe in a rag. From the lobby we descended into the sloping yard all covered by a wooden building, with the lower story of brick. The stench in this yard was very strong. The centre of this stench was the privy, around which always, every time I passed, people were crowding. The privy itself was not the place where people relieved themselves, but it served to indicate the place around which it had become customary to relieve oneself. Passing through the yard it was impossible not to notice that place; it always felt stifling when one entered the acrid atmosphere of the smell that came from it.

The lad, careful of his white trousers, cautiously led me past that place over the frozen filth, and made his way to one of the buildings. The people passing through the yard and along the galleries all

* In the class of tavern referred to (a 'traktír') the waiters always wore white cotton blouses and trousers, Russian style.

stopped to look at me. Evidently a cleanly dressed man was a prodigy in these parts.

The lad asked a woman whether she had not seen where the Census-takers were, and three or more men immediately answered his question; some said they were above the well, but others said that they had been there but had left and had gone to Nikíta Ivánovich. An old man with nothing over his shirt, who was adjusting his clothes near the privy, said they were in No.30. The boy decided that this information was the most probable, and led me to No. 30 under the penthouse of the basement story, into darkness and stench different from that of the yard. We descended into the lower story and went along the earth floor of a dark corridor. While we were passing along the corridor one of the doors opened abruptly and from it emerged a drunken old man with nothing over his shirt, who was apparently not a peasant. A washerwoman with bared and soapy arms was driving and pushing this man out with shrill screams. Ványa, my conductor, pushed the drunken man aside and reproved him. 'It won't do to make such scenes,' said he, 'and you an officer too!'

We came to the door of No.30. Ványa pulled at it. The door came unstuck with a smacking sound, opened, and we became aware of an odour of soapy steam and an acrid smell of bad food and tobacco. We entered into complete darkness. The windows were on the other side; but here were boarded corridors to right and left, with small doors at various angles leading into rooms roughly constructed of thin whitewashed boards. In a dark room to our left a woman was seen washing clothes at a trough. From a small door on the right an old woman looked out. Through another open door a hairy red-faced peasant in bast-shoes was seen sitting on a board fixed to the wall, which did duty for a bed: he had his hands on his knees, swung his feet in his bast-shoes, and looked at them gloomily.

At the end of the corridor was a little door leading into the room where the Census-takers were. This was the room of the landlady of the whole of No.30; she rented the whole of it from Iván Fedótych and let it out to the tenants and night-lodgers. In that tiny room of hers, under a tinfoil icon, sat a student Census-taker with his cards, and like an investigating magistrate questioned a peasant in a shirt and waistcoat. This was a friend of the landlady, who was answering the questions on her behalf. There also was the landlady—an old woman—and two inquisitive lodgers. When I had entered, the room was quite crowded. I squeezed up to the table. The student and I exchanged greetings, and he continued his questions. But I began to observe and to interrogate the lodgers who were living there, for my own purpose.

It turned out that in this first lodging I did not find a single person on whom to expend my beneficence. The landlady, in spite of the poverty, smallness, and dirt of her lodging, which struck me after the mansions in which I live, had a sufficiency even in comparison with the poor of the town; and in comparison with village poverty, which I knew well, she was living in luxury. She had a feather bed, a quilted coverlet, a samovár, a warm coat, and a cupboard with crockery. Her friend had a similarly comfortable appearance. He even had a watch and chain. The lodgers were poor, but not one of them was in immediate need of assistance. Help was asked by the woman washing clothes at the wash trough, who had been left by her husband with children on her hands; by an old widow-woman who said she had nothing to live on; and by the peasant in bast-shoes who told me he had not eaten that day. But on inquiry it appeared that none of these people was particularly in need, and that in order to aid them one would have to get to know them well.

When I offered to place her children in a children's home, the woman abandoned by her husband grew confused, considered a bit, thanked me very much, but evidently did not want that: she would have preferred a gift of money. The eldest girl helped her with the washing and the middle one took care of the little boy. The old woman begged hard to be put in an alms-house, but when I looked at the corner she lived in I saw that she was not destitute. She had a small trunk with goods in it, a teapot with a tin spout, two cups, and boxes that had held sweets and now had tea and sugar in them. She knitted socks and gloves and had a monthly allowance from a benefactress. What the peasant for his part evidently wanted was not something to eat but something to drink, and all that might be given him would go to the gin-shop. So that in that lodging there were none of those with whom, as I fancied, the house overflowed—people whom I could make happy by a gift of money. They were, it seemed to me, poor people of a dubious kind. I noted down the old woman, the woman with children, and the peasant, and decided that they would have to be attended to, but only after I had attended to those specially unfortunate ones whom I expected to find in that house. I decided that in the help we were going to distribute there must be a sequence: first would come the most unfortunate, and afterwards these people. But in the next and the next lodging it was the same thing. All the people were of the same kind, cases one would have to look into more carefully before helping them. I did not find any unfortunates who could be made fortunate by a mere gift of money. Ashamed as I am to admit it, I began to feel disappointed at not seeing in these houses anything like what I had expected. I thought I should find people of an exceptional kind, but when I had been to all the lodgings I became convinced that the inhabitants of these houses are not at all exceptional, but are just such people as those among whom I live. Among them, as among us, there were some more or less good and more or less bad, more or less happy and more or less miserable; and the unhappy were just such as exist among ourselves; people whose unhappiness depends not on external conditions but on themselves—a kind of unhappiness bank-notes cannot cure.

CHAPTER VI

THE DWELLERS IN THESE HOUSES form the lowest layer of the town population, of whom there are in Moscow probably more than a hundred thousand. Here in this house were representatives of all sections of this population: small employers and artisans, bootmakers, brushmakers, carpenters, joiners, cobblers, tailors, and smiths, and here too were cabmen and men trading on their own account, also women who kept stalls, washerwomen, dealers in old clothes, petty money-lenders, day-labourers, and people with no fixed occupation, as well as beggars and dissolute women.

Many of the very people I had seen at the entrance to Lyápin House were here, but here they were distributed among many workers. And moreover, whereas I had then seen them at their most wretched time when they had eaten and drunk all they possessed, and when, cold, naked, and driven from the taverns, they were waiting, as for heavenly manna, for admission into the free Night-Lodging-House, to be taken thence to the promised land of prison and sent under police escort back to their villages—here I saw them scattered among a large number of workers and at a time when one way or other they had obtained three or five kopeks to pay for a night's lodging, or perhaps even had some rubles to spend on food and drink.

Strange as it may seem to say so, I did not here experience anything like the feeling I had at Lyápin House. On the contrary, during the first round both I and the students had an almost pleasant feeling. Why do I say, 'almost pleasant'? That is untrue—the feeling produced by intercourse with these people, strange as it seems to say so, was simply a very pleasant one.

The first impression was that the majority of those who lived here were working people, and very good-natured ones.

We found most of them at work: washerwomen at their troughs, carpenters at their benches, bootmakers on their stools. The narrow lodgings were full of people, and brisk, cheery work was going on. The place smelt of workmen's perspiration, and at the bootmaker's of leather, and at the carpenter's of shavings. One often heard singing, or saw sinewy bare arms quickly and skilfully performing accustomed movements. Everywhere we were greeted cheerily and kindly: almost everywhere our intrusion into the daily life of these people was far from evoking the pretension or desire to show off and reply curtly which was evoked by the Census-takers' call at the houses of most of the wealthy families, but on the contrary these people replied to all our questions properly, without attaching any special importance to them. Our questions merely gave them occasion to make merry and joke about how the return should be filled in, who ought to count as two, and which two as one, and so forth.

We found many of them at dinner or tea, and every time in reply to our greeting: 'Bread and salt' or 'Tea and sugar',* they replied 'Please to join us', and even moved up to make room for us. Instead of the haunt of constantly changing inhabitants we thought we should find here, it turned out that in this house there were many lodgings in which people had lived a long time. One carpenter with his workmen, and a bootmaker with his assistants, had been there for ten years. At the bootmaker's it was very dirty and crowded, but all the people at work were very cheerful. I tried to talk with one of the workmen, wishing to hear from him of the misery of his position and of his being in debt to his master, but the workman

* Customary Russian folk-greetings to people having a meal.

did not understand me and spoke very well of his master and of his own life.

In one lodging an old man lived with his old wife. They sold apples. Their room was warm, clean, and full of goods. The floor was spread with straw sacking which they got at the wholesale apple-dealers. There were trunks, cupboards, a samovár, and crockery. In the corner were many icons, with two little lamps burning before them; on the walls hung warm overcoats covered up with sheets. The old woman, who had star-shaped wrinkles, was affable, talkative, and apparently pleased at her own quiet well ordered life.

Iván Fedótych, the landlord of the tavern and the lodgings, came from the tavern and went along with us. He jested good-humouredly with many of the lodgers, calling them all by their Christian names and patronymics,* and gave us brief sketches of them. They were all people of ordinary types, Martin Semënoviches, Peter Petróviches, Mary Ivánovnas—people who did not consider themselves unfortunate, but considered themselves, and really were, like anyone else.

We came prepared to see nothing but horrors; and instead of horrors we were shown something good that involuntarily evoked our respect. There were so many of these good people that the tattered, fallen, idle ones, scattered here and there among them, did not destroy the general impression.

The students were not so much struck by this as I was. They had come simply to do something they considered to be of scientific value, and were incidentally making casual observations; but I was a philanthropist and came to help the unfortunate, perishing, depraved people I expected to find here. And instead of unfortunate, perishing, depraved people, I saw a majority of tranquil, contented, cheerful, kindly and very good working people.

I felt this most vividly when in these lodgings I really came on some cases of crying need such as I was prepared to help.

When I discovered such need I always found that it had already been met, and that the help I wished to render had already been given: given before I came, and by whom? By those same unfortunate depraved creatures I was prepared to save; and given in a better way than I could have done.

* This is a usual Russian practice, but indicates some amount of familiarity with the lodgers on the part of the landlord.

In one cellar lay a lonely old man, ill of typhus. He had no connections. A widow with a little daughter—a stranger to him but his neighbour (occupying another corner of the room he lived in) was looking after him. She gave him tea, and bought medicine for him out of her own money. In another room lay a woman suffering from puerperal fever. A woman of the town was rocking the baby, had made it some pap wrapped in a rag to suck, and for two days had not gone out to ply her trade. A little girl who had been left an orphan had been taken into the family of a tailor who had three children of his own. So there remained only those unfortunate idle people: officials, copyists, footmen out of places, beggars, drunkards, prostitutes, and children, whom it was impossible to help at once with money, but whom it would be necessary to get to know well, to think about, and to find places for. I looked for people unfortunate merely from poverty and whom we could help by sharing our superfluity with them; and by some peculiar mischance (as it seemed to me) I did not find any such, but found only unfortunates of a kind to whom it would be necessary to devote much time and care.

CHAPTER VII

THE UNFORTUNATES I had noted down seemed to me to fall naturally into three classes: first, those who had lost advantageous positions and were awaiting a return to them (there were such both from the lower and higher ranks); then dissolute women, of whom there were very many in these houses; and thirdly, children. Most of all I found and noted people of the first class, who had lost their former advantageous position and wished to return to it. People of that kind, especially from among the gentry and officials, were very numerous. In almost all the tenements to which we went with the landlord, Iván Fedótych, he told us: 'Here there will be no need for you to fill in the list of lodgers yourselves. There is a man here who can do all that, if only he is not drunk to-day.'

And Iván Fedótych would call the man out by name, and he was always one of those who had fallen from a better position. At Fedótych's call there would creep out from some dark corner a once rich gentleman or official, usually drunk and always half-undressed. If not drunk he always readily undertook the task offered him: nodding with an air of importance, knitting his brows, and introducing learned terminology into his remarks, and holding with careful tenderness the clean, printed, red card in his trembling, dirty hands, he would look round on his fellow lodgers with pride and contempt as if triumphing now, by his superior education, over those who had so often humiliated him. He was evidently glad to come into touch with the world in which red cards are printed—the world to which he once belonged. Almost always in reply to my enquiries about his life the man would begin, not only readily but with enthusiasm, to tell the story, fixed in his mind like a prayer, of the misfortunes he had endured and especially of that former position which by his education he felt ought to be his.

There are very many such people scattered in various corners of Rzhánov House. One tenement was entirely taken up by them—men and women. When we approached it Iván Fedótych told us: 'Now here are the gentry.' The lodging was quite full: they were almost all (some forty persons) at home. In the whole house there were none more degraded and unhappy than these: the old shrivelled, and the young pale and haggard. I talked with some of them. The story was almost always the same, differing only in degree of development. Each of them had been rich, or had a father, brother, or uncle who had been or still was rich, or his father or he himself had had an excellent place. Then a misfortune occurred, caused either by some envious people or by his own imprudent good-nature, or by some accident, and now he had lost everything and had to perish in these unsuitable, hateful surroundings—lousy and tattered, amid drunken and debauched people, feeding on bullock's liver and bread, and holding out his hand for alms. All the thoughts, wishes, and memories of these people were turned solely to the past. The present appeared to them unnatural, abhorrent, and unworthy of attention. None of them had a present. They had only recollections of the past and expectations of a future, which might at any moment be realized and for the realization of which very little was needed, but that little was always just beyond their reach, so their life was wasting in vain. One had been in this plight for a year, another for five, and a third for thirty years. One of them need only be decently dressed to go to see a well-known person favourably disposed towards him; another need only be dressed, pay some debts, and get to the town of Orël; a third need only redeem his things from pawn and find a little money to continue a lawsuit he is bound to win, and then all would again be well. They all say they only need some external thing in order to resume the position they consider natural and happy for themselves.

Had I not been befogged by my pride as benefactor, I need only have looked a little into their faces—young and old—generally weak and sensual but good-natured, to understand that their misfortune could not be repaired by external means and that unless their views of life were changed they could not be happy in any position; and that they were not peculiar people in specially unfortunate circumstances, but were just such people as surround us and as we are ourselves. I remember that I found intercourse with this kind of unfortunates particularly trying, and I now understand why. In them I saw myself as in a looking-glass. Had I thought of my own life and that of the people of our circle, I should have seen that between us and these people there was no essential difference.

If those now about me do not live in Rzhánov House, but in large apartments or houses of their own in the best streets, and if they eat and drink dainty food instead of only bread with bullock's liver or herrings, this does not prevent their being similarly unfortunate. They too are dissatisfied with their position, regret the past and want something better; and the better positions they desire are just like those the dwellers in Rzhánov House want: namely, positions in which they can do less work and make others do more for them. The difference is merely in degree. Had I then reflected, I should have understood this; however, I did not reflect, but only questioned these people and noted them down, intending, after learning the details of their various circumstances and needs, to help them later on. I did not then understand that such men can only be helped by changing their outlook on life; and to change another man's outlook one must oneself have a better one and live in accord with it; and I was myself living according to the view of life that had to be altered before these people could cease to be unhappy.

I did not see that, metaphorically speaking, they were unhappy not because they lacked nourishing food but because their digestions were spoilt, and that they were demanding not what was nourishing but what excited their appetites. I did not see that the help they needed was not food, but a cure for their spoilt digestions. Though I anticipate, I will here remark that of all the people I noted down

I really helped none, though what they asked—and what seemed as though it would set them on their feet—was done for some of them. Of these I know three particularly well. All three, after being repeatedly set on their feet, are now again just in the same position as they were three years ago.

CHAPTER VIII

THE SECOND CATEGORY OF UNFORTUNATES whom I also hoped to help later on were the loose women, of whom there were very many of all sorts in Rzhánov House—from young ones who looked like women, to terrible and horrible old ones who had lost human semblance. The hope of being able to help these women, whom at first I had not had in view, came to me from the following incident.

It was in the midst of our round. We had already formed a systematic plan for doing our business.

On entering each new tenement we at once inquired for its master. One of us then sat down and cleared a place to write at, while another went round from corner to corner and questioned each person in the lodgings separately, bringing the information to the one who wrote.

On entering one basement-lodging a student went to find the master, while I began to question those in the lodging. The lodging was arranged thus: in the middle of a square fourteen-foot room was a brick stove. From it ran four partitions star-wise, forming four separate lodgings or cubicles. In the first of these, a passage partition which contained four bunks, were two people—an old man and a woman. Straight through this was a long cubicle occupied by the landlord of the tenement, a very pale young man dressed respectably in a drab cloth coat. To the left of the first cubicle was another in which was a sleeping man (probably drunk) and a woman in a pink blouse loose in front and tight behind. The fourth cubicle was beyond a partition; the entrance to it was through the landlord's cubicle.

The student went into the landlord's cubicle, while I remained in the first one questioning the old man and the woman. The man was a working printer, now without means of livelihood. The woman was a cook's wife. I went into the third cubicle and asked the woman in the blouse about the sleeping man. She said he was a visitor. I asked her who she was. She said she was a Moscow peasant-woman. 'What is your occupation?' She laughed and did not reply. 'How do you get your living?' I repeated, thinking she had not understood my question. 'I sit in the tavern,' said she. I did not understand her, and again asked, 'What do you live on?' She did not reply, but laughed. From the fourth cubicle, which we had not yet entered, there also came the sound of women's laughter. The landlord came out of his cubicle and joined us. He had evidently heard my questions and the woman's replies. He looked severely at her, and addressing me said: 'She's a prostitute,' evidently pleased that he knew this word used by the officials, and could pronounce it correctly.* Having said this to me with a scarcely perceptible smile of respectful satisfaction, he turned to the woman. As soon as he spoke to her his whole face changed; and with a peculiar, contemptuously rapid utterance such as people use to a dog, he said without looking at her:

'Why talk nonsense? "I sit in a tavern," indeed! If you sit there, then speak plainly and say you're a prostitute.' Again he used that word and added, 'She doesn't know what to call herself.'

His tone exasperated me. 'It is not for us to shame her,' said I; 'if we all lived godly lives there would not be any such as she.'

'Yes, that's the way of it,' said the landlord with an unnatural smile.

'Then it is not for us to reproach them but to pity them. Is it their fault?'

I don't remember exactly what I said; but I know that the contemptuous tone of this young landlord of a lodging full of women he called prostitutes, revolted me; and I felt sorry for the woman, and expressed both feelings. And hardly had I spoken, before in the room from which the laughter had come, the boards of the bunks creaked and above the partition (which did not reach to the ceiling) appeared the dishevelled curly hair and small swollen eyes of a woman with a shiny red face, and then a second, and a third. They had evidently got up on their bunks and were all three stretching their necks with bated breath and strained attention, silently looking at us.

* 'Prostitute' is a hard, foreign word, little used by common people in Russia.

An awkward silence ensued. The student who had been smiling became serious; the landlord lowered his eyes abashed; and the women, not drawing a breath, looked at me and waited. I was more abashed than any of them. I had not at all expected that a word casually dropped would produce such an effect. It was as when Ezekiel's field of death strewn with bones quivered at the touch of the spirit and the dead bones moved. I had spoken a chance word of love and pity, and it had acted on all as though they had only been waiting for that word to cease to be corpses and to become alive. They all looked at me and waited for what would follow. They waited for me to speak the words and do the deeds that would cause the bones to come together and be covered with flesh and come to life again. But felt I had no words or deeds with which to continue what I had begun. In the depth of my soul I felt that I had lied: that I was myself like them and that I had nothing more to say; and I began to write on the card the names and occupations of all the people in the lodging. This incident led me into a fresh error: that of supposing that it would be possible to help these unfortunates also. It seemed to me then, in my self-deception, that this would be quite easy. I said to myself: Let us note down these women also, and afterwards, when we have noted everybody down, we (who these 'we' were, I did not stop to consider) will attend to them. I imagined that we (those very people who have for several generations led, and are still leading, these women into that condition) could one fine day take it into our heads suddenly to rectify it all. Yet had I but remembered my talk with the loose woman who was rocking the child whose mother was ill, I might have understood how insensate such an undertaking was.

When we saw that woman with the child we thought it was her own. In reply to the question, Who are you? she said simply that she was a wench. She did not say, 'A prostitute'. Only the landlord of the lodging used that terrible word. The supposition that she had a child of her own suggested to me the thought of extricating her from her position. So I asked:

'Is that your child?'

'No, it's this woman's.'

'How is it you are rocking it?'

'She asked me to. She is dying.'

Though my supposition had proved erroneous, I continued to speak to her in the same sense. I began to ask her who she was and how she came to be in such a position. She told me her story willingly and very simply. She was of Moscow birth, the daughter of a factory workman. She had been left an orphan, and an aunt (now dead) had taken charge of her. From her aunt's she began to frequent the taverns. When I asked whether she would not like to change her way of life, my question evidently did not even interest her. How can the suggestion of anything quite impossible interest anybody? She giggled and said: 'Who would take me with a yellow ticket?'*

'Well, but suppose we found you a place as cook somewhere?' said I.

That idea suggested itself to me because she was a strong, flaxen-haired woman with a kindly, round face. There are cooks like that. My words obviously did not please her. She said:

'A cook! But I can't bake bread!' and she laughed. She said she could not, but I saw by the expression of her face that she did not wish to be a cook and despised that position and calling.

This woman, who like the widow in the Gospels had quite simply sacrificed her all for a sick neighbour, considered, as her companions did, that the position of a worker was degrading, and she despised it. She had been brought up to live without working and in the way that was considered natural by those around her. Therein lay her misfortune: this misfortune had led her into her present position and kept her there. That was what led her to sit in taverns. And which of us—man or woman—can cure her of that false view of life? Where among us are people who are convinced that an industrious life is always more to be respected than an idle one—people convinced of this and who live accordingly: valuing and respecting others on the basis of that conviction? Had I thought of this, I might have understood that neither I nor any one of those I knew could cure this disease.

I should have understood that those surprised and attentive faces that peered over the partition showed merely surprise at hearing sympathy expressed for them, but certainly not any hope of being cured of their immorality. They do not see the immorality of their lives. They know they are despised and abused, but cannot understand why. They have lived from childhood among other such women,

* The passport issued to a prostitute by the police.

29

who they know very well have always existed and do exist, and are necessary for society: so necessary that Government officials are appointed to see that they exist properly.* They know moreover that they have power over men and can often influence them more than other women can. They see that their position in society, though they are always abused, is recognized both by women and men and by the Government, and so they cannot even understand what there is for them to repent of and wherein they ought to amend. During one of our rounds a student told me of a woman in one of the lodgings who traded in her thirteen year-old daughter. Wishing to save the girl, I purposely went to that lodging. The mother and daughter were living in great poverty. The mother, a small, dark, forty-year-old prostitute, was not merely ugly but unpleasantly ugly. The daughter was equally unpleasant. To all my indirect questions about their way of life the mother replied curtly and with hostile distrust, evidently regarding me as an enemy. The daughter never answered me without first glancing at her mother, and evidently trusted her completely. They did not evoke in me cordial pity—rather repulsion; but yet I decided that it was necessary to save the daughter, and that I would speak to some ladies who take an interest in the wretched position of such women, and would send them here. Had I but thought of the long past life of that mother: of how she bore, nursed, and reared that daughter—in her position assuredly without the least help from others, and with heavy sacrifices—had I thought of the view that had been formed in her mind, I should have understood that in her action there was absolutely nothing bad or immoral: she had done and was doing all she could for her daughter—that is to say, just what she herself considered best. One might take the daughter from the mother by force, but one could not convince the mother that it was wrong of her to sell her daughter. To save her one ought long ago to have saved her mother—saved her from the view of life approved by everybody, which allows a woman to live without marriage, that is without bearing children and without working, serving only as a satisfaction for sensuality. Had I thought of that I should have understood that the majority of the ladies I wished to send here to save that girl themselves live without bearing children and without work, serving merely to satisfy sensuality and deliberately educate

* This is a reference to the licensing, inspection, and medical examination of brothels that was regularly carried on in Russia.

their daughters for such a life. One mother leads her daughter to the taverns, another takes hers to Court or to balls, but both share the same view of life: namely, that a woman should satisfy a man's lusts and that for that service she should be fed, clothed, and cared for. How then can our ladies save that woman or her daughter?

CHAPTER IX

STILL STRANGER was my relation towards the children. In my role of benefactor I noticed them too. I wished to save innocent beings from perishing in that den of depravity, and I wrote them down intending to occupy myself with them 'afterwards'.

Among them I was particularly struck by a twelve-year-old boy, Serëzha. He was a sharp, clever lad who had been living at a bootmaker's and was left homeless when his master was sent to prison. I was very sorry for the lad and wished to be of use to him.

I will tell how the help I gave him ended, for the story shows most clearly how false my position as a benefactor was. I took the boy home and put him in our kitchen. Was it possible to put a lousy boy taken from a den of depravity, among our own children? I considered myself very kind and good to let him inconvenience not me but our servants, and because we (not I but the cook) fed him, and because I gave him some cast-off clothes to wear. The boy stayed about a week. During that time I twice spoke a few words to him in passing, and while out for a walk called on a bootmaker I know and mentioned the boy to him as a possible apprentice. A peasant* who was staying with me invited the boy to live with him in the village as a labourer. The boy declined, and a week later disappeared. I went to Rzhánov House to inquire for him. He had been there, but was not at home when I called. That day and the day before he had gone to the Zoological Gardens, where he was hired for thirty kopeks a day to take part in a procession of costumed savages, who led an elephant about in some show they had on. I returned another day, but he was so ungrateful that he evidently avoided me. Had I then reflected on that boy's life and my own, I should have understood that he had been spoilt by learning the possibility of living an easy life

* Sutáev, of whom there is an account in Aylmer Maude's 'Life of Tolstoy'.

without work and by having become unaccustomed to work; and I, to benefit him and improve him, had taken him into my house where he saw—what? My own children—older than himself, and younger, and of his own age—never doing any work for themselves but giving all sorts of work to others: dirtying things, spoiling everything about them, overeating themselves with rich, tasty, and sweet food, breaking crockery, spilling things and throwing to the dogs food that to him appeared a delicacy. If I took him from a 'den' and brought him to a good place, he was right to assimilate the views of life existing in that good place; and from those views he understood that in a good place one must live merrily, eating and drinking tasty things without working. It is true he did not know that my children do the hard work of learning the declensions in Latin and Greek grammar, nor could he have understood the object of such work. But one cannot help seeing that had he understood that fact, the effect of my children's example on him would have been still stronger. He would then have understood that my children are being educated in such a way that without working now, they may be able in future, by the aid of their diplomas, to work as little as possible and command as much as possible of life's good things. And he understood this, and did not go with the peasant to tend cattle and live on potatoes and *kvas*, but went to the Zoological Gardens to dress as a savage and lead an elephant about for eightpence a day.

I might have understood how absurd it was of me, while educating my own children in complete idleness and luxury, to hope to correct other people and their children who were perishing from idleness in what I call the Rzhánov den, where at any rate three-fourths of the people work for themselves and for others. But I understood nothing of all that.

There were very many children in most wretched conditions in Rzhánov House: the children of prostitutes, orphans, and children who were taken about the streets by beggars. They were all very pitiful. But my experiment with Serëzha showed me that, living as I do, I could not help them. When Serëzha was living with us, I detected in myself a desire to hide our life, and especially our children's life, from him. I felt that all my efforts to guide him to a good industrious life were destroyed by the example we and our children set. To take a child from a prostitute or a beggar is very easy. It is very easy, when one has money, to have him washed, cleaned, and dressed in good clothes, well fed, and even taught various sciences; but for us who do not earn our own bread, to teach him to earn his bread is not merely difficult but impossible; for by our example, and even by that material bettering of his life which costs us nothing, we teach him the opposite. One may take a puppy, tend it, feed it, teach it to fetch and carry, and be pleased with it; but it is not enough to tend and feed a man and teach him Greek; one has to teach him to live: to take less from others and give more, but we, whether we take him into our house or put him into a Home founded for the purpose, cannot help teaching him the reverse.

CHAPTER X

THAT FEELING OF COMPASSION for people and aversion from myself that I had experienced at Lyápin House I no longer felt; I was quite filled with the wish to accomplish the business I had started—that of doing good to the people I met here. And strange to say, whereas it seemed that to do good—to give money to those in need—was a very good thing and should promote one's love of people, it turned out on the contrary that this business evoked in me ill-will towards people and condemnation of them. During the first round, in the evening, a scene occurred just like the one at Lyápin House; but it did not produce on me the same impression as at Lyápin House but evoked quite a different feeling.

It began when in one of the lodgings I really found an unfortunate who was in need of immediate aid. It was a hungry woman who had not had anything to eat for two days.

It was like this: in one very large, almost empty, night-lodging I asked an old woman whether there were any very poor people there, people who had nothing to eat. The old woman thought awhile, and then named two, but afterwards she seemed to remember something. 'Oh, yes, I fancy she is lying here,'said she, looking into one of the occupied bunks. 'Yes, this one, I fancy, has not had anything to eat.' 'Really? And who is she?' 'She was a strumpet, but nobody wants her now, so she gets nothing. The landlady has had pity on her, but now wants to turn her out. . . . Agáfya, eh, Agáfya!' cried the old woman.

We drew nearer and something on the bunk rose. It was a rather grey, dishevelled woman, lean as a skeleton, in a dirty, torn chemise, with particularly shining and fixed eyes. She looked past us with those fixed eyes; caught with her thin hand at a jacket lying behind her, in order to cover the bony breast exposed by her torn and dirty chemise, and ejaculated: 'What? What?' I asked her how she was getting on. It was long before she understood and replied: 'I don't myself know; they are turning me out.' I asked her—I am ashamed to write it down—whether it was true that she had not had anything to eat. With the same feverish rapidity she replied, still not looking at me: 'I did not eat yesterday and I have not eaten to-day.'

This woman's appearance touched me, but not at all as I had been touched at Lyápin House: there pity for those people made me at once feel ashamed of myself, while here I was glad to have found at last what I was looking for—someone who was hungry.

I gave her a ruble, and remember being very glad that others saw it. The old woman, seeing this, also asked me for money. It was so pleasant to give, that without considering whether it was or was not necessary, I gave to the old woman also. She then accompanied me on my way out, and some people standing in the corridor heard her thank me. Probably the questions I had asked about poverty had raised expectations, and some people were following us about. In the corridor again they began to ask me for money. There were among these people some evident drunkards who aroused an unpleasant feeling in me, but having given something to the old woman I had no right to refuse these and I began distributing money. While I gave, more and more people came up. Excitement arose in all the lodgings. On the staircases and in the galleries people appeared, watching me. As I came out into the yard a boy ran quickly down from one of the staircases, pushing through among the people. He did not see me and rapidly shouted, 'He gave Agáfya a ruble.' Having run down the stairs the boy joined the crowd that was following me. I went out into the street; various people walked with me and asked for money. I gave away what small change I had and went to a trading-stall there, asking the man who kept it to change ten rubles for me. And here there occurred what had happened at Lyápin House. A terrible confusion arose. Old women, broken-down gentry, peasants, and children, crowded to the stall holding out their hands; I gave them money and questioned some of them about their lives, entering them in my note-book. The owner of the stall, having turned in the fur corners of his winter overcoat, sat like a statue, occasionally glancing at the crowd and again directing his eyes past us. He evidently, like the rest, felt that it was stupid, but could not say so.

In Lyápin House I had been horrified by the wretchedness and degradation of the people and felt myself guilty, and felt a wish and a possibility of being better. But now a similar scene produced on me quite a different effect: I experienced, in the first place, a feeling of ill-will towards many of those who besieged me, and, secondly, I was uneasy as to what the shopkeepers and yard-porters thought of me.

On returning home that day I was ill at ease. I felt that what I was doing was stupid and immoral, and as always happens in consequence of an inner perplexity, I talked much about the business I had started, as though I did not at all doubt its success.

The next day I went alone to see those of the people I had noted down who seemed most to be pitied and whom I thought it would be easiest to help. As I have said, I did not really help any of them. To help them proved harder than I had expected. And whether because of my incompetence or because it really was impossible, I only disturbed them and did not help them. I visited Rzhánov House several times before the final Census-round was made, and the same thing happened each time. I was besieged by a crowd of suppliants among whom I was quite lost. I felt the impossibility of achieving anything because there were too many of them, and therefore felt angry with them for being so numerous; but besides that, taking them separately, they did not attract me. I felt that each of them was telling me lies or not telling the whole truth, and saw in me merely a purse from which money might be extracted. And it very often seemed to me that the money a man wheedled out of me would do him more harm than good. The oftener I went to the place and the more I got to know the people there the plainer the impossibility of doing anything became, but I did not abandon my enterprise till the last night of the Census.

I am particularly ashamed to remember that last visit. Previously I had gone alone, but now we went some twenty of us together. At seven o'clock those who wished to take part in this last night's round collected at my house. They were nearly all strangers to me: students, an officer, and two of my society acquaintances, who saying in the usual way '*C'est très intéressant!*' asked me to include them among the Census-takers.

My society acquaintances had dressed specially in shooting jackets and high travelling boots, a costume in which they went on hunting expeditions, and which in their opinion was adapted for a visit to the night-lodging-houses. They took with them peculiar note-books and extraordinary pencils. They were in that special state of excitement people are in when preparing for a hunt, a duel, or to start for the war. In their case the stupidity and falseness of our position was particularly noticeable, but the rest of us were in the same false situation. Before we started we held a consultation, like a council of war, as to how and with what to begin, how to divide our party, and so forth. The consultation was just like those which take place in councils, assemblies, and committees, that is to say, everybody spoke not because he had something that needed saying or because he wanted to learn something, but each devised something to say so as not to seem to lag behind the others. But in the course of these conversations no one referred to charity, of which I had spoken to them all so often. Abashed as I was, I felt that I must again refer to charity, that is to the need of entering up during our round all whom we found to be in a state of poverty. I had always felt ashamed to speak of this, but now, amid our excited preparations for the campaign, I could scarcely utter it. All listened to me as it seemed with regret, and at the same time all agreed verbally; but it was evident that they all knew it was folly and that nothing would come of it, and all immediately began to talk about something else. This continued till it was time to start and we drove off.

We arrived at the dark tavern, roused the attendants, and began to sort our papers. When we were told that the people had heard of our visit and were leaving the quarters, we asked the landlord to have the gates closed, and ourselves went out into the yard to reassure those who were leaving, telling them that no one would ask to see their passports.* I remember the strange and unpleasant impression those excited night-lodgers produced on me: tattered, half-dressed, by the light of the lamp in the dark yard all appearing to me to be tall; frightened and terrible in their fright they stood in a group near the stinking privy and heard our assurances but did not believe them.

* *To be without a passport, or to have a false one, was a serious offence in Russian law and police practice.*

Evidently, like hunted animals, they were ready for anything merely to escape from us. Gentlemen in various guises—as police-officers in town or country, as examining magistrates, and as judges—had harassed them all their lives in the towns and in the villages and on the highroads and in the streets and in taverns and dosshouses, and now suddenly these gentlemen had come and shut the gates on them merely to count them; it was as hard for them to believe this as it would be for hares to believe that dogs had come not to catch them but to count them. But the gates were closed, and the alarmed nightlodgers went back to their quarters, and having separated into groups we set to work. With me went the two society men and two students. Before us in the darkness went Ványa in overcoat and white trousers, carrying a lantern, and we followed him.

We visited lodgings I already knew and in which I also knew some of the lodgers, but most of the people were new and the spectacle was new and terrible—more terrible than I had seen at Lyápin House. All the lodgings were full, all the bunks were occupied, and often by two people. The sight was horrible from the way they were crowded together, and from the mingling of women and men. All the women who were not dead drunk were sleeping with men. Many women with children were sleeping with strange men on the narrow bunks. Terrible was the sight of these people's destitution, dirt, raggedness, and terror. And terrible, above all, was the immense number in this condition. One tenement, another, a third, a tenth, a twentieth, and no end to them! Everywhere the same stench, the same stifling atmosphere, the same overcrowding, the same mingling of the sexes, the same spectacle of men and women drunk to stupefaction, and the same fear, submissiveness, and culpability on all faces; and again I felt pained and ashamed of myself as I had done in Lyápin House, and I understood that what I had undertaken was horrid, stupid, and therefore impossible. And I no longer questioned anyone or took notes about anything, knowing that nothing would come of it.

I suffered profoundly. At Lyápin House I had been like one who happens to see a horrible sore on a man's body. He is sorry for the man and conscience-stricken at not having pitied him before, but he may still hope to help him. But now I was like a doctor who has come to the sufferer with his medicines, has uncovered his wound and chafed it, but has himself to admit that he has done it all in vain and that his medicine is of no use.

CHAPTER XI

THAT VISIT dealt the last blow to my self-deception. It became obvious to me that what I had undertaken was not merely stupid but horrid. Yet, though I knew this, it seemed to me that it would not do to throw up the whole affair at once. It seemed as if I was bound to go on, first, because by the article I had written and by my visits and promises I had raised hopes among the poor; and secondly, because I had also by my article and by conversations evoked the sympathy of charitable people, many of whom had promised to co-operate both with work and money. And I awaited applications from both classes, and meant to deal with them as best I could.

As to the needy, this is what occurred. I received more than a hundred letters and applications; these were all from the rich-poor, if I may use the expression. I went to see some of them, and to some I did not reply. Nowhere did I succeed in doing anything. All the applications were from people who had once occupied a privileged position (I mean a position in which a man receives from others more than he gives), had lost it, and wished to regain it. One wanted two hundred rubles to maintain his declining business and complete the education of his children; another wanted a photographic establishment; a third wanted his debts paid and to get his respectable clothes out of pawn; a fourth wanted a piano in order to perfect himself and to support his family by giving lessons. Most of them simply asked for help without defining how much money they wanted, but when one looked into what they wanted, it turned out that their needs grew in proportion to the amount of help available, and there was not and could not be any satisfying them. I repeat that this may have occurred because I did not know how to deal with them, but the fact remains that I helped nobody though in some cases I tried to.

As to the co-operation of the charitable, what happened seemed to me very strange and unexpected. Of all who promised me money for the poor and even fixed the amount, not one gave me a single ruble. From the promises given me I might have counted on receiving some three thousand rubles, but of all those people not one remembered the conversation or gave me a single farthing. Only the students gave

38

me what they received for their work on the census, which was, I think, twelve rubles. So that my whole undertaking, which was to have dealt with tens of thousands of rubles given by the rich and to have saved hundreds and thousands of people from poverty and vice, came merely to this: that I distributed haphazard some dozens of rubles to those who begged of me, and was left with twelve rubles in hand given by the students, and twenty five rubles allowed me by the Town Dúma for my work as organizer: which amounts I positively did not know what to do with.

The whole affair was at an end. On the Sunday of Carnival week, before leaving Moscow and going to the country, I went in the morning to Rzhánov House to get rid of those thirty-seven rubles by distributing them to the poor. I went to see those I knew in the tenements, and found only one sick man, to whom I gave something, five rubles I think. There was no one else there to give to. Of course many began begging. But I did not know them now any better than I had known them at first, and I decided to consult Iván Fedótych, the owner of the tavern, as to the disposal of the remaining thirty-two rubles. It was the first day of Carnival. Every one was dressed in his best, all had eaten enough, and many were tipsy. In the yard, by a corner of the house, in a torn peasant coat and bast-shoes, stood an old but still active rag-and-bone man sorting the booty in his basket, throwing the leather, iron, and other things, into different heaps, and trolling a merry song in a strong and excellent voice. I had a chat with him. He was seventy, lived by himself by his trade as rag-and-bone dealer, and not only did not complain, but said he had enough to eat and get drunk on. I asked him if there were any who were specially in need. He seemed vexed, and said plainly that none were in need except drunkards and lazybones, but on hearing of my aim, he asked me for five kopeks to get a drink with, and ran off to the tavern. I also went into the tavern to Iván Fedótych, to entrust him with the distribution of the remaining money. The tavern was full; gaudy and tipsy girls were going from door to door, all the tables were occupied, many were already drunk, and in a small room someone was playing a concertina and two people were dancing. Iván Fedótych out of respect for me ordered the dancing to cease, and sat down with me at a vacant table. I said that as he knew his lodgers and I was commissioned to distribute a little money, would he not point out to me those most in need? Good-natured Iván Fedótych (he died a year later), though busy with his trade, left it for a while to help me. He considered, and evidently felt puzzled. An elderly waiter heard what we were talking about and joined in our conference.

They began to go over the lodgers, some of whom I knew; but they could not agree. 'Paramónovna,' suggested the waiter. 'Yes, she goes hungry sometimes. But then she goes on the spree.' 'Well, what of that? All the same . . .' 'And Spiridón Ivánovich, he has children?' But Iván Fedótych had his doubts about Spiridón Ivánovich. 'Akulína? But she receives an allowance. How about the blind man?' To him I objected. I had just seen him. He was a blind man of eighty, without kith or kin. One would suppose no condition could be worse; but I had just seen him—he was lying drunk on a high featherbed and, not seeing me, he was abusing, in the filthiest language and in a terrible bass voice, the comparatively young woman with whom he co-habited. They then suggested a one-armed boy who lived with his mother. I noticed that Iván Fedótych was embarrassed owing to his conscientiousness, for he knew that at Carnival time whatever was given would all come back to him at the tavern. But I had to get rid of my thirty-two rubles, and I insisted, and somehow, well or ill, the money was at last disposed of. Those who received it were for the most part well dressed, and we had not to go far for them for they were there in the tavern. The one-armed boy appeared in high boots, a red shirt, and a waistcoat.

So ended my charitable activity, and I departed for the country, vexed with others—as is always the case—because I had myself done something stupid and bad. My charity came to nothing and quite ceased, but the flow of thoughts and feelings in me did not cease but went on with redoubled force.

CHAPTER XII

WHAT DID IT ALL MEAN?

I had lived in the country and had there been in touch with village poverty. Not out of humility which is more like pride, but to tell the truth which is necessary to make the whole trend of my thoughts and feelings comprehensible, I will mention that in the country I did very little for the poor, but the demands made on me there were so modest that even the little I did was of use to the people and created an atmosphere of love and satisfaction around me, amid which it was possible to soothe the gnawing consciousness of the wrongfulness of my way of life. When we moved to town I hoped to live in just the same way. But there I met poverty of quite a different kind. Town poverty was less truthful and more exacting and more cruel than village poverty. Above all, there was so much of it in one place that it produced a terrible impression on me. What I saw at Lyápin House made me at once realize the odiousness of my life. That feeling was sincere and very strong. But despite its sincerity and strength I was at first weak enough to fear the revolution it demanded in my life, and I compromised. I believed what everyone told me and what all have been saying since the world began, that there is nothing wrong in riches and luxury, which are God's gifts, and that one can help the needy without ceasing to be luxurious. I believed this and wished to do so. And I wrote the article in which I called on the rich for help. The rich all acknowledged themselves morally bound to agree with me, but evidently either did not wish or were unable to do anything, or give anything, for the poor. I began to visit the poor and saw what I had not at all expected. On the one hand in those dens—as I called them—I found people whom it was out of the question for me to help, for they were workers accustomed to work and to endure, and therefore possessed a far firmer hold on life than my own. On the other hand I saw unfortunates whom I could not help because they were just like myself. The majority of the unfortunates I saw were unfortunate only because they had lost the capacity, the wish, and the habit, of working for their bread. That is to say their misfortune consisted in being like me.

I could not find any unfortunates—sick, cold, or hungry—whom one could help at once, except the one starving woman Agáfya. And I became convinced that cut off as I was from the life of the people I wished to help, it would be almost impossible for me to find such unfortunates, for every case of real want was met by the very people among whom these unfortunates live, and above all, I became convinced that money would not enable me to alter the wretched life these people lead. I became convinced of all this, but from false shame at abandoning what I had begun, from self-deception as to my own beneficence, I continued for some time to go on with it till of itself it came to nothing, so that with much difficulty I managed somehow, with Iván Fedótych's aid, in the tavern in Rzhánov House, to get rid of those thirty-seven rubles which I did not consider belonged to me.

Of course I could have continued the affair and made of it a semblance of philanthropy. I could by persistency with those who had promised me money have obliged them to hand it over to me and could have collected still more, and could have distributed that money and consoled myself with my benevolent activity; but I saw on the one hand, that we rich people neither wish, nor are able, to set aside for the poor a part of our abundance (we have so many needs of our own), and that there is no one to give money to, if we wish only to do good and not merely to give away haphazard as I had done in the Rzhánov tavern. And I threw up the whole thing and with a feeling of despair left for the country.

There I wished to write an article about my experience and to explain why my undertaking had not succeeded. I wished to justify myself against the reproaches addressed to me concerning my article on the Census, and to indict society for its indifference and to state the causes which produce this urban poverty, and the need to counteract it, and also the means I saw for doing so.

I then began the article and thought it would contain much of value.

But try as I would, in spite of an abundance and superabundance of material, since I wrote under the influence of irritation, and had then not yet got rid of all that hindered my seeing the matter in a right light, and above all because I was not yet simply and clearly conscious of the cause of the whole matter (a very simple cause rooted in myself), I could not manage the article, and I did not finish it till the present year.*

In the moral sphere something occurs which is surprising and too little noticed.

If I tell a man who does not know it, anything I know of geology, astronomy, history, physics, or mathematics, he receives it as new information and never says to me: 'But what is there new about it? Everyone knows that and I have long known it'; but impart to a man the loftiest moral truth, expressed in the clearest and briefest form, as it has never before been expressed, and every ordinary man, especially one not interested in moral questions,

* The winter of 1885-6.

and especially one whom this moral truth strokes the wrong way, will certainly say: 'But who does not know that? That was known and uttered long ago.' It really seems to him that it was said long ago and in that very way. Only those to whom moral truths are serious and precious know how important and valuable they are, and by what prolonged efforts the simplification and elucidation of moral truth is reached—its transformation from dim, indefinitely conceived suppositions and wishes into firm and definite expressions inevitably demanding corresponding action.

We are all accustomed to think that moral teaching is a very empty and dull affair in which there can be nothing new or interesting, yet the whole life of man with all its complex and diverse activities—political, scientific, artistic, and commercial—which seem to be independent of morality, have no other purpose than the ever greater elucidation, confirmation, simplification, and diffusion, of moral truth.

I remember walking along a street once in Moscow and seeing a man come out of a shop, look attentively at the paving stones, select one of them, squat down over it and begin (as it seemed to me) to scrape or rub it with the greatest energy and ardour. 'What is he doing to the pavement?' thought I. Coming up to him I saw what he was doing. He was a lad out of a butcher's shop, and was whetting his knife on a paving stone. He was not thinking at all about the stones when he examined them, and was thinking still less about them while he was doing his job—he was simply whetting his knife. He had to sharpen his knife to cut meat with it, while it had seemed to me that he was doing something to the stones of the pavement. In just the same way, though it seems that mankind is occupied with commerce, treaties, wars, sciences, and arts, only one thing is important to humanity, and it is doing only that one thing: it is elucidating to itself the moral laws by which it lives. Moral laws exist; humanity merely elucidates them to itself, and this elucidation seems unimportant and insignificant to him who does not want moral law and does not wish to live by it. But this elucidation of the moral law is not only the chief, it is the sole business of humanity. This elucidation is unobserved, just as the difference between a dull knife and a sharp one may be unobserved. A knife is a knife, and for him who does not want to cut anything with that knife the difference between a dull and a sharp one passes unobserved. But for a man who has understood that his whole life depends on the dullness or sharpness of his knife, every whetting of it is important and he knows that there is no end to this sharpening, and that a knife is a knife only when it is sharp and can cut what needs cutting.

This happened to me when I began to write the present article. I thought I knew all and understood all about the questions evoked in me by the impressions received at Lyápin House and during the Census, but when I tried to realize and express them it turned out that the knife would not cut and had to be sharpened. And only now after three years do I feel that my knife has been sufficiently sharpened to enable me to cut what I want to. I have learnt very little that is new. My thoughts are the same, but they were duller, they dispersed easily and did not converge: they had no sting in them, and they did not unite into the one simplest and clearest conclusion, as they now do.

CHAPTER XIII

I REMEMBER that during the whole period of my fruitless attempt to aid the unfortunates in the town population I appeared to myself like one who wishes to draw another out of a bog but is himself standing in just such a bog. Each effort I made obliged me to realize the instability of the ground I stood on. I felt that I was myself in a bog, but this consciousness did not then cause me to examine more carefully beneath my feet to discover what I was standing on; I was all the time seeking external means of curing the evil around me.

I then felt that my life was bad and that it would not do to live so. But from the fact that my life was bad and that one must not live so, I did not draw the clear and simple conclusion that I must improve my way of life and live better, but drew the strange conclusion that to enable me to live better it was necessary to correct other people's lives; and so I began to correct them. I was living in town and wished to correct the life of other people living in the town, but I soon became convinced that I could not possibly do this, and I began to reflect on the nature of town-life and town-poverty.

'What is this town-life and town-poverty? Why, living in town, can I not help the town poor?' I asked myself. And I replied that I could do nothing for them, first, because there were too many there in one place, and secondly, because they were quite different from the poor in the villages. Why are there so many of them here, and in what do they differ from the poor of the villages? The reply to both questions was one and the same. There are many of them here because all who are unable to feed themselves in the villages collect here, around the rich, and their peculiarity is that they are people who have come from their village to feed themselves in the town.* (If there are any town poor who were born here and whose fathers and grandfathers were born here, those fathers and grandfathers came here to feed themselves.)

What is meant by 'feed oneself in town'? In the words 'to feed oneself in town' there is something strange, something resembling a joke, when one comes to consider it. How can people come from the country, that is, from where there are woods, and meadows, and grain, and cattle—all the wealth of the earth—to feed themselves in a place where trees, and grass, and even soil, are wanting, and where there are only stones and dust? What is meant by those words: 'feed oneself in the town', which are constantly used as though they were quite clear and comprehensible, both by those who are fed and by those who feed them?

I recall all the hundreds and thousands of town dwellers—some well off and some in poverty—with whom I talked about why they came there, and they all without exception said that

> Moscow neither sows nor reaps,
> But always has its wealth in heaps;

that there is plenty of everything in Moscow, and that therefore only in Moscow could they earn the money they needed in the country for grain, a cottage, a horse, and for articles of prime necessity. But yet the village is the source of all wealth and it is only there that real wealth is to be found: grain, and timber, and horses, and everything. Why come to town to obtain what is in the country? And why, above all, carry from the village to town what is needed by the villagers: flour, oats, horses, and cattle?

* *In English one would naturally say 'to get a living in the town', but it is here more convenient to use the Russian expression 'to feed themselves' because of what follows.*

Hundreds of times have I talked of this with peasants who were living in town, and from my talks with them and from my observation I have understood that the crowding of country folk into the towns is partly compulsory, because they cannot feed themselves otherwise, and partly voluntary, since the temptations of the town attract them. It is true that the condition of the peasant is such that to satisfy the demands made on him in the village he cannot avoid selling the grain and the cattle which he knows he will himself need, and so he is obliged, whether he likes it or not, to go to town to get his grain back again. But it is also true that the comparative ease with which money can be earned and the luxury of town-life attracts him thither, and that on the pretext of feeding himself in town he goes there to get easier work and to be better fed, to drink tea three times a day, to dress up, and even to get drunk and live dissolutely. The cause of both is the same: the passing of wealth from the producers into the hands of non-producers and its accumulation in towns. And really when autumn comes all the wealth is collected in the village. And immediately come demands for taxes, conscription, rents, and also the temptations of vodka, weddings, fêtes, itinerant pedlars, and other things; and in one way or another that wealth in its diverse forms—sheep, calves, cows, horses, pigs, fowls, eggs, butter, hemp, flax, rye, oats, buckwheat, peas, and hemp-seed and linseed—passes into the hands of other people and is carried to the towns and from the towns to the cities. The villager, obliged to part with all this to satisfy the demands and temptations presented to him, having given up his wealth remains in want and has to go to the place to which his wealth has been carried, and there he tries partly to secure the money he needs to get what is of prime necessity in the country, and partly, carried away by the temptations of the town, he himself with others indulges in what the town has to offer.

Everywhere in Russia, and I think not in Russia only but throughout the world, this goes on. The wealth of the country producers passes into the hands of dealers, landowners, officials, and manufacturers, and those who receive this wealth wish to enjoy it. And they can only enjoy it fully in town. In the village, on account of the distance at which people live, it is difficult, in the first place, to satisfy all the requirements of the rich; there are not all the workshops, stores, banks, restaurants, theatres, and all kinds of social amusements. Secondly, one of the chief pleasures furnished by riches—vanity, the desire to surprise and outshine others—is also difficult to secure in the country, again on account of the sparseness of the population. In the village connoisseurs of luxury are lacking—and there is no one to astonish. No matter what adornments of the house, what pictures or bronzes a dweller in the village may procure, or what carriages or toilets—there is no one to admire them or envy them—for the peasants do not understand anything about it. Thirdly, luxury in the country is even disagreeable and dangerous to a man who has a conscience and fear. It is uncomfortable and uncanny in the country to have a milk bath, or to feed puppies on milk, when near by there are children who need it; it is uncomfortable and uncanny to build pavilions and lay out gardens among people who live in huts surrounded by manure, and who lack fuel. In the village there is no one to keep the stupid peasants in order, who in their ignorance may destroy all this.

And so the rich people gather together in the towns and settle near other rich people who have similar tastes: where the gratification of every luxurious taste is carefully guarded by numerous police. The core of such town-dwellers are the government officials; around them all sorts of workmen and traders have settled down, and they are joined by the rich. There a rich man only wishes for anything and it will be supplied. There too it is pleasanter for a wealthy man to live because there he can satisfy his vanity, there is someone to vie with in luxury, someone to astonish and to outshine. Above all, it is better for a rich man in town because formerly, in the village, he was uncomfortable and felt ill at ease on account of his wealth, but now on the contrary it would be uncomfortable not to live luxuriously as all the people around him do. What seemed frightening and awkward in the country, here seems to him quite proper. The rich assemble in town and there, under the protection of the authorities, calmly demand all that has been brought thither from the country. The villager is partly obliged to go where this continual holiday of the rich is going on and where what has been taken from him is being used up, in order to feed on the crumbs that fall from the rich man's table, and partly—seeing the easy and luxurious life of the rich which is approved and defended by everybody—he wants to arrange his own life so as to work less and enjoy the labour of others more.

So he makes his way to town and looks round where the rich people are, and tries by all means to get back from them what he needs, submitting to all the conditions they impose on him. He assists in the satisfaction of all their whims; and he or she attends on the rich in the baths, in the restaurants, as cabman, or as prostitute, and makes carriages, and toys, and fashionable dresses, and gradually learns from the rich man to live like him not by work but by obtaining from others by various expedients the riches they have accumulated—and so he becomes perverted and perishes. And it was this population perverted by city-wealth which forms the town-poverty I wished to aid but was unable to deal with.

And indeed one need but consider the position of those country folk who come to town to earn money for bread or for taxes, when they see everywhere around them the insanely squandered thousands and the easily acquired hundreds, while they themselves have to earn kopeks by heavy toil, to be surprised that any of them remain working people, and that they do not all turn to the easier ways of obtaining money, by trading, cattle-dealing, mendicancy, vice, fraud, or even robbery.

You know it is only we who share in the unceasing orgy that goes on in the towns, who can be so accustomed to it that it seems to us natural for one person to live in five enormous rooms heated by fuel enough to cook the food and warm the lodgings of twenty families; to employ two horses and two attendants to carry us half a mile; to cover our parquet-floors with rugs, and to spend, I will not say five or ten thousand rubles on a ball, but say twenty-five rubles on a Christmas Tree, and so on. But a man who needs ten rubles for bread for his family, or whose last sheep is being taken to pay a seven-ruble tax and who cannot obtain the money even by heavy toil, cannot get accustomed to it. We think it all seems natural to the poor. There are even people naïve enough to say that the poor are very grateful to us for feeding them by our luxury. But being poor does not deprive men of reason, and they reason as we do. When *we* hear of a man losing or squandering ten or twenty thousand rubles, we immediately think, 'What a foolish and good-for-nothing fellow he is to squander so much money uselessly, and how well I could have used that money for a building I have long wanted, or to improve my farm,' and so forth; and the poor reason just in the same way when they see wealth senselessly wasted, and they do it the more insistently since they need the money not to satisfy some caprice but to supply things they urgently need. We are much mistaken when we think that the poor can fail to see this, and can calmly look at the luxury surrounding them.

They never have admitted and never will admit that it is right for some to have a continual holiday while others must always fast and work. At first it astonishes and angers them to see it. Then they grow accustomed to it; and seeing that such arrangements are considered legitimate, they themselves try to avoid work and to share in the perpetual holiday. Some succeed and become such ever-feasting folk, others gradually insinuate themselves into an approach to that position, others again break down without having attained their aim, and having lost the habit of working, fill the brothels and doss-houses.

Two years ago we took a peasant lad from the village as a manservant. He did not get on with the footman and was dismissed. He found a place with a merchant, satisfied his master, and now goes about in showy boots and wearing a chain across his waistcoat. In his place we engaged a married peasant. He took to drink and lost some money. We engaged a third man. He was intemperate, and having drunk all his clothes, loafed for a long time about the doss-houses. An old man-cook took to drink in town and fell ill. A footman who used to drink desperately, but who in the country had avoided vodka for five years, took to drink again last year while living in Moscow without his wife who used to restrain him, and he ruined his whole life. A lad from our village is living with my brother as manservant. His grandfather, a blind old man, came to me while I was staying in the country and asked me to shame his grandson into sending ten rubles towards the payment of the taxes, as otherwise he would have to sell his cow. 'He always says: one has to dress properly,'said the old man; 'well, he has got himself boots and that is enough, or else what is it he wants? Does he want to have a watch?'said the grandfather, expressing by those words the insanest proposition he could think of. The proposition was indeed senseless if one knew that the old man had gone through the whole of Lent without being able to afford any oil with his food, and that he was losing the wood he had cut because he was unable to pay a ruble and twenty kopeks he owed; but it turned out that the old man's insane jest was an actual fact. The lad came to me in a black overcoat of good cloth and wearing boots for which he had paid eight rubles. A few days earlier he had taken ten rubles in advance from my brother and had bought the boots. And my children, who have known the lad since childhood, tell me that he really considers it necessary to provide himself with a watch. He is a very good-natured lad, but he thinks he will be laughed at till he has a watch. So a watch is necessary. This year in our house a housemaid, a girl of eighteen, had an affair with the coachman. She was dismissed. Our old nurse, with whom I spoke about it, reminded me of another poor girl whom I had forgotten. She too during our short stay in Moscow ten years ago had an affair with a footman. She also was dismissed, and ended in a brothel, dying of syphilis in the hospital before she was twenty. We only need look around us to be horrified at the infection which—not to speak of the factories and workshops that serve our luxury—we by our luxury directly and immediately diffuse among the very people we afterwards wish to help.

And so looking into the nature of the town poverty I was unable to help, I saw that its first cause was that I collect what the country folk need and take it to town. The second cause was that here in town, by means of what I have collected in the country, I by my insensate luxury tempt and corrupt those country folk who follow me to town in order to get back somehow or other what was taken from them in the village.

CHAPTER XIV

FROM QUITE AN OPPOSITE SIDE I came to the same conclusion. Remembering all my relations with the city poor during that period, I saw that one reason I was unable to help them was that they were insincere and untruthful with me. They all regarded me not as a man but as a means. I could not get into touch with them: perhaps, thought I, I do not know how to; but without sincerity it was impossible to help them. How can one help a man who does not tell one his whole position? At first I blamed them for this (it is so natural to blame others), but a single word from a remarkable man—namely, Sutáev,* who was staying with me at the time, explained the case to me and showed me where the cause

* Sutáev (previously alluded to) was a peasant sectarian whom Tolstoy held in high esteem.

of my failure lay. I remember that Sutáev's remark struck me forcibly even then, but I only understood its full significance later. It was at the time when my self-delusion was at its height. I was sitting at my sister's; Sutáev also was there and my sister was asking me about my enterprise. I began telling her and, as always happens when one is not sure of what one is doing, I told her with great enthusiasm, warmth, and verbosity, both what I was doing and what might come of it. I told her how we were going to look after the orphans and old folk, to send back to their villages peasants who could not get on in town; how we should make the path of reform easy for the vicious, and how, if only this affair succeeded, not a single man in Moscow would be left without help. My sister sympathized with me and we talked about it. During this conversation I glanced at Sutáev. Knowing his Christian life and the importance he attaches to charity, I expected his approval and spoke so that he should understand me. I addressed my sister, but what I said was meant rather for him. He sat immovable in his blacktanned sheepskin coat which, peasant-fashion, he wore indoors as well as out of doors, but he seemed not to hear us and to be absorbed in his own thoughts. His small eyes were dim as though directed inwards. Having said my say, I turned to him and asked what he thought of it.

'It's all useless,' said he.

'Why?'

'The whole Society you're starting will be no use, and no good will come of it,' repeated he with conviction.

'Why not? Why will it be no use to help thousands, or even hundreds, of unfortunates? Is it wrong to clothe the naked and feed the hungry as the Gospel tells us to?'

'I know, I know! But you're not doing the right thing. Is that the way to help? You go out walking and a man asks you for twenty kopeks. You give it. Is that charity? Give him spiritual charity, teach him! But what have you done? Merely got rid of him!'

'No, that's not what we are talking about. We want to find out the need that exists, and to help with money and work and find employment for those who require it.'

'You won't do anything with those people that way.'

'What do you mean? Are they to be left to die of cold and hunger?'

'Why should they die? Are there so many of them?'

'Many of them!' said I, thinking he treated the matter so lightly because he did not know what an immense number there were. 'Do you know that in Moscow alone there are, I suppose, some twenty thousand cold and hungry people? And in Petersburg, and in other towns . . .!'

He smiled.

'Twenty thousand! And how many homes are there in Russia alone? A million?'

'Well, what of it?'

'What of it!' His eyes gleamed, and he became animated. 'Why, let us divide them among us. I am not rich, but I will at once take two. There is that lad you had in your kitchen. I have asked him, but he won't come. If there were ten times as many we could place them all. You take one, I'll take another. We could go to work together. He would see how I work, and would learn how to live. We would sit at one table and he would hear a word now from me and now from you. That is charity, but your scheme is quite useless.'

This simple remark struck me. I could not but acknowledge its justice; but it then seemed to me that, though it was true, what I had begun might perhaps also be useful. But the farther I went with the affair and the more I came in contact with the poor, the oftener I remembered those words and the more significance for me did they acquire. Indeed, I drive up in an expensive fur coat, or in my own carriage; or a man who has no boots sees my two thousand ruble lodgings, or even merely sees that I give away five rubles without regret because it comes into my head to do so; and he knows that if I give away rubles like that, it is because I have collected many and have a lot of superfluous ones I have not given away but on the contrary have extracted with ease from other people. What can he see in me but a man who has taken what ought to be his? And what feeling can he have towards me but a desire to get back as many as possible of the rubles I have taken from him and from others? I want to get into touch with him, and complain that he is not frank; but I fear to sit on his bed lest I should get lice or be infected, and I dare not let him into my room. When he comes, hungry, to see me, he has to wait in the hall (if he is lucky) or in the porch. Yet I say he is to blame that I cannot get into touch with him and that he is not frank!

Let the most cruel of men try to gorge himself on five-course dinners among people who have eaten little and eat only black bread.

No one will find it possible to eat and see the hungry folk licking their lips. So, to be able to eat tasty food where there are hungry people, it is first of all necessary to hide oneself from them and eat where they cannot see one. And that is just what we do first of all.

And I looked more simply at our life and saw that to come in close touch with the poor is not difficult for us just by accident, but that we purposely arrange our life so as to make such contact difficult.

More than this, standing on one side to look at our life—the life of the rich—I saw that all that is considered as welfare in our life, consists in, or at any rate is inseparably bound up with, what separates us as far as possible from the poor. Indeed all the efforts of our wealthy life, beginning with food, clothes, dwellings, our cleanliness, and even our very education—have as their chief aim to segregate us from the poor. And on thus dividing ourselves—separating ourselves with impassable walls—from the poor, at least nine tenths of our wealth is spent. The first thing a man who gets rich does is to cease to eat out of the common bowl;* he gets crockery, and separates himself from the kitchen and the servants.

He feeds his servant well that her saliva may not flow at sight of his tasty food, and he eats by himself: but as it is dull eating alone, he devises ways of improving the food and decorating the table, and the very manner of taking our food (dinners) becomes a subject of vanity and pride; and the way of partaking of food becomes a way of separating himself from others. It is unthinkable for a rich man to invite a poor man to his table. One must know how to take a lady to table, how to bow, to sit, to eat, to use a finger-bowl, and only the rich know how to do all that. The same occurs with clothes. If a rich man wore simple clothes merely to protect his body from the cold: an overcoat, a sheepskin, felt and leather boots, a peasant coat, trousers, and shirt—he would need very little, and he could not, if he had two sheepskins, refuse to give one to a man who had none; but a rich man begins by having apparel made for him which consists of several articles and is only suitable for special occasions and therefore will not do for a poor man. He has dress-coats, vests, pea-jackets, patent leather shoes, capes, shoes with French heels, fashionable clothes composed of small pieces, hunting dress, travelling jackets, and so forth, which

* In a Russian peasant family it is usual for all to eat out of one common family bowl, each with his own wooden spoon.

are suitable only in conditions remote from poverty. Thus clothes also become a means of separation from the poor. Fashion makes its appearance, which is just what separates the rich from the poor. It is the same, even more clearly, with our dwelling places. In order to live alone in ten rooms it is necessary that this should not be seen by those who are living ten in a room. The richer a man is the more difficult it is to make one's way to him—the more porters there are between him and the poor, and the less possible is it to take a poor man over his carpets and seat him in a satin chair. It is the same with means of conveyance. A peasant driving in a cart or on a carrier's sledge must be very harsh not to give a lift to a traveller on foot—there is room and opportunity for him to do so. But the finer the carriage the more remote the possibility of giving a lift to anyone. Some of the smartest vehicles are even named 'sulkys'.

The same is true of the whole manner of life expressed by the word cleanliness.

Cleanliness! Who does not know people, especially women, who make a great virtue of this cleanliness? And who does not know the devices of this cleanliness, which are endless when obtained by the labour of others? Who among those who have become rich does not know by experience with what difficulty and trouble he accustomed himself to this cleanliness, which only confirms the proverb, 'White hands love other people's work'?

To-day cleanliness consists in changing one's shirt every day; to-morrow in changing twice a day. To-day in washing one's neck and hands every day; to-morrow one's feet also, after tomorrow one's whole body each day and with some special friction besides. To-day one has a table-cloth for two days; to-morrow a fresh one every day; and then two a day. To-day the footman's hands must be clean; to-morrow he must wear clean gloves, and in clean gloves must bring in a letter on a clean tray. And there are no limits to this cleanliness when it is obtained by other people's labour—and which is of no use to anyone except as a means of separating oneself from others and making intercourse with them impossible.

More than that, when I looked into the matter I became convinced that the same thing is true of what is generally called education.

Language does not deceive; it calls by its true name what people understand by that name. What the common folk call 'education' is, fashionable dress, refined conversation, clean hands, and a particular kind of cleanliness. Of such a man in contradistinction to others, they say that he is an 'educated man'. In a rather higher circle they mean by 'education' the same that is meant among the people, but to the conditions of 'education' are added piano-playing, a knowledge of French, ability to write a Russian letter without mistakes in spelling, and yet more external cleanliness. In a still higher circle by 'education' is meant all this, with the addition of a knowledge of English, and a diploma from one of the higher educational institutions, and a yet higher degree of cleanliness. But the first, the second, and the third kind of education are essentially one and the same. 'Education' consists of those forms and that knowledge which will separate a man from others. Its object is the same as that of cleanliness—to separate us from the mass of the poor, in order that those cold and hungry people may not see how we make holiday. But to hide oneself is impossible, and they do see.

And thus I became convinced that the reason it was impossible for us, the rich, to help the town poor, lay also in the impossibility of coming into close touch with them, and that this impossibility we ourselves create by our whole life and by the whole use we make of our wealth. I became convinced that between us—the rich—and the poor there stands a wall of cleanliness and education that we have erected and reared by our wealth, and to be able to aid the poor we have first of all to destroy that wall, so that we might apply Sutáev's method of distributing the poor among us. And from this side, too, I reached the same conclusion to which the course of my reflections on town poverty had brought me: that the cause of that poverty is our wealth.

CHAPTER XV

I BEGAN TO EXAMINE the matter from yet another side—the purely personal one. Among the things which particularly struck me during the time of my philanthropic activity there was a very strange one, for which I was long unable to find an explanation. It was this: every time it chanced, in the street or at home, that I gave some small coin to a pauper without talking to him, I saw, or it seemed to me that I saw, pleasure and gratitude on his face and I myself experienced a pleasant sensation at such times. I saw that I had done what the man wanted and expected of me. But if I stopped to speak to the man, and questioned him sympathetically about his former and his present life, entering more or less into detail, I felt that I could not give him three or twenty kopeks, and I began rummaging in my purse, doubting how much to give, and always gave him more, and always saw that the man went away dissatisfied. If I entered into still closer communication with him my doubts as to how much to give increased still more, and no matter what I gave the man became yet more gloomy and more dissatisfied. As a general rule it turned out that if after closer contact with a poor man I gave him three rubles or more, I nearly always saw gloom, dissatisfaction, and even resentment on his face, and it even happened that when I had given ten rubles he went away without even saying thank you, as though I had offended him. And on such occasions I always felt ill at ease, ashamed of myself, and guilty. If I kept in touch with a poor man for weeks, months, and years, and helped him, told him my views, and came into close touch with him, my relations with him became a torment and I saw that the poor man despised me. And I felt that he was right to do so.

If I go along the street and he, standing there, begs three kopeks of me among others walking or driving past, and I give it him, I am for him a passer-by and a good, kindly passer-by—one who gives a thread towards making a shirt for the naked. He expects nothing more than a thread, and if I give it he blesses me sincerely. But if I stop with him, talk to him as to a fellow man, and show that I wish to be more than a passer-by to him; if as often happens he weeps while telling me his woe, he no longer regards me merely as a passer-by, but sees what I want him to see in me—a kindly man. But if I am a kindly man my kindness cannot stop at twenty kopeks, or at ten rubles, or at ten thousand. It is impossible to be good-natured only a little. Suppose I have given him much—set him up, clothed him, put him on his feet so that he may live without depending on others, but for some reason—misfortune or his own weakness and viciousness—he again lacks the overcoat, linen, and money which I gave him—is again hungry and cold and has again come to me—why should I refuse him? If the reason of my activity is to attain a certain material result: to give him so many rubles or such and such an overcoat, I might, once I had given them, be at rest; but the reason of my activity is not that, its reason is that I wish to be a kindly man, that is to say I wish to see myself in every other man. Everyone understands kindliness in this way and not otherwise. And therefore if he drinks all you give him twenty times over, and if he is again cold and hungry, you—if you are a kindly man—cannot help giving to him again, and can never cease giving if you have more than he has. And if you draw back, you thereby show that all you did you did not because you were a kindly man, but because you wished to seem kindly in his eyes and in the eyes of others.

And with such people, from whom I had to draw back and cease giving and thereby renounce kindliness, I experienced a tormenting sense of shame.

What was that shame? I felt it at Lyápin House, and before and after that in the village whenever I happened to give money or other things to the poor, and during my visits to the town poor.

One recent instance of this shame vividly reminded me of it and supplied me with an explanation of the shame I experienced when giving money to the poor.

It occurred in the country. I wanted twenty kopeks to give to a pilgrim, and sent my son to borrow them from someone; he brought the pilgrim the money and told me he had got it from our man-cook. A few days later some more pilgrims came and I again wanted twenty kopeks. I had a ruble, and remembering that I owed money to the cook, I went to the kitchen hoping to get change. I said: 'I borrowed twenty kopeks of yours, here's a ruble. . . .' Before I had finished speaking he called his wife from the next room and said: 'Take it, Parásha.' Thinking she understood what I wanted, I handed her the ruble. I must mention that the cook had been with us only a week and though I had seen his wife I had never spoken to her. Just as I was going to ask her for the change, she quickly bent over my hand and wished to kiss it,* evidently supposing that I was giving her the ruble. I muttered something, and left the kitchen. I felt ashamed—more painfully ashamed than I had done for years. I even writhed and was conscious of making grimaces, and I groaned with shame as I ran out of the kitchen.

* A common way of expressing gratitude in Russia.

This shame, which seemed to me quite undeserved and unexpected, startled me, especially as it was long since I had experienced such a feeling, and because it seemed to me that I, as an old man, was living in a way that did not deserve such shame. It struck me very much. I mentioned the occurrence to my family and to some acquaintances, and they all agreed that they would have felt as I did. And I began to ask myself why it had made me feel ashamed. An incident that had happened to me previously in Moscow supplied me with the answer.

I pondered on that incident, and the shame I had felt with the cook's wife became intelligible, and all the feelings of shame experienced during my period of Moscow charity, and which I now constantly experience when I happen to give people anything more than such petty contributions to mendicants and pilgrims as I am accustomed to give and consider not as charity but as decency and politeness. If a man asks you for a light, you must light a match for him if you have one. If a man asks for three or twenty kopeks, or even for a few rubles, you must give it if you have it. It is a matter of politeness and not of charity.

The incident was this: I have already mentioned two peasants with whom, two years ago, I used to saw wood. One Saturday evening, in the dusk, I was walking with them to town. They were going to their master to get their wages. Near the Dragomílov Bridge we met an old man. He asked for alms and I gave him twenty kopeks. As I gave it I thought that my charity would have a good effect on Semën, with whom we had been talking of divine things. Semën was that Vladímir peasant who had a wife and two children in Moscow. He also stopped, turned up the skirt of his long coat, drew out his purse, and rummaging in it, took out a three-kopek piece which he gave to the old man, asking for two kopeks change. The old man showed that he had two three-kopek pieces and a one-kopek. Semën looked at these, and was on the point of taking the one kopek, but changed his mind, took off his cap, made the sign of the cross, and went on, leaving the old man the three kopeks. I knew Semën's position. He had no house and no property. His earnings up to the day when he gave those three kopeks amounted to six rubles and fifty kopeks. So that six rubles and fifty kopeks represented his total savings. My savings equalled about six hundred thousand rubles. I had a wife and children and so had Semën. He was younger than I and had fewer children; but his children were young while I had two already old enough to work, so that apart from our savings our positions were alike; perhaps mine was even somewhat the better. He gave three kopeks, I gave twenty. What had he and what had I given? What ought I to have given to match his gift? He had six hundred kopeks: he gave one of them, and then two more. I had six hundred thousand rubles. To do what he did, I should have given three thousand rubles and asked for two thousand rubles change, and if there was no change I should have left those two thousand rubles also, made the sign of the cross, and gone on my way; quietly talking of how factory hands live and of the price of liver on the Smolénsk market. I thought of this at the time, but only much later was I able to draw from that instance the conclusion inevitably flowing from it. That conclusion seems so unusual and strange that despite its mathematical certainty one needs time to grow accustomed to it. It always seems as if there must be some mistake about it, but there is none. There is only the terrible fog of delusion in which we live.

That deduction, when I reached it and recognized its certainty, explained to me my feeling of shame with the cook's wife and with all the poor people to whom I gave, or give, money.

What indeed is this money I give to the poor, and which the cook's wife thought I was giving to her? In most cases it is such a small fraction of my property that it cannot be expressed in figures intelligible to Semën or to the cook's wife; it is generally about a one-millionth part. I give so little that for me it is not and cannot be a deprivation; it is only a diversion indulged in when and as I please. And that was how the cook's wife understood me. If I give a ruble or a twenty-kopek piece to a man from the street, why should I not give her a ruble? To give away money like that is in her eyes the same as for gentlefolk to throw gingerbreads among a crowd to be scrambled for; it is an amusement for those who possess much 'mad money'. I was ashamed because the mistake she made showed me plainly how she, and all poor people, must regard me: 'He throws mad (that is, unearned) money about.'

What indeed is my money, and where has it come from? Part of it I have got from the land I inherited from my father. A peasant sells his last sheep or cow to pay it to me. The other part of my money

I have got for my writings, for books. If my books are harmful I only place temptation in the path of those who buy them and the money I receive is ill-gotten; but if my books are of use the case is still worse. I do not give them to people, but say, 'Give me seventeen rubles,* and then I will let you have them.' And as in the former case the peasant sold his last sheep, so here a poor student, a teacher, or any poor man, deprives himself of things he needs, to give me that money. And I have thus got together much money, and what do I do with it? I bring it to town and give some of it to the poor if they also come to town and obey my whims and clean the pavement and my lamps and boots, and work for me in factories. For this money I get all I can out of them: that is, I try to give them as little, and to take as much, as possible. And quite unexpectedly, without any particular reason, I suddenly begin giving away this same money to those same poor people; not to all of them, but to some whom I select. How can each of them help thinking that perhaps he may have the luck to be one of those with whom I shall amuse myself when I distribute my mad money?

That is how they all regard me, and how the cook's wife also regarded me. And I was so greatly deluded that I called 'doing good', this chucking away farthings with one hand to those whom it pleased me to select, while gathering thousands from the poor with the other! It is not surprising that I felt ashamed.

Yes, before doing good I must myself stand aside from evil, in conditions where one may cease to do evil. For my whole life is evil. I might give away a hundred thousand rubles and still not be in a position to do good, for I should still have five hundred thousand left. Only when I have nothing left shall I be in a position to do even a little good, if but as much as the prostitute who for three days looked after the sick woman and her baby. And that had seemed to me so little! And I dared to think of doing good! What I felt from the first at the sight of the hungry and cold people at Lyápin House: namely, that I was to blame for it, and that one could not, could not, *could not* go on living as I was doing, was the one thing that was really true!

What then must we do? To this question, if anyone still needs an answer, I will, God willing, furnish a detailed reply.

* *The price of Tolstoy's collected works at that time.*

CHAPTER XVI

IT WAS HARD for me to realize this, but when I came to it I was horrified at the delusion in which I had been living. I was up to my ears in the mire, yet thought I could drag others out of it.

What indeed do I want? I want to do good, to arrange that people should not be cold or hungry but should live in a way fit for human beings.

I want this, and I see that by violence, extortion, and various devices in which I participate, the workers' bare necessities are taken from them, while the non-workers (of whom I am one) consume in superfluity the fruits of the labour of those who toil.

I see that this exploitation is so arranged that the more cunning and complex the devices a man employs (or which those from whom he inherits have employed) the more he commands of the work of others and the less he works himself.

First comes a Stieglitz,* a Derviz,* a Morózov,† a Demídov,‡ a Yusúpov,** and then the great bankers, merchants, landowners, and officials. Then the middle-sized bankers, merchants, officials, and landowners—of whom I am one. Then the lower order of petty traders, inn-keepers, usurers, police officers and constables, school teachers, chanters, and business clerks; then the houseporters, footmen, coachmen, water-carriers, cabmen, and pedlars; and then at last come the working people, the factory-hands and peasants, who in number are to the others as ten to one. I see that the life of nine-tenths of the people—the workers—demands by its nature strain and labour as all natural life does, but that in consequence of the various devices which deprive these people of necessities and make their life hard, it becomes worse and more full of privations

* *Prominent financiers and railway concessionaires in Russia when Tolstoy was writing this book.* † *The Morózovs were very wealthy cotton-mill owners, of peasant origin.* ‡ *The Demídovs were the enormously wealthy founders of the mining industry in Russia.* ** *The Princes Yusúpov were very large landowners, having held important official positions from the time of Peter the Great. They are descendants of a Khan of the Nogáy tribe.*

year by year, while our life—the life of the nonworkers—by the help of science and art directed to that aim, becomes each year more superabundant, attractive, and secure.

I see that in our time working folk, especially the old men, women, and children, simply perish from intense labour and insufficient nourishment, and that they are not sure of obtaining even the most elementary necessities; while side by side with this the non-working class, of which I am a member, is year by year more and more provided with superfluities and luxuries, becomes yet more and more secure, and has finally, among its lucky members (of whom I am one), reached such a degree of security as in olden times people only dreamt of in fairy tales. We have reached the condition of the owner of the magic inexhaustible purse; that is to say, a condition in which a man is not only completely freed from the law of labour for the support of life, but is able without labour to avail himself of all life's bounties and to hand on that magic inexhaustible purse to his children or to whom he pleases. I see that the produce of man's toil passes more and more from the labouring people to those who do no labour, and that the pyramid of the social structure is, as it were, reconstructed so that the foundation stones pass to the top, and the rapidity of this movement increases almost in geometrical progression. I see that what is happening is as though in an ant-hill the society of ants were to lose its sense of a common law, and some ants began to carry the produce of toil from the bottom of the heap to the top, ever narrowing the base and enlarging the top and so compelling the other ants to shift from the base to the top. I see that the ideal of an industrious life has been replaced by the ideal of a magic purse. The rich, and I among them, have by various devices obtained that magic purse for themselves, and to enjoy it we move to town—that is, to the place where nothing is grown but everything is consumed. The poor labouring man who is plucked that the rich man may have this magic purse, tries to follow him to town, and there also takes to tricks, and either secures a position in which while working little he obtains much, thus laying yet more burdens on the working folk; or, not reaching such a position, he perishes and becomes one of those cold and hungry inmates of the night-lodging-houses—who are increasing in number with extraordinary rapidity.

I belong to the class who by various devices deprive the working people of necessities, and who by these devices have provided a magic purse for themselves which is a temptation to those same unfortunates. I want to aid people, and therefore it is clear, above all, that I should not pluck them as I am doing, and on the other hand I should not tempt them. Otherwise, by most complex cunning and cruel devices, which have been elaborated through the ages, I have arranged for myself the condition of any owner of a magic purse, that is, a condition which enables me, without ever doing any work, to compel hundreds and thousands of people to work for me—as I am doing; and I imagine that I pity people and wish to help them. I sit on a man's back, choking him and making him carry me, and yet assure myself and others that I am very sorry for him and wish to ease his lot by all possible means—except by getting off his back.

It is really so simple. If I want to aid the poor, that is, to help the poor not to be poor, I ought not to make them poor. But as it is, at my own choice I give away to the poor who have strayed from the path of life, rubles, or tens or hundreds of rubles; but of exactly such rubles I take thousands from people who have not yet strayed from the path, and thus make them poor and also pervert them.

It is very plain; yet it was terribly difficult for me to understand it fully without any compromises or excuses which would justify my position; but as soon as I acknowledged my guilt all that had before seemed strange, complicated, obscure, and insoluble, became quite intelligible and simple. Above all, my own path of life resulting from this explanation became simple, clear and agreeable, instead of being tangled, insoluble, and tormenting, as it had been before.

Who am I who wish to help people? I wish to help people and—having got up at noon, after playing bridge with four candles on the table—enfeebled, pampered, needing the aid and service of hundreds of people, I came to help – whom? People who rise at five o'clock, sleep on boards, feed on bread and cabbage, are able to plough, to mow, to fix an axe-handle, to plane, to harness a horse, and to sew—people who in strength, endurance, skill, and abstemiousness are a hundred times superior to me who come to help them! What else but shame could I experience on coming into contact with these people? The weakest among them—a drunkard living in Rzhánov House, whom they call a loafer—is a hundred times more industrious than I; his balance (so to say), that is, the proportion between what he takes from people and what he gives to them, is a thousand times superior to my balance if I reckon what I take from people as against what I give to them.

And those are the people I go to help. I go to help the poor. But who is poor? Not one of them is poorer than I am. I am a quite enfeebled, good-for-nothing parasite, who can only exist under most exceptional conditions found only when thousands of people labour to support a life that is of no value to anyone. And it is I, an insect devouring the leaf of the tree, who wish to aid the growth and health of that tree and wish to heal it.

I spend my whole life in this way: I eat, talk, and listen; I eat, write, or read, that is again talk and listen; I eat and play; I eat and again talk and listen; I eat and go to bed; and so it is every day, and I am unable, and do not know how, to do anything else. And that I may do this it is necessary that from morning to evening the porter, the peasant, the man and woman cook, the footman, the coachman and laundress, should work; to say nothing of those working people who are needed that these coachmen, cooks, footmen and the rest should have utensils and the things with which and on which they work for me: axes, barrels, brushes, crockery, furniture, glasses, blacking, paraffin, hay, wood-fuel, and meat. And all these people work hard every day and all day, that I may be able to talk, eat, and sleep. And it was I, this wretched man, who imagined that I could help others—help the very people who were supporting me.

It is not surprising that I did not help anyone and that I felt ashamed, but it is surprising that such an absurd idea could have occurred to me. The woman who tended the sick old man helped him; the peasant woman who cut a bit of bread from the loaf she had obtained from the soil, helped a beggar; Semën, who gave three kopeks he had earned, helped the beggar, because those three kopeks really represented work he had done; but I had served no one, had worked for no one, and knew well that my money did not represent work I had done.

And I came to feel that in money itself, in the very possession of it, there is something evil and immoral; and that money itself, and the fact that I possess it, is one of the chief causes of the evils I saw around me—and I asked myself: What is money?

CHAPTER XVII

MONEY! WHAT IS MONEY?

Money represents work. I have even met educated people who declare that money represents the work of him who possesses it. I confess that in an obscure way I formerly shared that opinion. But I felt it necessary to know what money really is, and to find this out I turned to science.

Science says that there is nothing unjust or harmful in money, but that it is a natural condition of social life, necessary: (1) for convenience of exchange, (2) for fixing a measure of value, (3) for savings, and (4) for payments. The obvious fact that if I have three surplus rubles in my pocket which I can spare, I can at a whistle call together in any civilized town a hundred people who for those three rubles will perform most laborious, repulsive, and degrading tasks, is not due to the nature of money but to the very complex conditions of our economic life. The power some people have over others does not arise from money, but from the fact that the labourer does not receive the full value of his labour. That he does not receive the full value of his labour results from the nature of capital, rent, and wages, and from complex relations between these and the items of production, distribution, and consumption, of wealth. In plain Russian it results that those who have money can twist those who have none into ropes. But science says that the truth of the matter does not lie in that. Science says that three factors enter into every kind of production: land, stored up labour (capital), and labour. From different interactions of these factors on one another, and because the first two factors—land and capital—are not in the hands of the workers but in those of other people—and from very intricate combinations arising from this, the enslavement of some people by others results. From what does the dominion of money, which amazes us by its injustice and cruelty, arise? Why do some people rule over others by means of money? Science says that this is due to the division of the factors of production, and from combinations that result therefrom and oppress the labourers. This reply always seemed to me strange, not merely because it leaves out one part of the question—namely, the significance of money in the matter—but also by its division of the factors of production, which at first sight always strikes one as artificial and not in accord with the facts. It is asserted that in all production three factors are always engaged: land, capital, and labour, and thereupon it is always assumed that wealth (or what represents it—money) is naturally subdivided among those who own these factors: the rent—the value of the land – belongs to the landlord; the interest to the capitalist; and wages—the payment for work—to the working man. Is that so? First of all, is it true that in all production these three factors are engaged?

Around me while I write this, hay is being produced. Of what is this production made up? I am told: of the land on which the grass has grown; of capital—the scythes, rakes, pitchforks, and carts necessary for gathering the hay; and of labour. But I see that this is not true. Besides the land—the sun, water, and the social organization (which preserves these fields from trespass), the workers' knowledge, and their ability to speak and to understand words, and many other factors which for some reason political economy does not take into account—all take part in the production of this hay.

The power of the sun is just such a factor of all production as the land, and is yet more necessary. I can imagine a condition (say in a town) in which people assume a right to shut off the sun from others by walls or trees; why is it not included among the factors of production? Water is another factor as essential as land. So is the air also. And I can again imagine people deprived of water and of pure air because other people claim an exclusive right to the water and the air that is needed. Social security is another such essential factor, and food and clothing for the workers are also such factors of production, as some economists admit. Education and the ability to speak, which make it possible to apply various kinds of work, are other such factors. I could fill a whole volume with such omitted factors of production. Why then have just these three factors of production been selected and put at the basis of the science? Sunlight and water can be reckoned as separate factors of production just as land is; the labourers' food and clothing, knowledge, and its transmission, can be reckoned as separate factors of production, just like the labourers' implements. Why are sunbeams, water, food, and knowledge not reckoned as separate factors of production, but only land, implements, and labour? Is it merely because only in rare instances do people claim rights in sunbeams, water, air, or the right to speak and to listen, while in our society such rights are constantly claimed in the use of land and the implements of labour? There is no other basis for it, and so I see, first, that the division of the factors of production into three only is quite arbitrary and does not rest on the nature of things. But perhaps this division is so natural to people that wherever economic relations are formed these three, and only these three, factors of production come to the front. Let us see whether that is so. I look first of all around myself at the Russian settlers, of whom there are and have been millions. These settlers come to some new land, settle down on it, and begin to work; and it does not enter any of their heads that a man who does not work the land can have any right to it, and the land does not advance any separate claims of its own, on the contrary the settlers regard the land as a common possession and consider that every man has a right to mow and plough where he pleases and as much as he can manage. The settlers bring implements for the cultivation of the land, for growing vegetables, and for building their houses, and again it does not occur to anyone that the tools of labour can of themselves produce an income nor does that capital make any claim, but on the contrary the settlers consciously recognize that any profit charged for the loan of implements or for a loan of grain—that is, for capital—is unjust. The settlers work on free land with their own tools or with tools lent to them without interest, each on his own account, or all together at a common task, and in such a commune it is impossible to find rent, interest on capital, or wages. In speaking of such communes I am not inventing, but am describing what has taken place everywhere and happens now, not only among Russian settlers but everywhere, as long as nothing infringes man's natural habits. I describe what appears to every one natural and reasonable. People settle on the land and each one sets to work at what is natural to him; and each, having prepared what he needs for it, does his own work. If it is more convenient for them to work together they form an association, an *artél*; but neither in their separate farming nor in the *artéls* are the factors of production separated, but there is only labour and the necessary conditions of labour: the sun which warms all, the air which people breathe, the water they drink, the land on which they work, clothes for their bodies, food for their stomachs, the crowbar, the spade, the plough, and the engine, with which people work; and it is evident that neither the sun, the air, the water, the land, nor the clothes for the body, nor the crowbar with which they work, nor the spade, nor the plough, nor the engine which they use in the *artél*, can belong to anyone but to those who make use of the rays of the sun, breathe the air, drink the water, eat the bread, cover their bodies, and work with the spade or the engine; because all these are needed only by those who use them. And when people act so, we all see that they act as is proper for men and as is reasonable. And so, observing the economic relations among men at the time of their formation, I do not see that the division of the factors of production into three is natural to man. On the contrary I see that it is unnatural and irrational. But perhaps it is only in primitive societies that the division into those three factors does not take place, while it is inevitable with an increase in population and the development of culture, since this division has taken place in European society and we cannot help acknowledging the accomplished fact. Let us see whether that is so. We are told that in European society the division of the factors of production has been completed, that is, that some people possess the land, others the implements of production, and a third set is deprived of land and implements. The workers are deprived of land and of the implements of production. We are so accustomed to this assertion that we are no longer struck by its strangeness. But if we consider that expression, we at once perceive its incorrectness and even senselessness. There is an inner contradiction in the very expression. The conception of a labourer includes the conception of the land on which he lives and of the tools he works with. If he did not live on the land and had no implements of labour he would not be a labourer. There never has been or could be a labourer without land or implements. There cannot be an agricultural labourer without land on which to work, and without scythe, cart, and horse; nor can there be a shoemaker without a house on the land, without water, air, and implements of toil with which he works. If a peasant has no land, horse, or scythe, or a shoemaker has no house, water, or awl, this means that someone has driven him off the land and taken from him, or cheated him out of, his scythe, cart, horse, or awl, but it does not mean that there can be an agricultural labourer without a plough, or a shoemaker without tools. As a fisherman on land and without tackle is unthinkable unless someone has driven him off the water and taken his tackle, so is a peasant or shoemaker unimaginable without the land on which he lives and without implements of labour, unless someone has deprived him of land and taken away his tools.

There may be people who are driven from one spot to another and from whom their implements of toil have been taken, and who are compelled to work with other people's tools at articles they do not need, but that does not indicate that such is the nature of production; it only means that there are cases when the natural conditions of production are infringed. If one accepts as the factors of production everything of which the worker may be deprived by other people's violence—why not consider a claim on a slave's person to be a factor of production? Why not regard a claim to the sun's rays, to the air, to the water, as being such factors? A man may appear who, having built a wall, shuts out the sun from his neighbour; there may be someone who diverts the water of a river into a pond and so pollutes the water; or someone may appear who regards another as his possession; but neither the first, nor the second, nor the third pretension, even if forcibly carried into effect, can be admitted as a basis for a division of the factors of production, and it is as incorrect to accept an imaginary right to the land and to the implements of toil as separate factors of production as it would be to reckon the imaginary right to control the rays of the sun, the air, the water, or the person of another man, as being such factors. There may be people who claim a right to the land and to a worker's implements of toil, as there have been men who claimed a labourer's person, and as there may be men claiming an exclusive use of the sun, of water, or of the air, and there may be men who drive the worker from place to place and forcibly take from him the produce of his toil as soon as it is made, as well as his implements of labour, and who compel him to work for a master and not for himself, as is done in factories—all this is possible; but there can still be no workman without land and without tools, just as a man cannot be another's chattel despite the fact that men long declared that it was so.

Just as the assertion of a right of property in another man's person cannot deprive a slave of his innate right to seek his own welfare rather than that of his owner—so now the assertion of a right of property in land and in other men's implements of production, cannot deprive the labourer of each man's innate right to live on the land and with his personal or communal tools to produce things he considers useful for himself. All that science, observing the present economic conditions, can say is that there exist claims made by certain people to the workers' land and tools, in consequence of which for some of those workers (by no means for all) the conditions of production natural to man are violated in such a way that the workers are deprived of the land and of the implements of production and compelled to use other people's tools; but it cannot be said that this casual infringement of the law of production is itself the law of production.

By affirming that this division of the factors of production is the basic law of production, an economist does what a zoologist would do who, seeing a great many greenfinches with clipped wings in little cages, should conclude that a little cage and a small water-pail drawn up along rails, are the essential conditions of the life of birds and that the life of birds is composed of these three factors. However many finches there may be with clipped wings in cardboard cages, the zoologist should not consider cardboard cages a natural condition of birds. However many workers may be driven from their places and deprived of their produce and of the implements of their toil, the natural characteristic of a worker to live on the earth and produce with his own implements the things he needs will remain the same. There are the claims made by some people to the earth and to the labourers' implements of toil, just as in the ancient world there were the claims of some men to own the persons of others; but as there cannot be a division of people into owners and slaves, such as people wished to establish in the ancient world, so there cannot be a division of the factors of production into land and capital, such as economists in present-day society wish to establish. But these unjustifiable encroachments by some men on the freedom of others, men of science call natural factors of production. Instead of taking its bases from the natural characteristics of human society, science has taken them from a specific case and, wishing to justify that specific case, has admitted one man's right to the land whereon another feeds himself, and to the tools of labour with which another works; that is, it has admitted a right which never existed and never can exist and which bears a contradiction in its very expression, for the right a man claims to land he does not work on is really nothing but the right to use land I do not use, and the right to the tools of labour is nothing but the right to work with tools I do not work with. Science by its division of the factors of production asserts that the natural condition of the workman is the unnatural condition in which he finds himself, just as in the ancient world, by the division into citizens and slaves, people asserted that the unnatural condition of the slaves was a natural characteristic of man. That division, accepted by science merely to justify an existing evil which it has adopted as the basis of its investigations, has resulted in science vainly trying to furnish some kind of explanation of existing facts, and while denying the clearest and simplest answers to the questions presented, giving answers that amount to nothing.

The question for economic science is this: What is the cause of the fact that some people who have land and capital are able to enslave those who have no land or capital? The reply which common sense presents is that this results from money, which has the effect of enslaving people. But science denies this, and says that it does not result from the nature of money but from the fact that some people have land and capital and others have not. We ask: Why can people who have land and capital enslave those who have none?—and we are told: 'Because they have land and capital.' But that is what we were asking about. To be deprived of land and of the tools of production is enslavement. It is the old reply: *facit dormire quia habet virtus dormitiva.** But life does not cease to present its essential question, and even science itself sees this and tries to give a reply, but cannot do so as long as it starts from the basis it has chosen and revolves in a vicious circle. To be able to do it, science should first of all renounce its false division of the factors of production, that is, should cease to take the results of phenomena for their causes, and should first seek the nearest, and then the more remote, causes of those phenomena which form the subject of its investigation. Science should reply to the question: What is the reason of the fact that some people are deprived of the land and of the implements of production, while others possess them? Or what is the reason of the alienation of the land and the implements of labour from those who cultivate the land and use the implements? And as soon as science sets itself that question quite new considerations present themselves, turning upside down all the assumptions of the former quasi-science which revolved in a vicious circle of assertions that

* *It causes sleep because it has a sleep-giving quality.*

the poverty of the workers results from the fact that they are poor. To plain men it seems indubitable that the proximate cause of the enslavement of some people by others is money. But science denies this, and says that money is only an instrument of exchange which has nothing in common with the enslavement of people. Let us see whether that is so.

CHAPTER XVIII

WHERE DOES MONEY COME FROM? Under what conditions does a nation always have money, and under what conditions do we know nations not using it? A tribe lives in Africa or Australia, as in olden times the Scythians or the Drevlyans* lived. Such a tribe lives, ploughing, raising cattle, and growing fruit. We hear of them at the dawn of history, and history begins with the incursion of conquerors. The conquerors always do one and the same thing: they take from the tribe all they can take, cattle, grain, woven stuffs, and even male and female prisoners, and carry it all off. Some years later the conquerors return, but the tribe has not yet recovered from its ruin and there is but little to be taken from it, so the conquerors devise other better ways of exploiting the tribe. These ways are very simple and occur naturally to everyone. The first method is personal slavery. This involves the inconvenience of having to direct the whole working force of the tribe and feed them all; so a second method naturally presents itself—that of leaving the tribe on its land, while claiming for oneself the ownership of the land and dividing it among one's followers in order through them to exploit the people's labour. But this method too has its inconveniences. The followers have to manage all the productive operations of the tribe; and a third method, as primitive as the others, is introduced—that of demanding a certain periodic tribute from the conquered. The conqueror's aim is to take as much as possible of the people's produce. Obviously, to do this, he must take the things that have the highest value among the tribesmen and that at the same time are not bulky but can conveniently be stored, such as skins and gold.

* A Slavonic tribe mentioned in early Russian history.

So the conqueror usually imposes on the family or tribe a periodic tribute in skins and gold and by this means exploits the toil of the people in the way most convenient to himself. The skins and the gold having been almost all taken from the tribe, the conquered people to obtain gold have to sell to one another and to the conqueror and his followers everything they have, both their property and their work. This same process went on in the ancient world and in the Middle Ages, and goes on still. In the ancient world, with the frequent conquest of one nation by another and in the absence of recognition of the equality of man, personal slavery was the most usual method by which some people enslaved others, and the centre of gravity of that enslavement rested on chattel slavery. In the Middle Ages the feudal system—that is, the property in land bound up with it, and serfdom—partly replaced chattel slavery, and the centre of gravity of the enslavement was shifted from the person to the land: in recent times, since the discovery of America and the development of trade and the influx of gold accepted as the general money standard, with the intensification of government power, money tribute has become the chief method of enslaving people and on it all the economic relations of man are based. In a volume of literary productions there is an article by Professor Yánzhul which gives the recent history of the Fiji Islands. If I wanted to invent a most striking illustration of the way in which the demand for money has become in our days the chief instrument by which some men enslave others, I could not invent anything more glaring and convincing than this true story, which is based on documentary evidence and occurred the other day.

The Fijians live in Polynesia on islands in the Southern Pacific Ocean. The whole group, Professor Yánzhul tells us, consists of small islands covering about 8,000 square miles. Only half of them are inhabited, by a population of 150,000 natives and 1,500 whites. The native inhabitants, who emerged from savagery long ago, are distinguished among the natives of Polynesia by their ability, and are capable of work and of development, as they have proved by rapidly becoming good farmers and cattle-breeders. They were thriving, but in 1859 the kingdom found itself in a desperate position. The Fijians and their King Thakombau needed money. They needed $45,000 for contributions or indemnities demanded by the United States of America for violence said to have been inflicted by Fijians on some citizens of the American republic.

To collect this sum the Americans sent a squadron, which suddenly seized some of the best islands as security and even threatened
to bombard and destroy the settlements unless the contribution was
paid to the American representatives by a given date. The Americans
had been among the first white men to settle in Fiji with missionaries.
Selecting or seizing under one pretext or another the best plots of
land on the islands and laying out cotton and coffee plantations they
hired whole crowds of natives, whom they bound by contracts the
savages did not understand, or obtained through contractors who
dealt in live chattels. Conflicts between such planters and the natives,
whom they regarded as slaves, were inevitable, and a conflict of that
kind served as pretext for the American demand for compensation.
Despite its prosperity Fiji till then had been in the habit of making
payments in kind, as was customary in Europe till the Middle Ages.
The natives did not use money, and their trade was entirely done
by barter; goods were exchanged for goods, and the few public or
government levies were collected in country produce. What were
the Fijians and their King Thakombau to do when the Americans
categorically demanded $45,000 under threat of dire consequences
in case of non-payment? For the Fijians the figure itself was incomprehensible, not to speak of the money, which they had never seen
in such quantities. Thakombau consulted with the other chiefs, and
decided to turn to the Queen of England. At first he asked her to take
the islands under her protection, and later on asked her simply to
annex them. But the English treated this petition cautiously and were
in no hurry to rescue the semi-savage monarch from his difficulties.
Instead of a direct reply they fitted out a special expedition, in 1860,
to investigate the Fiji Islands, in order to decide whether it was worth
spending money on satisfying the American creditors and annexing
the islands to the British dominions.

Meanwhile the American government continued to insist on payment, took possession, as security, of some of the best positions,
and having observed the prosperity of the people, raised its demand
from $45,000 to $90,000, and threatened to raise it still further if
Thakombau did not pay promptly. So, pressed on all sides, poor
Thakombau, who was ignorant of European methods of arranging
credit transactions, began, on the advice of European settlers, to seek
money from Melbourne merchants on any terms, even if he had to
yield his whole kingdom to private persons. And so in Melbourne, in

response to Thakombau's appeal, a trading Company was formed. This Company, which took the name of the Polynesian Company, concluded an agreement with the Fiji rulers on terms very favourable to itself. Undertaking to meet the debt to the American government and engaging to pay it by certain fixed dates, the Company under its first agreement obtained 100,000, and later 200,000 acres, of the best land at its own selection, with freedom for all time from all taxes and duties for its factories, operations, and colonies, and for a prolonged period the exclusive right to establish banks in Fiji with the privilege of unlimited issue of bank-notes. Since the signing of that contract, finally concluded in 1868, the Fijians were confronted, side by side with their own government under Thakombau, by another power—the influential trading Company with great landed possessions on all the islands and a decisive influence in the government. Till then Thakombau's government for the satisfaction of its needs had contented itself with what it obtained by various tributes in kind and by a small customs duty on imported goods. With the conclusion of this agreement, and the establishment of the powerful Polynesian Company, its financial position changed. An important part of the best land in its dominions passed over to the Company and so the taxes diminished; on the other hand, as we know, the Company had a right to the free import and export of goods, as a result of which revenue from the customs was also reduced. The natives, that is to say ninety-nine per cent of the population, had always been but poor contributors to the customs revenue, for they hardly used any European goods except a little cotton stuff and some metal ware; and now, when through the Polynesian Company the wealthier European inhabitants escaped the payment of customs dues, King Thakombau's revenue became quite insignificant and he had to bestir himself to increase it. And so Thakombau consulted his white friends as to how to escape from his difficulties, and they advised him to introduce for the first time in the country direct taxation, and, no doubt to facilitate matters for him, it was to be in the form of a money-tax. The levy was instituted in the form of a general poll-tax of £1 on each male and four shillings on each woman in the islands.

Even to the present day in the Fiji Islands, as we have already mentioned, the cultivation of the soil and direct barter prevails. Very few natives have any money. Their wealth consists entirely of various raw produce and of cattle, but not of money. Yet the new tax demanded, at fixed dates and at all costs, a sum of money which for a native with a family came to a very considerable total. Till then a native had not been accustomed to pay any personal dues to the government except in the form of labour, while the taxes had all been paid by the villages or communes to which he belonged, from the common fields out of which he, too, drew his chief income. He had only one way out of the difficulty: to obtain money from the white colonists, that is, to go either to a trader or a planter who had what he needed—money. To the first he had to sell his produce at any price, since the tax-collector demanded it by a given date, or he was even obliged to borrow money against future produce, a circumstance of which the trader naturally took advantage to secure an unscrupulous profit; or else he had to turn to a planter and sell him his labour, that is to become a labourer. But it turned out that wages on the Fiji Islands, in consequence probably of much labour being offered simultaneously, were very low, not exceeding, according to the report of the present administration, a shilling a week for an adult male, or £2 12s a year; and consequently merely to obtain the money to pay his own tax, not to mention his family's, a Fijian had to abandon his home, his family, his own land and cultivation, and often to move far off to another island and bind himself to a planter for half a year, in order to earn the £1 needed for the payment of the new tax; while for the payment of the tax for a whole family he had to seek other means. The result of such an arrangement can easily be imagined. From his 150,000 subjects Thakombau only collected £6,000; and then an intensive demand, previously unknown, began for taxes, and a series of compulsory measures. The local administration, previously honest, soon came to an understanding with the white planters who had begun to manage the country. The Fijians were taken to court for non-payment and sentenced, besides the payment of costs, to imprisonment for not less than half a year. The role of prison was played by the plantation of the first white man willing to pay the tax and legal costs for the prisoner. In this way the whites obtained cheap labour to any desired extent. At first this handing over to compulsory labour was permitted for a period of six months only, but later on the venal judges found it possible to sentence men even to eighteen months' labour and then to renew the sentence. Very soon, in a few years, the picture of the economic condition of the inhabitants of Fiji had completely changed. Whole flourishing districts had become half-depopulated and were extremely impoverished. The whole male population, except the old and the feeble, were working away from home for the white planters to obtain money needed for the payment of the tax, or to satisfy sentences of the court. Women in Fiji do hardly any agricultural labour, and so, in the absence of the men, the land was neglected or totally abandoned. In a few years half the population of Fiji had become slaves to the white colonists. To improve their condition the Fijians again turned to England. A new petition appeared, to which were appended the names of many of the most notable persons and chiefs, begging to be made British subjects, and it was presented to the British consul. By this time England, thanks to its scientific expeditions, had not only studied but had even surveyed the islands and was well aware of the natural wealth of that beautiful corner of the globe. For these reasons the negotiations this time were crowned with full success, and in 1874, to the great dissatisfaction of the American planters, England officially entered into possession of the Fiji Islands, adding them to its colonies.

Thakombau died and a small pension was assigned to his heirs. The government of the islands was entrusted to Sir Hercules Robinson (Lord Rosmead), the Governor of New South Wales. During the first year of its annexation to England Fiji was without a government of its own, but Sir Hercules Robinson appointed an administrator. On taking the islands in hand the English government had a hard task to solve in fulfilling all that was expected of it. In the first place, the natives expected the abolition of the hateful poll-tax; the white colonists (who were partly American) either regarded the British rule distrustfully or (the British section) expected from it all kinds of benefits, for instance, the recognition of their dominion over the natives and the legalization of their claims to land they had seized, and so forth. The English government, however, proved competent to deal with the problem, and its first act was to abolish for ever the poll-tax which occasioned the enslavement of the natives for the profit of a few colonists. But here Sir Hercules Robinson was confronted by a serious dilemma. It was necessary to annul the poll-tax to escape from which the Fijians had appealed to the British government, but at the same time, by the rules of English colonial policy, the colony had to pay its own way, that is to say, had to find means to meet the expenses of its administration. Yet with the abolition of the poll-tax the whole income of Fiji (from the customs dues) did not exceed £6,000, whereas the expenses of the administration demanded at least £70,000 a year. So Robinson, having abolished the money tax, devised a labour tax, that is, imposed obligatory labour on the Fijians, but this did not bring in the £70,000 required for his own and his assistants' maintenance. And matters did not progress till the appointment of a new Governor, Sir A. M. Gordon (Baron Stanmore), who, to obtain from the inhabitants the money needed for his own and his assistants' support, devised the plan of not demanding money until there should be enough of it in circulation on the islands, but of collecting produce from the natives and selling it himself.

This tragic episode in the life of the Fijians is the clearest and best indication of what money is and of its significance. Here all is expressed: the first basis of slavery—cannon, threats, murder, the seizure of land, and also the chief instrument—money, which replaces all other means. What has to be followed through the course of centuries in an historic sketch of the economic development of nations, is here, when the various forms of monetary coercion have been fully developed, concentrated into a single decade. The drama begins with the American government sending ships with loaded cannon to the shores of the islands whose inhabitants it wishes to enslave. The pretext for the threat is monetary, but the drama begins with cannon directed against all the inhabitants: women, children, the aged, and the innocent: an occurrence now being repeated in Africa, Chinia, and Central Asia. That was the beginning of the drama: 'Your money or your life,' repeated in the history of all the conquests of all the nations; $45,000 and then $90,000, or a massacre. But there were no $90,000 available. The Americans had them. And then the second act of the drama begins: brief, bloody, terrible and concentrated slaughter has to be postponed, and changed for less noticeable, but more prolonged, sufferings. And the tribe with its ruler seeks means to substitute monetary enslavement—slavery, for the massacre. It borrows money, and then the monetary forms of the enslavement of men are organized.

These forms at once begin to act like a disciplined army and within five years the whole work is done: the people are not only deprived of the right to use the land, and of their property, but also of their liberty; they are slaves.

The third act begins: the situation is too hard and the unfortunate people hear rumours that it is possible to exchange masters and go into slavery to someone else. (Of emancipation from the slavery imposed by money there is no longer any thought.) And the tribe calls in another master, to whom it submits with a request to mitigate its condition. The English come, see that the possession of these islands will make it possible for them to feed the drones of whom they have bred too many, and the English government annexes these islands with their inhabitants, but does not take them as chattel slaves and does not even take the land and distribute it to its own supporters. Those old methods are now unnecessary. All that is necessary is that a tribute should be exacted; one large enough on the one hand to keep the slaves in slavery, and sufficient on the other to feed a multitude of drones.

The inhabitants had to pay £70,000 sterling. That is the fundamental condition on which England agreed to rescue the Fijians from their American slavery, and at the same time this was all that was necessary for the complete enslavement of the natives. But it turned out that under the conditions they were in the Fijians could not possibly pay £70,000. The demand was too great. The English modify the demand for a time, and take part of the claim in produce, in order, in due course, when money should be in circulation, to raise their exaction to its full amount. England did not act like the former Company, whose procedure may be compared to the first arrival of savage conquerors among a savage people, when all they want is to seize what they can get and to go away again, but England acts as a far-seeing enslaver: it does not at once kill the hen that lays the golden egg, but will even feed it, knowing the hen to be a good layer. At first she slackens the reins for her own advantage, in order later to pull them in and reduce the Fijians to the state of monetary enslavement in which the European and civilized world finds itself, and from which no emancipation is in sight.

Money is a harmless medium of exchange, only not when at the shores of a country loaded cannon are directed against its inhabitants. As soon as money is forcibly exacted at the cannon's mouth, then inevitably that is repeated which occurred on the Fiji Islands and has been repeated, and is repeated, everywhere and always: in the case of the old Princes of Russia and the Drevlyans, and with all governments and their subjects. People who have the power to coerce others will do it by the forcible demand of such a quantity of money as will oblige the coerced to become the slaves of the coercers. And besides this, what happened in the case of the English and the Fijians always happens, namely that the coercers, in order to hasten the enslavement, will in their demands for money always exceed rather than understate the limit of what is needed for the purpose. They will reach that limit without exceeding it only if a moral feeling is present, and even if that feeling does exist, they will always reach it when they are themselves in want. But governments will always exceed that limit, first because a government has no moral feelings, and secondly because, as we know, governments are themselves in extreme want, due to wars and to the need of paying their support-ers. Governments are always irredeemably in debt and, even if they wished to, could not help following the rule expressed by a Russian statesman of the eighteenth century, that 'one must shear the peasant and not let him get overgrown'. All governments are irredeemably in debt, and this debt in its totality (apart from fortuitous diminutions in England and America) increases from year to year in a terrifying progression. Similarly do the budgets grow, that is, the necessity of struggling with other aggressors and making payments of money and land to those who aid its own aggressions, and therefore the charges on land grow in the same way. Wages do not grow—not on account of the law of rent, but because there is an exaction by violence, of payments to the state and for the land, which has the purpose of taking from people all their surplus so that to satisfy this demand they must sell their labour: for the exploitation of that labour is the object of the imposition of the taxes. But the exploitation of that labour is only possible when, in the aggregate, more is demanded than the workers can pay without depriving themselves of nourish-ment. Raising the scale of wages would destroy the possibility of this slavery, and therefore, while there is violence, it never can be raised. And this simple and intelligible action of one set of men on another, economists have called the 'iron law'; while the instrument by means of which this action is produced they call a 'medium of exchange'.

Money—this harmless medium of exchange—is needed by men in their mutual intercourse. But why has there never been, or could there be money in its present-day significance where no forcible demand for money-taxes exists? And why has there always been, and always will be—as there is among the Fijians, the Kirgiz, the Africans, the Phoenicians, and in general among people who do not pay taxes—either the direct exchange of things for things, or else the use of casual tokens of value, such as sheep, furs, skins, or shells? Any particular kind of money only obtains currency among people when it is forcibly demanded of them all. Only then does it become necessary to everyone that he may ransom himself from violence, and only then does it obtain a constant exchange value. And what then acquires value is not what is most convenient as a medium of exchange but what the government demands. If gold is demanded, gold will have value; if knuckle-bones were demanded, knuckle-bones would have value. If this were not so, why has the emission of this medium of exchange always formed, and why does it form, a prerogative of government? People—let us say the Fijians—have established a medium of exchange; well then let them exchange as they please, and you who have power—that is who have means to inflict violence—should not interfere with that exchange. But as it is, you coin money, forbidding anyone else to coin it, or else (as among us in Russia) you merely print bits of paper with the Tsar's head on them and sign them with a particular signature, exacting penalties for any imitation of this money, and you distribute it to your assistants, and in payment of state and land taxes demand just these coins or these bits of paper with just that signature, and so much of it that a workman has to give his whole labour to obtain these same bits of paper or coins, and you assure us that we need this money—as a 'medium of exchange'. Men are all free and they do not oppress one another, do not hold one another in slavery, only there is this money in use and an iron law according to which rent rises and wages dwindle to a minimum! The fact that half (and more than half) the Russian peasants are enslaved as labourers to landowners and to mill-owners, on account of direct and indirect taxes and land dues, does not at all mean, what is obvious, that the compulsory exaction of direct, indirect, and land taxes paid in money to the government and to its assistants—the landowners—compels workmen to go into slavery to those who take the money, but it means that money exists—a medium of exchange—and that there is an iron law!

Before the serfs were emancipated I could compel Vánka to do any kind of work, and if he refused I sent him to the rural police and they whipped his bottom till Vánka submitted. At the same time if I made Vánka overwork himself or did not give him land or food, the matter went before the authorities and I had to answer for it. Now men are free, but I can make Vánka, Sidórka, or Petrúshka do any kind of work, and if he refuses I do not give him money for his taxes and they will whip his bottom till he submits; besides which I can make a German, a Frenchman, a Chinaman, or a Hindu, who lacks land and bread, work for me by not giving him money to hire land or buy bread unless he submits to me. And if I make him work without food beyond his strength, and if I kill him with work, no one will say a word to me, and if in addition I have read books on political economy I may be firmly convinced that all men are free and that money does not occasion slavery. The peasants have long known that 'a ruble hits harder than an oak cudgel'. But the economists do not wish to see this. To say that money does not cause slavery, is just like saying half a century ago that the serf-law did not produce slavery. Economists say that despite the fact that the possession of money enables one man to enslave another, money is a harmless medium of exchange. Why should one not have said half a century ago, that despite the fact that the serf-law could enslave a man, the law was not a means of enslavement but a harmless medium of mutual service? Some people gave rough labour, others attended to the physical and mental welfare of the slaves and organized their work. I even think that that used to be said.

CHAPTER XIX

IF THIS PSEUDO-SCIENCE, political economy, were not occupied, like all the juridical sciences, with devising excuses for violence, it could not avoid taking note of the strange fact that the distribution of wealth—the circumstance that some people are deprived of land and capital and that some men enslave others—is all dependent on money, and only by means of money does one set of men now exploit the labour of others, that is, enslave others.

I repeat: a man who has money can buy up all the corn and starve another and make a complete slave of him through his need of bread. And this is done before our eyes on an enormous scale. It would seem necessary to seek the connection between the phenomena of slavery and money; but science asserts with full confidence that money has nothing to do with the enslavement of men.

Science says: money is a commodity like any other the value of which is fixed by its cost of production, the only difference being that this commodity has been chosen as most convenient to serve as a standard of values, for savings, as a means of exchange, and to effect payments: one man makes boots and another grows grain, while a third raises sheep; and more conveniently to exchange their produce they introduce money which represents a proportionate amount of work, and by its means they can exchange leather soles for sheep's ribs and ten pounds of flour.

The exponents of this pseudo-science are very fond of imagining such a state of affairs to themselves, but it never existed in the world. Such a conception of society is like the conception of a primitive uncorrupted perfect human society that philosophers used to be fond of devising. But there never was such a state. In all human societies where money has existed as such, violence has always been exerted by the strong and well armed against the weak and unarmed; and where there was violence the standard of values, money—whatever it may have been: cattle, hides, furs, or metals—inevitably lost that significance and became merely a means of ransom from violence. Money certainly has the innocuous qualities science enumerates, but they would be its essential qualities only in a society where there was no violence of man to man—in an ideal society; and in such a society money as money—a common measure of values—would not exist at all, just as it has not existed and could not exist in any society not subjected to general governmental violence. But in all societies known to us where money exists it has obtained importance as a medium of exchange only because it has served as an instrument of violence. And its chief significance is not as a medium of exchange but as an instrument of violence. Where there is violence money cannot be a regular medium of exchange because it cannot be a standard of values. It cannot be a standard of values because as soon as one man in a society can deprive another of the products of his labour, this standard is at once infringed. If horses and cows are brought to market some of which have been reared by their owners while others have been forcibly taken from those who reared them, it is plain that the price of horses and cows in that market will not correspond to the cost of rearing the stock, and that the prices of all articles will be altered as a consequence of this alteration, and money will not have fixed the price of those articles. Moreover if one can acquire a cow, a horse, or a house, by force, it is also possible to take money itself by force and with that money to obtain all kinds of produce. But if money itself is obtained by violence and used to purchase commodities, it quite loses every semblance of a medium of exchange. The oppressor, when he seizes the money and gives it for things produced by labour, does not exchange, but by means of money takes whatever he wants.

But even if such an imaginary and impossible society had existed in which, without any general governmental violence exercised over men, money—silver or gold—had the significance of a standard of values and a medium of exchange, even then as soon as violence was introduced money would at once lose that significance. An oppressor makes his appearance in such a society as a conqueror. This man, let us suppose, seizes cows, horses, clothing, and the houses of the inhabitants, but finds it inconvenient to deal with all these, and so it naturally occurs to him to take from these people whatever among them represents all kinds of values and can be exchanged for all kinds of articles, namely, money. Money at once ceases to have significance as a standard of values in that society, because the value of all articles will depend on the caprice of the oppressor. The article the oppressor needs most and for which he will give most money, will become the most valuable, and vice versa. So that in a society subjected to violence money at once acquires the predominant significance of a means whereby the oppressor exercises his violence, and it will retain significance as a medium of exchange among the oppressed only in so far and to such an extent as is convenient to the oppressor.

Let us imagine matters in such a society. Serfs furnish their owner with linen, poultry, sheep, and day-labour. The owner substitutes money dues for these payments in kind and fixes prices for the various articles brought him. Anyone who can supply no linen, corn, cattle, or day-labour, may pay a fixed sum of money. Evidently among this owner's serfs the price of articles will always depend on the arbitrary will of the serf owner. He uses the articles he receives; and some he needs more and others less, and accordingly fixes higher or lower prices for them. Evidently his whims or needs will decide the prices of these articles among those who have to pay him. If he needs grain he will fix a higher payment for not furnishing the allotted quantity of grain and a cheaper rate for not furnishing linen, cattle, and day-labour; and so those who have no grain will sell their produce, labour, linen, or cattle, to others, in order to be able to buy grain to satisfy the proprietor. If the serf-owner decides to put all these obligations on a money basis, again the price of the commodities will not depend on their labour value but, first, on the amount of money the estate owner demands, and, secondly, on the question which of the articles produced by the peasants he most needs and for which therefore he will pay more, and for which less, money. The exaction by the estate-owner of money from the peasants would only fail to influence the price of articles among those peasants themselves—first, if the serfs of this owner lived in isolation from others and had no intercourse except among themselves and with their owner; and, secondly if he used the money not to purchase commodities in his own village, but outside it. Only under such conditions would the prices of the commodities, though nominally altered, remain relatively true, and money would have the significance of a standard of values and of exchange; but if the peasants had economic relations with the surrounding population, the estate-owner's greater or lesser demand for money would heighten or lower the price of the articles they produced, in relation to their neighbours. (If less money were demanded of their neighbours than of them, their produce would be sold more cheaply than that of their neighbours and vice versa.) And, secondly, only if the money he collected were not used to purchase the productions of his own peasants would the estate-owner's exaction of money from the peasants fail to influence the value of their produce. But if he uses the money to buy things his peasants produce, it is evident that among them the relation of prices between various commodities will constantly change according to the estate-owner's purchases of this or that commodity. Let us suppose that one estate-owner charged very highly for permission to allow his serfs to work or trade on their own account, while a neighbouring proprietor made a small charge for the same privilege, it is plain that within the domain of the former all commodities will be cheaper than in the domain of the second, and that prices in the one domain and the other will depend directly on the increase or decrease of the dues the serfs have to pay.

Such is one of the influences of violence on price. Another, resulting from the former, will consist in the relation between the values of the different products. Let us suppose that one estate-owner is fond of horses and pays well for them, while another likes towels and pays well for them. Evidently in the domain of both these owners the price for horses and towels will be high, and the price of these commodities will be out of proportion to that of cows and grain. Next day the man fond of towels dies, and his successor is fond of poultry: evidently the price of linen will fall and the price of poultry will rise. Where the violent coercion of one man by another exists in a society, the significance of money as a standard of values at once succumbs to the arbitrary will of the oppressor, and its significance as a medium for the exchange of the products of toil gives way to its significance as the most convenient means of exploiting the labour of others. The oppressor needs the money not as a means of exchange, nor to fix the standard of values—he fixes that himself—but only for convenience in his oppression, since money can be stored up and money affords the easiest method of keeping the greatest number of people in slavery. To seize all the animals, in order always to have as many horses and cows and sheep as may be wanted, is inconvenient, for they have to be fed; and it is the same with grain, which may spoil; and it is the same with labour and the corvée: at one time a thousand labourers are wanted, at another time not even one. Money demanded from those who have none makes it possible to avoid all these inconveniences and always to have everything that is wanted, and just for this purpose does the oppressor need it. Besides that, money is required by the oppressor in order that his power to exploit the labour of others may not be limited to certain people but may extend to all who need money. If there was no money each estate-owner could exploit only the labour of his own serfs; but when two of them agree to take from their serfs money which those serfs do not possess, they can both equally exploit all the forces on the two estates.

And so an oppressor finds it more convenient to make his demands on other people's work by means of money, and he needs money simply for this purpose. And for a man subjected to violence—a man from whom his work is taken— money is not necessary either for exchange (he exchanges without money as all nations without governments have done) or to fix a standard of values, for that fixing is done apart from him; or for savings, for a man from whom the produce of his labour is taken cannot save; or for payments, because a man who is oppressed will have to pay out more than he receives or, if he does receive, the payments made him are not in money but in goods (in cases where he receives payment for his work directly from his employer's stores) and the same is practically the case if all he earns is spent on articles of primary necessity in outside shops. Money is demanded of him and he is told that if he does not pay it he will get no land or grain, or his cow or his house will be taken from him and he will be hired out to labour or will be put in prison. From this he can escape only by selling the produce of his labour and his labour itself at prices fixed not by fair exchange but by the power which demands the money of him.

And under such conditions—the influence on values of tribute or of taxes, which is seen always and everywhere: with land-owners on a small scale and in kingdoms on a large scale—under these conditions, when the cause of the change in prices is as plain as the reason why marionettes move their limbs is plain to him who looks behind the wings—under these conditions to speak of money as representing a medium of exchange and a standard of values is, to say the least, amazing.

CHAPTER XX

EVERY ENSLAVEMENT OF ONE MAN BY ANOTHER is based entirely on the fact that one man can deprive another of life, and while maintaining that menacing position can compel the other to obey his will.

One may say with confidence that if there is any enslavement of man, if, that is, one man at the will of another and contrary to his own desire performs actions undesirable to the doer, the cause of this is simply violence and is based on a threat to the man's life. If a man gives his whole work to others, gets insufficient nourishment, hands his little children over to hard labour, leaves the land and devotes his whole life to hateful labour on things he does not himself want—as occurs before our eyes in our world (which we call cultured, because we live in it), it is safe to say that he does this only because he is threatened with death if he does not do it. And so in our cultured world, where the majority of people do work that is hateful and unnecessary to them under terrible privations, the majority of people are in a state of slavery based on threats to their lives. In what does this enslavement consist? And wherein lies the threat to their lives?

In ancient times the method of enslavement and the threat to life were obvious: a primitive method of enslaving people was employed. It consisted in a direct threat to kill them by the sword. The armed man said to him who was unarmed: I can kill you, as you see I have just killed your brother, but I do not wish to—I spare you because, first of all, it will be more advantageous both for you and for me if you work for me than if you are killed. So do everything I order, for if you refuse I shall kill you. And the unarmed man submitted to him that was armed and did all he commanded. The unarmed man worked, the armed man threatened. That was the personal slavery that first appeared among all peoples and is still to be met with among primitive tribes. That form of enslavement comes first, but as life becomes more complex it changes its form. As life becomes more complicated that method presents great inconvenience to the oppressor. To exploit the labour of the weak it is necessary to clothe and feed them—that is, to keep them so that they are fit for work—and this of itself limits the number of the slaves; besides, this method obliges the oppressor to stand always over the slaves threatening them with death. And so another method of enslaving them is devised.

Five thousand years ago, as is written in the Bible, Joseph in Egypt invented this new, more convenient, and broader method of enslaving people. It is the same that in modern times is employed for taming unruly horses and wild beasts in menageries. It is—hunger.

This is how this invention is described in the Book of Genesis, in the Bible:

> (Chapter XLI, verse 48) And he gathered up all the food of the seven [fruitful] years which were in the land of Egypt, and laid up the food in the cities: the food of the field, which was round about every city, laid he up in the same.
> (49) And Joseph laid up corn as the sand of the sea, very much, until he left numbering; for it was without number.

(53)   And the seven years of plenty, that was in the land of Egypt, came to an end.

(54)   And the seven years of famine began to come, according as Joseph had said: and there was famine in all lands; but in all the land of Egypt there was bread.

(55)   And when all the land of Egypt was famished the people cried to Pharaoh for bread: and Pharaoh said unto all the Egyptians, Go unto Joseph; what he saith to you, do.

(56)   And the famine was over all the face of the earth: and Joseph opened all the storehouses, and sold unto the Egyptians; and the famine was sore in the land of Egypt.

(57)   And all countries came into Egypt to Joseph for to buy corn; because the famine was sore in all the earth.

Joseph, employing the primitive method of the enslavement of people by threat of the sword, collected the grain in the fruitful years, in anticipation of bad years which usually follow good ones, as everyone knows even without Pharaoh's dream, and by that means—hunger—he enslaved both the Egyptians and the inhabitants of the surrounding countries by methods more powerful and more convenient to Pharaoh. When the people began to hunger, he arranged matters so as to keep them permanently in his power—by hunger. This is described in Chapter XLVII:

(13)   And there was no bread in all the land; for the famine was very sore, so that the land of Egypt and the land of Canaan fainted by reason of the famine.

(14)   And Joseph gathered up all the money that was found in the land of Egypt, and in the land of Canaan, for the corn which they bought: and Joseph brought the money into Pharaoh's house.

(15)   And when the money was all spent in the land of Egypt, and in the land of Canaan, all the Egyptian came unto Joseph, and said, Give us bread: for why should we die in thy presence? for our money faileth.

(16)   And Joseph said, Give your cattle; and I will give you for your cattle, if money fail.

(17)   And they brought their cattle unto Joseph: and Joseph gave them bread in exchange for the horses, and for the flocks,

and for the herds, and for the asses: and he fed them with bread in exchange for all their cattle for that year.

(18) And when that year was ended, they came unto him the second year, and said unto him, We will not hide from my lord, how that our money is all spent; and the herds of cattle are my lord's; there is nought left in the sight of my lord, but our bodies, and our lands:

(19) wherefore should we die before thine eyes, both we and our land? buy us and our land for bread, and we and our land will be servants unto Pharaoh: and give us seed, that we may live, and not die, and that the land be not desolate.

(20) So Joseph bought all the land of Egypt for Pharaoh; for the Egyptians sold every man his field, because the famine was sore upon them: and the land became Pharaoh's.

(21) And as for the people, he removed them to the cities from one end of the border of Egypt even to the other end thereof.

(22) Only the land of the priests bought he not: for the priests had a portion from Pharaoh, and did eat their portion which Pharaoh gave them; wherefore they sold not their land.

(23) Then Joseph said unto the people, Behold, I have bought you this day and your land for Pharaoh: lo, here is seed for you, and ye shall sow the land.

(24) And it shall come to pass at the in-gatherings, that ye shall give a fifth unto Pharaoh, and four parts shall be your own, for seed of the field, and for your food, and for them of your households, and for food for your little ones.

(25) And they said, Thou hast saved our lives: let us find grace in the sight of my lord, and we will be Pharaoh's servants.

(26) And Joseph made it a statute concerning the land of Egypt unto this day, that Pharaoh should have the fifth; only the land of the priests alone became not Pharaoh's.

Previously Pharaoh, to exploit the labour of the people, had to compel them to work by force; but now, when the stores and the land were Pharaoh's, he only had to guard those stores by force, and hunger enabled him to compel them to work for him.

The land is all Pharaoh's and the stores (the part he collects) are always his, and so, instead of driving with the sword each man individually to work, it is only necessary to use force to guard the stores, and the people are enslaved not by the sword but by hunger.

In a year of famine all may be starved at Pharaoh's will, and in a year of plenty those who owing to some mishap are short of grain can be starved.

And the second method of enslavement is instituted not directly by the sword, that is, not by the strong man driving the weaker man to work by threats of killing him, but by the oppressor, having taken the supplies and guarded them with the sword, compelling the weaker man to labour for his food.

Joseph says to the hungry: 'I can starve you to death as I have the corn, but I spare you on condition that, for the grain I give you, you will do whatever I command.'

For the first method of enslavement the man in power needs only warriors constantly riding about among the people and, by threats of death, seeing that his orders are obeyed. For the first method the oppressor need only divide up with his warriors. But under the second method, besides warriors, the oppressor needs another kind of assistants to preserve the stores of grain and the land from the hungry people—he needs great and little Josephs, managers and distributors of the grain. And the strong man has to divide up with them, and to give Joseph a vesture of fine linen, a gold ring, and servants, and grain, and silver for his brethren and his relatives. Besides, by the nature of the case, under the second method not only the managers and their relatives but all those who have stores of grain become sharers in the advantage of the violence used. As under the first method founded on sheer force, everyone who had arms became a participant in the violence employed, so under the second method based on hunger, all who have supplies share in the benefits of the oppression and lord it over those who have none.

For the oppressor the advantage of this method over the former is that, first and chiefly, he is no longer obliged to coerce the workers by force to do his will, but they come themselves and sell themselves to him; secondly, a smaller number escape his coercion. The only disadvantage of this method for the oppressor is that it obliges him to share with a larger number of people. The advantage of this method for the oppressed is that they are no longer subject to coarse violence, but are left to themselves and can always hope under fortunate conditions to pass over from the ranks of the oppressed to the ranks of the oppressors; the disadvantage for them is that they can never more escape from some measure of coercion. This new method of enslavement generally comes into use together with the old method, and the strong man reduces the one and extends the other as may be required. But this method of enslavement still does not fully satisfy the strong man's desire—to take as much as possible of the produce of their labour from the greatest number of workers and to enslave as great a number of people as possible—and does not keep pace with the increasing complexity of life's conditions, and a still newer method of enslavement is devised. The new, and third, method is that of tribute. This method like the second is based on hunger, but to the method of enslaving people by deprivhing them of bread is added that of depriving them also of other necessaries. The oppressor demands from the slaves such a quantity of monetary tokens, which he himself possesses, that to obtain them the slaves are obliged to sell not only more than the fifth of their store of grain that Joseph fixed, but also articles of prime necessity: meat, skins, wool, clothes, fuel, even buildings, and thus the oppressor always holds the slaves in subjection not only by hunger, but also by thirst, want, cold, and all other kinds of privation.

And a third form of slavery is organized—the monetary, which consists in the strong man saying to the weak one: I can do what I like with each of you separately, I can simply take a gun and shoot each of you, or I can kill you by taking the land that feeds you; I can, with the money you have to bring me, buy up all the grain that feeds you, and I can sell it to other people and starve you all at any moment, and I can take from you all that you have: cattle, dwellings, and clothes; but that is inconvenient and unpleasant for me, and therefore I allow you all to arrange your own work and your own production as you please—only bring me so many pieces of money, the demand for which I will assess either per head or according to the land you hold, or by the quantity of food and drink you have, or by your clothes, or your buildings. Bring me these money tokens and arrange matters among yourselves as you please, but know that I shall defend and protect not widows, nor orphans, nor the sick, nor the old, nor those who have suffered from fires, but only the regularity of circulation of these money tokens. That man only will be justified before me and protected by me who regularly brings me the required number of money tokens I demand. But how he gets them is a matter of indifference to me.

And the strong man only issues these tokens as receipts for the fulfilment of his demands.

The second method of enslavement is that by taking a fifth part of the crops and laying up stores of grain, Pharaoh, besides personal enslavement by the sword, obtains in common with his assistants the possibility of ruling all the workers in times of famine and some of them whenever calamity befalls them.

The third method is, that Pharaoh demands of the workers more than would pay for the fifth of the crops which he formerly took from them, and with his assistants obtains a new means of ruling over the workmen not only in time of famine and casual misfortune but at all times. Under the second method the people kept some supplies of grain, which enabled them without surrendering themselves to slavery to bear small failures of harvest and casual mishaps, but under the third method, when the exactions are greater, their supplies of grain and all other supplies of prime necessities are taken from them and at the slightest mishap the worker, having no reserves of grain or other supplies which he could exchange for grain, has to go into slavery to those who have money. For the first method the oppressor need only have soldiers and need only divide with them; for the second, besides guards over the land and the stores of grain, he also requires collectors and clerks to distribute the grain; under the third method he can no longer himself own all the land, but besides warriors to guard the land and the wealth, he must also have landowners and tax-collectors, officials to allot the taxes and assess them per head or according to the articles used; inspectors, customs-officers, revenue officers and assessors. The organization of the third method is much more complex than that of the second; under the second method the collection of the grain can be farmed out as was done in ancient times and is still done in Turkey; but when the enslaved are taxed, a complex administration is needed to watch that the people or their taxable actions should not escape the tribute. And so under the third method, the oppressor has to share with a still greater number of people than under the second method; besides which, by the very nature of the case, all people either of that same or of other countries who have money become participants. The advantages for the oppressor of this method over the first or second methods are the following:

In the first place, by means of this method a greater amount of labour can be taken and taken in a more convenient manner, for a money tax is like a screw, it can be easily and conveniently turned to the utmost limit which does not kill the golden hen; so that it is not necessary to await a famine year as in Joseph's time—for the famine year can always be arranged.

Secondly, because under this method the coercion is extended to all those landless people who formerly escaped and gave only part of their labour for bread, but who are now obliged in addition to that part to give also part of their labour for taxes to the oppressor. The disadvantage for the oppressor is that under this method he has to share with a greater number of people: not only his immediate assistants but, first, with all those private landowners who usually appear where this system is adopted, and secondly, with all those people of his own or even of other nations who have such money tokens as are demanded from the slaves.

The advantage for the oppressed in comparison with the second method is only this, that he has still more personal independence from the oppressor; he can live where he pleases, do what he pleases, and sow or not sow grain; he is not obliged to account for his work, and if he has money he can consider himself quite free, and he can always hope, or actually attain if but for a time—when he has money to spare or has land bought for it—not merely a position of independence but even that of an oppressor. The disadvantage for him is that, under this third method, the position of the oppressed in general becomes far harder and they are deprived of the greater part of what they produce, since under this third method the number of people who live on the labour of others is still greater and therefore the burden of supporting them falls on a smaller number. This third method of enslavement is also a very old one, and comes into use together with the two previous ones without entirely excluding them. None of the three methods of enslavement has ever ceased to exist. All three methods may be compared to screws which press down a board that lies on the workers and squeezes them. The chief, fundamental, and central screw, without which the others cannot hold—the one which is first screwed down and never ceases to act—is that of personal slavery, the enslavement of one set of people by another by means of threats to kill them with the sword; the second—which is screwed down after the former—is the enslavement of people by depriving them of land and of stores of food, a deprivation supported by the personal threat of death; and the third screw is the enslavement of people by a demand for money tokens they have not got, and that too is supported by the threat of murder. All three screws are operated, and only when one is tightened are the others relaxed. For the complete enslavement of the workers all three screws—all three methods of enslavement—are needed, and in our society all three methods are constantly in use—all three screws are tightened.

The first method, enslaving men by personal violence and by threats to kill them by the sword, has never been abandoned, and will not be abandoned as long as there is any enslavement of man by man, because all enslavement depends upon it. We are all very naïvely confident that personal slavery has been abandoned in our civilized world, that the last remnants of it were abolished in America and in Russia, and that now only among savages is there slavery, but that we have none. We forget only one small circumstance, namely about those millions of men in standing armies without which no single government exists and with the abolition of which the whole economic structure of every government would inevitably go to pieces. But what are those millions of soldiers if not the personal slaves of those who rule over them? Are not they compelled to do the will of their owners under threat of torture and death—a threat frequently put into execution? The only difference is that the subjection of these slaves is not called slavery but discipline, and that while the others were slaves from birth to death, these are so for the period, more or less brief, of what is termed their 'service'. Personal slavery is not only not abolished in our civilized societies but with the introduction of universal military conscription it has of late been strengthened, and still remains what it always has been, though somewhat modified. And it cannot fail to exist, for as long as there is any enslavement of man by man there will be this personal slavery which by threat of the sword maintains the territorial and tax enslavement of men. It may be that this slavery, that of the army, may be very necessary, as is alleged, for the defence and glory of our fatherland, though this advantage is more than doubtful, for we see that in unsuccessful wars it often serves for the enslavement and degradation of the country; but what is evident is the suitability of this slavery for the maintenance of land and tax slavery. If the Irish or the Russian peasants seized the land from the estate-owners, the troops would come and take it back again. Build distilleries or breweries and fail to pay the excise dues, and soldiers come and close the establishment. Refuse to pay taxes and the same will happen.

The second screw is the method of enslavement by depriving people of land and therefore of their food supplies. This method of enslavement also has existed and does exist wherever people are enslaved, and however much its form may be altered it exists everywhere. Sometimes the land all belongs to the sovereign, as in Turkey, and a title of the harvest is taken for the treasury; sometimes only part of the land, and a tax is collected from it; sometimes again the land all belongs to a small number of people and part of the labour is taken for it, as in England; or a larger or smaller part of it belongs to great landowners, as in Russia, Germany, and France. But where there is enslavement there is also appropriation of land by means of enslavement. This screw for the enslavement of people is slackened or tightened in proportion to the strain on the other screws; thus, in Russia when personal enslavement extended to the majority of workmen, land slavery was superfluous; but the screw of personal slavery in Russia was only relaxed when the screws of land and tax enslavement were tightened. The people were all inscribed in communes, their migration or change of location was made difficult, the land was appropriated or given to private owners, and then the peasants were set 'free'. In England, for instance, the land enslavement is what chiefly acts, and the question of the nationalization of the land merely consists in tightening the tax screw in order to relax the screw of territorial enslavement.

The third method of enslavement—by tribute or taxation—also existed before, and in our time, with the diffusion of uniform money tokens in various states and the intensification of governmental power, it has acquired special force. This method has been so elaborated in our time that it bids fair to replace the second—the territorial—method of enslavement. It is the screw with the tightening of which the land-screw relaxes, as is evident in the economic condition of all Europe. Within our own memory, we have lived through two transitions of slavery from one form to another in Russia: when we freed the serfs and left the proprietors in possession of most of the land, the proprietors feared that their power over the slaves would slip away; but experience showed that when letting go of the old chain of personal slavery they only had to seize the other, that of land-ownership. The peasant lacked bread to eat and the proprietor had the land and the stores of grain, and therefore the peasant remained a slave as before. The next transition was when government demands greatly tightened the other screw—that of taxation, and most of the labourers were obliged to sell themselves into bondage to the estate-owners or to the factories. And the new form of slavery held the people yet more thoroughly, so that nine-tenths of the Russian working classes work for proprietors and factory owners only because they are compelled to do so by the demands for State and land taxes. This is so obvious that were the government to try the experiment of not collecting direct, indirect, and land taxes for a year, all the work on other people's land and at the factories would come to a standstill. Nine-tenths of the Russian people hire themselves out when the taxes are being collected, and on account of those taxes.

All three methods of enslavement have existed continuously and still exist; but people are inclined not to notice them as soon as new justifications are alleged for them. And what is strange is that this very method on which at the present time everything is based, the screw holding everything together, is just what is not noticed.

When in the ancient world the whole economic structure was based on personal slavery, the greatest intellects did not notice it. To Xenophon and Plato and Aristotle and to the Romans it seemed that things could not be otherwise, and that slavery was an inevitable and natural outcome of wars, without which the existence of humanity was unthinkable. So also in the Middle Ages, and even down to recent times, people did not see the significance of land-ownership and the slavery resulting from it, on which the whole economic structure of the Middle Ages rested. And just in the same way now, no one sees or even wishes to see that in our time the enslavement of the majority of people depends on money-taxes—State and land taxes—demanded by the governments and their dependants and collected by the administration and the army—the very administration and army that are paid for out of those taxes.

CHAPTER XXI

WHAT IS SURPRISING is not that the slaves themselves—subjected to slavery from of old—are not conscious of their condition and consider the slavery in which they have always lived to be a natural condition of human life, and regard a change in the form of slavery as an alleviation; nor is it surprising that slave-owners sometimes sincerely think they are emancipating their slaves by loosening one screw when another is already screwed tight. Both slaves and owners are accustomed to their position, and the slaves, not knowing freedom, only seek alleviation or a mere change of the form of their slavery, while the slave-owners—desiring to hide their injustice—wish to attribute a special significance to the new forms of slavery they impose on the people in place of the old. But it is surprising that science, which is called liberal, can when investigating the economic conditions of a people's life avoid seeing what is at the base of the whole economic condition of the people. One would think it the business of science to discover the connection between phenomena and the common cause of a series of phenomena. But political economy does just the opposite: it carefully conceals the connection of the phenomena and their significance and carefully avoids answering the simplest and most essential questions; like a lazy and restive horse it only goes well down hill when there is nothing to pull, but as soon as it is necessary to pull, it swerves, pretending that it has to go aside to do its own business. As soon as a serious essential question presents itself to science, a learned discussion is at once begun on irrelevant matters, merely with the purpose of distracting attention from the question at issue.

You ask: What is the cause of the unnatural, abnormal, irrational, and not merely useless but harmful phenomenon—that some men cannot eat or work except by the will of others? And science, with most serious mien, replies: Because some people control the work and the nourishment of others—such being the law of production.

You ask: What is this right of property on the basis of which some people appropriate the land, food, and instruments of labour of others? Science answers with most serious mien: This right is based on the protection of a man's work; that is, that the protection of the work of one set of men expresses itself by seizing the work of other men.

You ask: What is this money that is everywhere coined and printed by governments, that is, by the authorities, and which is forcibly demanded of the workers in such enormous quantities, and in the form of national debts is imposed on future generations of labourers? You ask whether this money exacted as taxes in quantities increased to the utmost possibility, has not an effect on the economic relations of the payers towards the receivers. And science with most serious face replies: Money is a commodity like sugar or chintz, and is distinguished only by the fact that it is the most convenient medium of exchange, but taxes have no influence on the economic condition of the people: the laws of the production, exchange, and distribution of wealth are one thing, while taxes are another.

You ask whether the circumstance that government can at its pleasure raise or lower prices, and by increasing taxes can bind in slavery all who do not possess land, has not an influence on economic conditions. And science with most serious face replies: None at all! The laws of production, distribution, and exchange are one science; taxes and State affairs in general are another science—that of finance.

You ask, finally, about the whole people being in slavery to the government, about the government being able at its own will to ruin everybody, to take all the produce of their labour and even to tear the men themselves from their work, putting them into military slavery; you ask whether this circumstance has no influence on economic conditions. To this science does not even take the trouble to reply: this is quite a separate matter—State law. Science most seriously examining the laws of the economic life of the people whose every function and whole activity depends on the oppressor's will, and regarding this influence of the oppressor as a natural condition of people's life, does what an investigator of the economic conditions of the life of personal slaves of various owners would do if he did not take into account the influence exerted on the lives of those slaves by the will of the owner who at his own caprice obliges them to do this or that work and drives them at will from place to place, feeds them or leaves them unfed, and kills them or lets them live.

We should like to think that science does this out of stupidity, but one only has to penetrate and examine the propositions of the science to convince oneself that it is not due to stupidity but to great ingenuity.

This science has a very definite aim, which it attains. That aim is to maintain superstition and deception among the people and thereby hinder the progress of humanity towards truth and welfare. There has long existed, and still exists, a terrible superstition which has done almost more harm than the most fearful religious superstitions. And it is this superstition which so-called science maintains with all its might and main. This superstition is quite similar to the religious superstitions: it consists in the assertion that, besides man's duty to man, there exist yet more important obligations to an imaginary being. For theology this imaginary being is God, but for political science it is the State. The religious superstition consists in this, that sacrifices, sometimes of human lives, to this imaginary being are necessary, and men may and should be brought to them by all means, not excluding violence. The political superstition consists in this, that besides the duties of man to man there exist more important duties to the imaginary being, and that sacrifices, very often of human life, offered up to this imaginary being, the State, are also necessary, and that men may and should be brought to them by all possible means not even excluding violence. This superstition, formerly supported by the priests of various religions, is now supported by so-called science. Men are thrust into a most terrible slavery, worse than ever before; but science tries to assure people that this is necessary and cannot be otherwise.

The State must exist for the good of the people and must carry on its business: govern the people and defend them from enemies. For this the State needs money and soldiers. The money must be supplied by all the citizens of the State, and therefore all the relations of men must be viewed under the necessary conditions of statehood.

'I want to help my father in his farm work,' says a simple ignorant man; 'I want to marry, but they take me, and send me for six years to Kazán as a soldier. I leave the army and want to plough the land and support my family, but for a hundred versts around me I am not allowed to plough unless I pay money, which I have not got, to people who do not know how to plough and who demand so much money for it that I have to give them all my labour; but for all that I earn something and want to give what I have saved to my children; but an official comes to me and takes away my savings for taxes; again I earn something, and again it is all taken away from me. All my economic activity, all of it without exception, is dependent on the demands of the State, and it seems to me that an improvement in my condition and in that of my brothers must come from our emancipation from the demands of the State.'

But Science says: Your conclusions are the result of your ignorance. Learn the laws of the production, distribution, and exchange of wealth, and do not confuse economic with political questions. The facts you refer to are not infringements of your liberty but necessary sacrifices which you, like other people, must bear for your own freedom and welfare. 'But, you see, they have taken my son, and promise to carry off all my sons as soon as they grow up,' again replies the simple man. 'They took him by force and have driven him under fire into some strange land of which we had never heard and for aims we cannot understand. And, you see, the land we are not allowed to plough and for want of which we starve is owned by a man we have never seen and whose usefulness we cannot even comprehend. And the taxes, for which the policeman took the cow from my children by force, will for all I know go to that same policeman who took the cow, and to various members of Commissions and Ministries whom I do not know and in whose utility I do not believe. How can all this violence secure my liberty, and all this evil promote my welfare?'

It is possible to compel a man to be a slave and to do what he considers bad for himself, but it is impossible to make him think that while suffering violence he is free and that the evident evil he endures forms his welfare. That seems impossible, but is just what has been done in our time by the aid of science.

The government, that is armed men using force, decide what they must take from those whom they coerce: like the English in dealing with the Fijians, they decide how much labour they require of their slaves, decide how many assistants they need to collect this labour, organize their assistants as soldiers, as landed proprietors, and as tax-collectors. And the slaves yield up their labour and at the same time believe that they give it up not because their masters wish it, but because, for their own freedom and welfare, service and bloody sacrifice offered to a divinity called 'the State' are essential, and that while paying this service to this divinity they remain free.

They believe this because formerly religion and the priests said so, and now science and the learned people talk that way. But we need only cease to believe blindly what others, calling themselves priests and learned men, say, for the absurdity of such assertions to become evident. People who do violence to others assure them that this violence is necessary for the State, and that the State is necessary for the freedom and welfare of the people: it turns out that the oppressors oppress the people to promote their freedom, and harm them for their good. But men are rational beings that they may understand wherein their welfare lies and may promote it freely. And affairs the goodness of which is unintelligible to people and to which they are driven by force, cannot be good for them, for a rational being can regard as good only what presents itself to his reason as being so. If from passion or lack of sense men are drawn towards evil, all that others who do not commit the same errors can do is to persuade them to do what accords with their real welfare. People may be persuaded that their welfare will be greater if they all become soldiers, are all deprived of land, and give their whole labour for taxes; but until all men regard this as their welfare and therefore do it voluntarily, it cannot be called the general good of man. The sole sign of the goodness of an undertaking is that people do it of their own free will, and man's life is full of such affairs.

Ten workmen provide themselves with cooper's tools in order to work together, and doing this they do what is certainly for their common welfare; but it is not possible to suppose that these workmen if they compel by violence an eleventh man to participate in their association, could affirm that what was their common good would also be good for this eleventh man.

So also with gentlemen who give a dinner to a friend of theirs; it is impossible to assert that this dinner will be good for someone from whom they take ten rubles by force for it. So also with peasants who decide to dig a pond for their convenience. For those who consider the existence of the pond a benefit worth more than the cost of labour expended upon it, the making of it will be a common good, but for him who considers the existence of this pond as less important than the harvesting of a field with which he is behind-hand, the digging of this pond cannot be considered a good. So also of roads people make, and of churches, and museums, and a great variety of social and political affairs. All these things can be a good only for those who regard them as such and engage on them freely and willingly, as in the case of the purchase of the cooper's tools for the association, the dinner given by the gentlemen, or the pond dug by the peasants. But undertakings to which people have to be forcibly driven cease to be a common good just on account of that violence.

This is all so clear and simple that if people had not so long been deceived it would not be necessary to explain anything. We live, let us suppose, in a village, and we, all the villagers, have decided to build a bridge across a bog into which we sink. We have agreed or promised to give so much money, or timber, or so many days' work from each household. We have agreed to do this because this bridge will be worth more to us than its building will cost. But among us there are some for whom it is better not to have the bridge than to spend money on it, or who at least think that this is so.

Can coercing these people to take part in building the bridge make it a benefit to them? Evidently not, for those who considered free participation in the building of the bridge disadvantageous will consider it yet more disadvantageous when it is compulsory. Let us even suppose that we all without exception agreed to build this bridge and promised to contribute so much money or labour from each household for the work, but it so happens that some of those who promised to contribute have not done so because their circumstances changed, causing them to think it better to be without a bridge rather to spend money on it; or simply they have changed their minds; or even reckon on others building the bridge without their contribution and on still being able to use it. Can the compelling of these people to take part in building the bridge make their compulsory sacrifice a benefit to them? Evidently not, for if they did not fulfil their promise owing to altered circumstances which made it harder for them to contribute to the bridge than to do without a bridge, obligatory contributions will be only a greater evil to them. And if the refusers aimed at taking advantage of the labour of others, still, compelling them to make sacrifices will merely be a punishment for their intention, and a quite unproven intention punished before it had been carried into effect; but in neither case will compulsion to participate in an undesired affair be an advantage to them.

So it is when sacrifices are undertaken for an affair intelligible to everyone and of evident and undoubted utility, such as a bridge across a bog all have to cross. How much more unjust and senseless will it be to compel millions of people to make sacrifices for an aim that is unintelligible, intangible, and often indubitably harmful, as is the case with military service and the payment of taxes. But according to science what appears to everyone an evil is a common good; it seems that there are people, a tiny minority, who alone know wherein the common good lies, and, though all the rest of the people consider this common good to be an evil, this minority, while compelling all the rest to do this evil, can consider to be a common good.

Therein lies the chief of superstition and chief of deception hindering the progress of humanity towards truth and welfare. The maintenance of this superstition and this deception is the aim of political sciences in general, and of what is called political economy in particular. Its aim is to hide from people the condition of oppression and slavery in which they are. The means it employs for this purpose are, when dealing with the violence that conditions the whole economic life of the enslaved, purposely to treat this violence as natural and inevitable, and thus to deceive people and divert their eyes from the real cause of their misery.

Slavery has long been abolished. It was abolished in Rome, and in America, and in Russia, but what was abolished was the word and not the thing itself.

Slavery consists in some men freeing themselves from labour (needed for the satisfaction of their wants) which is compulsorily put upon others; and where there is a man not working, not because others work for him lovingly but because instead of working himself he is able to compel others to work for him—there slavery exists. And where, as in all European countries, there are people utilizing the labour of thousands of others by means of violence and believing that they have a right to do so—while others submit to this coercion and regard it as their duty to do so—there slavery of terrible dimensions exists.

Slavery exists. In what does it consist? In that in which it has always consisted and without which it can never exist—the violence of the strong and armed towards the weak and unarmed.

Slavery in its three fundamental methods of personal violence—military service; land tribute enforced by soldiery; and tribute imposed on inhabitants in the form of direct and indirect taxes and maintained by that same soldiery—exists just as it used to. We do not see it only because each of the three forms of slavery has received a new justification, hiding its meaning from us.

The personal violence of the armed towards the unarmed has been justified as the defence of the fatherland against its imaginary foes; in reality it has its old meaning, namely the subjection of the vanquished by oppressors. The violence exerted in depriving the workers of the land they work has received justification as a reward for services supposed to have been rendered to the common good, and it is confirmed by the right of inheritance; in reality it is the same deprivation of land and enslavement of the people, effected by the army (the authorities).

The last, the monetary coercion of taxation—the strongest and now the chief method—has received the most amazing justification, namely that people are deprived of their property and freedom and of their whole good for the sake of freedom and general welfare. In reality it is nothing but the same slavery, except that it is impersonal.

Where violence is legalized, there slavery exists. Whether the violence is expressed by incursions made by princes and their retainers, killing women and children and burning the villages; or by slave-owners taking work or money from their slaves for land and in case of non-payment calling in armed forces; or by some people laying tribute on others and riding armed through the villages; or by the Ministry of the Interior collecting money through Provincial Governors and the rural police, and in case of refusals to pay sending in the military—in a word, so long as there is violence supported by bayonets, there will not be a distribution of wealth among the people, but all wealth will go to the oppressors.

A striking illustration of the truth of this conclusion is supplied by Henry George's project for nationalizing the land. George proposes to recognize all land as belonging to the State, and therefore to replace all taxes, both direct and indirect, by a ground rent. That is to say, every one making use of land should pay to the State the rental-value of such land.

What would result? Agricultural slavery would be abolished within the bounds of the State, that is, the land would belong to the State: England would have its own, America its own, and the slave-dues a man had to pay would be determined by the amount of land he used.

Perhaps the position of some of the workers (agrarian) would be improved, but as long as the forcible collection of a rent tax remained—there would be slavery. An agriculturalist unable after a failure of crops to pay the rent forcibly demanded of him, to retain his land and not lose everything would have to go into bondage to a man who had money.

If a bucket leaks there is certainly a hole in it. Looking at the bottom of a bucket it may seem that the water leaks out of several holes, but however much we may stop up these imaginary holes from outside, the water will still leak out. To stop the flow we must find the place where the water escapes from the bucket and stop it up from inside. The same must be done with measures proposed for stopping the ill-distribution of wealth—for stopping up the holes through which wealth leaks away from the people. People say: 'organize workers' associations, make capital public property, make the land public property!' All this is only external plugging of the places from which the water seems to leak. To stop the leakage of the workers' wealth into the hands of the leisured classes it is necessary to find from within the hole through which this leakage takes place. This hole is the coercion armed men exert on the unarmed; the violence of troops by means of which the people themselves are taken from their work, and the land and the produce of people's toil taken from the people. As long as there exists a single armed man arrogating to himself the right to kill any other man whatever, so long will the irregular distribution of wealth exist, that is, slavery.*

* In the Appendix the reader will find some pages which in other editions have appeared as the conclusion of this twenty-first chapter. They are really an earlier version, which Tolstoy replaced by the four preceding chapters on money. Though he struck those pages out of his final version and they are not needed for the sequence of the argument—but are a repetition of it—they seem sufficiently interesting to be worth preserving in an Appendix.

CHAPTER XXII

I AM ALWAYS SURPRISED by the oft-repeated words: 'Yes, in theory that is so, but how is it in practice?' Just as if theory were some nice phrases needed for conversation but not in order that practice, that is one's whole activity, should necessarily be based on it. There must have been a terrible number of stupid theories in the world for such a remarkable opinion to be generally accepted. Theory is what a man thinks on a subject, and practice is what he does. How then can it be that a man thinks he should do a thing this way and then does it the opposite way? If the theory of bread-baking is that it has first to be kneaded and then set to rise, no one knowing the theory, except a lunatic, will do the reverse. Yet with us it has become the fashion to say, 'In theory that is so, but how is it in practice?'

In the matter with which I am engaged, what I had always thought was the case has been confirmed, namely, that practice inevitably follows theory and, I will not say justifies it, but cannot be different, and that if I have understood a matter about which I have thought, I cannot do it otherwise than as I understand it.

I wished to help the poor just because I had money and shared the common superstition that money represents work, or is in general a legitimate and good thing. But when I began giving away money I saw that I was giving drafts I had collected—which were drawn on the poor. I was doing what many land-owners used to do, making some serfs serve other serfs. I saw that every use of money, whether by purchase of anything, or as a free gift of it to someone, is the issuing for collection of a draft on the poor, or the giving of it to someone for collection from the poor. And therefore the absurdity of what I wished to do—help the poor by exactions on the poor—became plain to me. I saw that money in itself is not merely not a good, but is an evident evil, depriving people of the greatest blessing—that of labouring and utilizing the fruits of one's own exertions—and that I cannot transmit this blessing to anyone, because I myself lack it: I do not labour and have not the happiness of utilizing my own labour.

It might seem that there was nothing particular in this abstract reflection on the question, What is money? But this reflection, which

I entered upon not as a mere reflection but to solve a question of my life and sufferings, gave me the answer to the question, What must we do?

As soon as I understood what riches are and what money is, it not only became clear and indubitable to me what I must do, but also what everybody ought to do, and what they will, therefore, inevitably do. In reality I merely understood what I had long known—the truth transmitted to mankind in remote times by Buddha, and Isaiah, and Lao-tsze, and Socrates, and to us particularly clearly and indubitably by Jesus Christ and his forerunner John the Baptist. In reply to the people's question: What then must we do? John the Baptist replied simply, briefly, and clearly: 'He that hath two coats, let him impart to him that hath none; and he that hath food, let him do likewise' (Luke III. 10, 11). The same was said by Christ many times and yet more clearly. He said, 'Blessed are the poor, and woe unto ye that are rich.' He said, 'Ye cannot serve God and mammon.' He forbade his disciples to take money or even two coats. He told the rich young man that because he was rich, he could not enter the kingdom of God, and that it is easier for a camel to go through the eye of a needle than for a rich man to enter the kingdom of God. He said that he who will not renounce all—house, and children, and fields, to follow him, is not his disciple. He spoke the parable of the rich man, who like our rich men did nothing bad but merely clothed himself well and ate and drank sumptuously, and thereby ruined his soul, and of the pauper Lazarus, who did nothing good, but was saved just by the fact that he was a pauper.

That truth had been known to me well enough, but the false teaching of the world had so obscured it that it had become to me merely a 'theory' in the sense people like to give that word, that is to say, it was mere empty words. But as soon as I succeeded in destroying in my consciousness the sophistries of the worldly teaching, theory merged with practice and the reality of my own life and of the life of all men showed up as its inevitable consequence.

I understood that man, besides living for his personal welfare, must necessarily serve the welfare of others: that if we are to draw a comparison from the world of animals, as some people are fond of doing when defending violence and strife by the struggle for existence in the animal kingdom, we should draw it from the social animals, such as bees, and that therefore man, to say nothing of his reason or innate love of his fellow man, is called on by his very nature to serve others and to serve the common human ends. I understood that that is the natural law of man under which alone he can fulfil his destiny and so be happy. I understood that this law has been infringed, and is infringed, by the fact that people, like robber bees, forcibly avoid toil and exploit the labour of others and direct their toil not to the common good but to the personal gratification of ever-spreading passions (lusts), and themselves, like the robber bees, perish thereby. I understood that men's misfortunes come from the slavery in which some hold others. I understood that the slavery of our time was produced by the violence of militarism, by the appropriation of the land, and by the exaction of money. And having understood the meaning of all three instruments of the new slavery, I could not but wish to free myself from taking part in it.

When I was a serf-owner and understood the immorality of that position, I tried to liberate myself from it, like others who understood it. Considering my rights as slave-owner to be immoral, I tried (until it should be possible to free myself completely from that position) to exert those rights as little as possible and to live and let others live as if those rights did not exist; and at the same time I tried by all means to instil into other slave-owners a sense of the wrongness and inhumanity of our imaginary rights. I cannot but do the same in regard to the present slavery. Until I can completely renounce the rights given me by the possession of landed property and money, which are maintained by military violence, I can but exact my rights as little as possible and at the same time do all that I possibly can to make plain to others the illegitimacy and inhumanity of those pseudo-rights. The participation of a slave-owner in slavery consists in making use of other people's labour, whether that slavery rests on his right to the slave or on his possession of land or money.

And therefore if a man really dislikes slavery and does not wish to be a participant in it, the first thing he will do will be not to use other people's labour, either by owning land, by accepting government employment, or by money.

And the rejection of all the customary means of exploiting other people's labour will inevitably make it necessary for such a man, on the one hand to restrict his needs, and, on the other, to do for himself what others formerly did for him.

This very simple and inevitable deduction enters into all the details of my life, immediately alters it all, and at once releases me from the moral sufferings I experienced at the sight of the miseries and depravity of men, and destroys all those three causes which made it impossible to help the poor and which I had encountered when seeking the causes of my failure.

The first cause was the crowding of the people into the towns and the consumption in towns of the wealth of the villages. It is only necessary for a man to wish not to exploit other people's labour by means of government service, land-ownership, or money—and to wish therefore to satisfy his needs himself to the best of his strength and ability, for it never to enter his head to leave the village, where it is easiest to satisfy one's needs, for the town where everything is the product of someone else's labour and everything has to be bought. Then, in the village, he will be in a position to help the needy, and will not experience the feeling of helplessness I experienced in town when I tried to help people not by my own labour but by other people's labour.

The second cause was the separation of the rich from the poor. It is only necessary for a man not to wish to exploit other people's labour by means of state service, land-ownership, or by money, for him to find himself obliged to satisfy his wants himself, and immediately the wall separating him from the working people will disappear of itself, and he will blend with them and stand shoulder to shoulder with them, and it will become possible for him to help them.

The third cause was shame, based on consciousness of the immorality of my possession of the money with which I wanted to help others. We only need cease to wish to exploit other people's work by means of government service, ownership of land, or by money, and we shall never have that superfluous mad money, my possession of which evoked in others, who had none, the demands I was unable to satisfy, and evoked in me a consciousness of being in the wrong.

CHAPTER XXIII

I SAW THAT THE CAUSE of men's sufferings and depravity was that some are in slavery to others, and so I drew the simple conclusion that if I wish to help others I must first of all cease causing sufferings I wish to relieve, that is, must not take part in the enslavement of men. But what drew me to enslave people was that from childhood I had been accustomed not to work but to make use of the labour of others, and I had lived, and still live, in a society that is not merely accustomed to this enslavement, but justifies it by all sorts of artful and artless sophistries. And I came to the following simple conclusion, that in order not to cause suffering and depravity I must make as little use as possible of the work of others and must myself work as much as possible. By a long path I reached the inevitable conclusion reached thousands of years ago by the Chinese in the saying: 'If there is one idle man, another will be starving.' I came to the simple and natural conclusion that if I pity a tired horse on which I am riding, the first thing I must do if I am really sorry for it, is to get off and walk on my own feet.

That reply, which gives full satisfaction to our moral feelings, was clear to my eyes and is clear to the eyes of us all, but we look aside and do not see it.

In our search for a cure of our social evils we seek on all sides—in governmental, anti-governmental, scientific, and philanthropic superstitions, and do not see what strikes everyone's eyes.

We use a close-stool and want others to carry it out for us, and we pretend to be very sorry for them and to want to make it easier for them, and we invent all kinds of devices except the very simple one of carrying it out for ourselves if we want to use the stool in the house, or of going outside to do our business.

For him who sincerely suffers at seeing the sufferings of those about us, there is a very clear, simple, and easy means, the only possible one for the cure of the evils surrounding us and to enable us to feel that we are living legitimately—the same that John the Baptist gave in reply to the question: 'What then must we do?' and which Christ confirmed: not to have more than one coat and not to have money, that is, not to make use of other people's labour and therefore, first, to do all we can with our own hands.

This is so simple and so clear. But it is simple and clear when the needs are simple and clear and when a man is still fresh and not spoilt to the marrow of his bones by laziness and idleness. I live in a village and lie on the stove,* and I order a neighbour who is in debt to me, to chop wood and heat my stove. It is very clear that I am lazy and am taking my neighbour from his work; and I shall feel ashamed, and it will be tiresome to be always lying down, and if my muscles are strong and I am accustomed to work I shall go and chop the wood myself.

But the temptation of slavery of all kinds has existed so long and so many artificial wants have grown up on it, there are so many people bound up one with another who are accustomed in various degrees to these wants, and people have been so spoilt and pampered for generations, and so complex are the temptations and the justifications that have been devised for luxury and idleness, that for a man at the top of the ladder of idle people it is far from being as easy to understand his sin as it is for a peasant who makes his neighbour heat his stove.

It is terribly hard for people who are on the upper rungs of that ladder to understand what is demanded of them. Their heads are made dizzy by the height of the ladder of lies they stand on, when they see the place below to which they must descend in order to live their life not entirely well but even not quite inhumanly; and therefore this simple and clear truth seems strange to them.

For a man with ten servants, liveries, coachmen, a chef, pictures, and pianos, it certainly seems strange and even ridiculous to do what is the simplest and first action of anyone who is, I will not say a good man but merely a man and not an animal: himself to chop the wood with which his food is cooked and with which he is warmed; himself to clean the boots and goloshes with which he has carelessly stepped into some dirt; himself to bring the water with which he keeps himself clean, and carry out the dirty water in which he has washed.

But besides the remoteness of people from the truth, there is another cause which keeps them from seeing that it is obligatory for

* *In Russian peasant huts the brick stove is built so as to heat the hut and to serve as an oven, and its flat top furnishes a warm and convenient place to sleep on.*

them to undertake the simplest and most natural physical work: this is the complexity of the circumstances and inter-connected interests of those among whom a rich man lives.

This morning I went out into the corridor where the stoves are lighted. A peasant was heating the stove that warms my son's room. I went into his room; he was still asleep. It was eleven o'clock. Today is a holiday; and so excuses—there are no lessons.

A plump eighteen-year-old lad with a beard, who has eaten much the evening before, sleeps till eleven o'clock. But a peasant of his own age has got up in the morning, has already done a lot of things and is heating the tenth stove, while my son sleeps. 'Better let the peasant not heat the stove to warm that sleek lazy body!' thought I. But at once I remembered that this stove warms also the housekeeper's room, who is a woman of forty and till three in the morning prepared everything for the supper my son ate, and then put away the dishes, but who still got up at seven. She could not heat the stove for herself, she would not have time. The peasant was heating for her also, and on her account the lazy fellow gets warmed.

It is true that the interests of all are interwoven, but with no prolonged reckoning each man's conscience tells him on whose side is the labour and on whose the idleness. And not only does conscience tell it, it is told most clearly of all by his account-book. The more money anyone spends the more he obliges others to work for him; the less he spends the more he works.

But industry, public works, and finally that most terrible of words: culture—the development of science and art?

CHAPTER XXIV

LAST YEAR,* in March, I was returning home late one evening. Turning from Zúbov Street to Khamóvniki side-street I saw some black spots on the snow of the Virgin's Field. Something was moving there. I should not have paid attention to it if a policeman standing at the entrance to the side-street had not shouted in the direction of the black spots:

'Vasíli! Why don't you bring her?'

* *That is, in 1884.*

'She won't come!'replied a voice from there, and after that the black spots moved towards the policeman.

I stopped and asked him what it was. He said:

'They have arrested the wenches at the Rzhánov House and taken them to the police-station. This one lagged behind, you see she won't move.'

A yard-porter in a sheepskin coat was fetching her. She walked in front and he kept pushing her from behind. We, the porter, the policeman, and I, were all wearing winter things, but she had only her dress on. In the dusk I could only make out a brown dress, and a kerchief on her head and neck. She was short, as starvelings are, with short legs and a disproportionately broad ill-shaped figure.

'Now, carrion, we're waiting for you. Get along, I say! I'll give it you!' shouted the policeman. It was plain he was tired and had lost patience with her. She went a few steps and again stopped. The elderly yard-porter, a good-natured fellow (I know him personally), pulled her by the arm:

'There, I'll teach you to stop! Go on!' he said, pretending to be angry. She staggered and began to speak in a grating voice. Every sound she uttered was a false note, hoarse and squeaking.

'Now then! What are you shoving for? I'll get there!'

'You'll freeze,' said the porter.

'Our kind don't freeze. I'm a hot'un.'

She meant it as a jest but it sounded like abuse. Near the lamp-post that stands not far from the gate of our house she again stopped and leant—almost fell—against the wooden fence of the yard, and began fumbling in her skirts with clumsy benumbed fingers. They again shouted at her, but she only muttered and went on with what she was doing. In one hand she held a cigarette bent like an arc, and in the other some sulphur matches. I stopped, ashamed to go past her though also ashamed to stand and look on. At last I made up my mind and went up to her. She leant with her shoulder against the wooden fence, and vainly trying to strike the sulphur matches against it threw them away. I looked at her face. She was a starveling, but it seemed to me no longer young. I supposed her to be about thirty. She had a dirty-coloured face, small, dim, and drunken eyes, a knob-shaped nose, crooked slobbering lips that turned down at the corners, and a short strand of dry hair showed from under her kerchief. Her figure was long and flat and her hands and feet stumpy.

I stopped opposite her. She looked at me and smirked, as if to say she knew what I was thinking about.

I felt I had to say something to her, and I wished to show her that I pitied her.

'Are your parents alive?' I asked.

She laughed hoarsely, then suddenly stopped and, raising her brows, looked at me.

'Are your parents alive?' I repeated.

She smirked with an expression which seemed to say: 'You have found a queer thing to ask about!'

'I have a mother,' she said. 'What is it to you?'

'And how old are you?'

'Over fifteen,' said she, promptly answering a question she was evidently accustomed to.

'Now, get on! We shall freeze to death with you here, blast you!' shouted the policeman, and she staggered away from the fence and swaying to and fro went down Khamóvniki street to the police-station, while I turned in at the gate, entered the house, and asked if my daughters had come home. I was told that they had been to a party, had enjoyed themselves very much, had returned, and were already asleep.

Next morning I wanted to go to the police station to learn what they had done with this unfortunate woman, and I was setting out rather early, when one of those gentry* whose weaknesses have caused them to fall from the comfortable life to which they are accustomed and who are now up and now down again, came to see me. I had known this one three years. During that time he had several times pawned everything he had, even to the clothes he was wearing. Such a misfortune had happened to him quite recently, and now he was spending his nights in one of the night-lodgings at Rzhánov House and coming to me in the daytime. He met me as I was going out and, without listening to what I wanted to say, at once began to tell me what had happened at Rzhánov House that night. Before he had half finished the story he, an old man who had seen all phases of life, burst into sobs, began to cry, and turned to the wall. This is what he told me. All he said was perfectly true. I afterwards verified it on the spot, and learnt additional details which I will add to his story.

* *This was A. P. Ivánov who for many years worked intermittently, between his fits of drinking, as a copyist for Tolstoy.*

In that doss-lodging on the ground floor, in Number 32 where my friend slept, among various transient night-lodgers, men and women who came together for five kopeks, there lived a washerwoman of about thirty years old, a blond woman, quiet and well-conducted but sickly. The landlady of the tenement is a boatman's mistress. In summer her lover keeps a boat, but in winter they make a living by letting bunks for the night, at three kopeks without a pillow or five kopeks with a pillow. The washerwoman had lived there for some months and was a quiet woman; but of late they had taken a dislike to her because her coughing prevented the lodgers sleeping. In particular a half-crazy old woman of eighty, who was also a permanent lodger there, took a violent dislike to the washerwoman and was always nagging at her for spoiling her sleep and for hawking all night like a sheep. The washerwoman kept silent; she was in debt for her lodging and felt guilty, and so she had to be quiet. She was less and less often able to go to work, her strength was failing, and so she could not pay the mistress of the room; for the last week she had not been out to work at all, and with her cough only poisoned the life of them all, especially of the old woman who also did not go out. Four days before, the mistress told her she could not remain there: she was already owing sixty kopeks and did not pay them, and there seemed little hope of their being paid; the bunks were all occupied, and the other lodgers complained of her coughing.

When the mistress told the washerwoman to leave unless she could pay, the old woman was delighted, and pushed her out into the yard. The washerwoman went away but returned an hour later; and the mistress had not the heart to drive her away again. And on the next and the third day the mistress did not drive her out. 'Where shall I go to?' said the washerwoman. But on the third day the landlady's lover, a Moscovite and one who knew town ways and regulations, went for the police. A policeman, with a sword and a pistol on a red cord, came to the lodging, and using only polite and proper words fetched the washerwoman out into the street.

It was a clear, sunny, but frosty, March day. Water was running down the gutters, and the yard-porters were breaking up the ice on the pavements. The sledges of the cab-drivers bumped over the crusted snow and screeched as they scraped on bare stones. The washerwoman went up the sunny side of the slope, came to the church, and sat down on the sunny side of its porch. But when the sun began to sink behind the house and the puddles began again to coat with ice, she felt cold and frightened. She got up and dragged herself along. . . . Where to? Home, to the only home she had had latterly. Before she got there, resting on her way, it was growing dark. She came to the gates, turned in at them, slipped, uttered an exclamation, and fell.

One man passed, and then another. 'Must be drunk.' Yet another man passed, stumbled over the washerwoman, and said to the yard-porter: 'Some drunken woman is lying in your gateway, I nearly broke my head tumbling over her. Get her moved away, can't you!'

The yard-porter went to see about it . . . but the washerwoman was dead. That is what my friend told me. It may be thought that I am selecting the facts—my meeting with the fifteen-year-old prostitute and the story of this washer-woman—but do not let that be supposed; it happened just so, in one night—I do not remember the date, but in March 1884.

And then having heard my friend's account I went to the police station, meaning to go from there to Rzhánov House to get further details about the washerwoman. The weather was fine, sunny, and in the shade between the frost-crystals the night frost had formed, running water was again visible, while in the blaze of the sun on the Khamóvniki square everything was thawing and the water was running. One heard a noise from the river. The trees of the Sans-Souci gardens showed up blue across the river, the browned sparrows, unnoticed in winter, caught one's eye by their merriment; and men too seemed to wish to be merry, but they all had too many cares. The sound of the church bells was heard, and against a background of these mingling sounds one heard that of firing in the barracks; the whistle of bullets and their smack against a target.

I came to the police station. In it were several armed men—they took me to their chief. He, too, was armed with a sword and pistol, and was busy giving directions about a ragged shivering old man who stood before him and was too feeble to answer clearly the questions put to him. When he had finished with the old man he turned to me. I asked about yesterday's girl. At first he listened to me attentively, but then smiled at my not knowing the regulations or why they are taken to the police-station,* and especially at my being surprised at her youth.

* For medical examination, as prostitutes.

'Why really, there are some twelve-year-old ones, and lots of thirteen and fourteen,' said he cheerfully.

In reply to my question about yesterday's girl, he explained that she had probably been sent to the Committee. (I think that was what he said.) And he replied vaguely when I asked where she had spent the night. He did not remember the particular girl I was asking about. There were so many of them every day.

At Rzhánov House, in Number 32, I found a church chanter already reading the Psalms over the deceased woman. She had been placed on what had been her bunk, and the lodgers (all quite poor people) had collected among themselves enough money to pay for the prayers, a coffin, and a shroud, and the old women had dressed her and laid her out. The church chanter was reading in the dim light, a woman in a cloak was standing with a wax taper in her hand, and another such taper was held by a man (a gentleman, I should say) who was standing in a clean overcoat with a good astrakhan collar, shining goloshes, and a starched shirt. This was her brother. They had traced and found him.

I went past the deceased woman to the mistress's corner and asked her all about it. She was frightened at my questions; she evidently feared she might be accused of something; but after a while she began to speak freely and told me everything. As I went out I looked at the dead woman. There is a beauty about all dead people, but this one was specially beautiful and touching in her coffin: her face clean and pale, with prominent closed eyes, sunken cheeks, and soft flaxen hair above the high brows; a tired kindly face, and not sad but surprised. And indeed, if the living do not see, the dead must be surprised.

The day I wrote this down, there was a great ball given in Moscow.

That evening I left home after eight o'clock. I live in a place surrounded by factories, and I left the house after the factory whistles had sounded, which after a week's incessant work let the men out for a holiday.

I passed, and was passed by, workmen making for the dram-shops and taverns. Many were already drunk and many had women with them.

I live amid factories. Every morning at five a whistle is heard, then a second, a third, a tenth, and others farther and farther away. This means that work has begun for women, children, and old men. At eight o'clock the whistle sounds again for half an hour's interval. At noon there is a third: this is an hour for dinner; and at eight a fourth sounds, for closing.

Curiously enough all the three factories around me produce exclusively articles needed for balls.

In the nearest one stockings are made; at another, silk stuffs; in the third, perfumery and pomades.

It is possible to hear those whistles and to attach to them no idea but that of time. 'Ah, there's the whistle already, so it is time for my walk'; but it is also possible to realize what really is the case: that the first whistle at five in the morning means that people—sleeping in a damp basement, often men and women side by side—get up in the dark and are hurrying to the buildings where the machines drone and taking their places at work—to which they foresee no end and for themselves no use; and so they work, often in hot, stuffy, dirty rooms, with very short intervals, for one, two, three . . . twelve and more hours a day. They sleep and again get up, and again and again continue the same work—which has no meaning for them and to which they are driven by sheer necessity.

And so week passes after week, with the intervention of holidays, and here I saw these workers let out for one of these holidays. They come out into the street: everywhere taverns, Imperial dram-shops, and wenches. And tipsily they drag one another along by the arm, and drag with them girls such as the one that was taken to the police station, and hire sledges, and drive or walk from tavern to tavern, swearing and staggering and saying they know not what. Formerly I had seen such staggering factory-hands and fastidiously avoided them and almost blamed them; but since I have heard those whistles every day and know their meaning, I am only surprised that all these men do not become roughs such as those of whom Moscow is full, and not all the women come to be like the girl I saw near my house.

So I walked about, watching these workmen making turmoil in the streets till about eleven o'clock. Then their movement began to quieten down. Only a few drunken ones remained, and here and there men and women who were taken to the police station. And now from all sides carriages began to appear all driving in one direction.

On the boxes were coachmen and footmen well-dressed and wearing cockades. The well-fed caparisoned trotters flew over the snow at fourteen miles an hour, and in the carriages were ladies wrapped in warm cloaks and careful of their flowers and coiffures. Everything—from the horses' harness, the carriages, the rubber tyres, and the cloth of the coachmen's warm coats, to the stockings, shoes, flowers, velvet, gloves, and perfumes—was made by those people some of whom are sprawling drunk in their bunks in the dormitories, some are with prostitutes in the dosshouses, or distributed in the lock-ups. Past them—on what was all theirs and in what was all theirs—drive those going to the ball; and it never enters their heads that there is any connection between the ball to which they are going and those drunkards at whom their coachmen shout so sternly.

These people with quiet consciences—in full confidence that they are doing nothing bad but something very good—amuse themselves at the ball.

Amuse themselves! Amuse themselves from eleven till six in the morning, through the very middle of the night, while others are tossing with empty stomachs in doss-houses, and some are dying like the washerwoman.

The amusement consists in married women and girls baring their breasts, padding themselves out behind, and showing themselves in this unseemly condition in which an unperverted girl or woman would not for the world wish to exhibit herself to a man; and in that semi-nude condition, with bare breasts protruding and arms uncovered to the shoulder, with bustles behind and dresses drawn tight to their hips, in the strongest illumination, women and girls, whose chief virtue has always been modesty, appear among strange men similarly clad in improperly close-fitting garments, whom to the sound of intoxicating music they embrace, and with whom they whirl around. The old women, often exposing their persons as much as the young ones, sit, look on, and eat and drink things that taste nice; the old men doing the same. No wonder this is done at night when the common people, being all asleep, do not see it. But that is not done to hide it; it seems to the doers that there is nothing it is necessary to hide, that it is very good, and that by this amusement in which they consume the painful labour of thousands, they not only injure no one, but actually feed the poor.

It may be very merry at balls. But how does this happen? When among ourselves we see that some one has not eaten or is cold, we are ashamed to be merry, and cannot be merry till he has been fed and warmed; and we do not understand people making merry with sports that cause others to suffer. We dislike and do not understand the mirth of cruel boys who squeeze a dog's tail in a cleft stick and make merry over it.

Then how is it that here in these amusements of ours blindness has befallen us, and we do not see the cleft stick in which we squeeze the tails of those who suffer for our amusement?

Not one of the women who drove to this ball in a one hundred and fifty ruble dress was born at the ball, or at Madame Minanquoit's,* and each of them has lived in the country and seen peasants, and knows her own nurse and lady's-maid who have poor fathers or brothers for whom to save a hundred and fifty rubles to build a hut is the aim of a long and laborious life. She knows this—how then can she be merry, knowing that at this ball she wears on her half-naked body the hut that is the dream of her good maid's brother? But granting that this may not have struck her—the fact that velvet, silk, sweets, flowers, laces, and dresses do not grow of themselves but are made by people, is one that it would seem she cannot but know—or what kind of people make these things, and under what conditions they make them, and why. She must know that the seamstress she scolded did not make that dress for her at all out of love of her, and so she cannot help knowing that it was all made for her under compulsion, and that, like her dress, the lace and flowers and velvet were made for the same reason. Perhaps, however, they are so befogged that they do not see even that. But the fact that five or six people, old, decent, often infirm, footmen and maids, have missed their sleep and been put to trouble on her account she cannot help knowing. She has seen their weary, gloomy faces. She cannot but know also that the frost that night reached thirty-one degrees below zero Fahrenheit, and that in that frost the old coachman sat on his box all night. But I know that they really do not see this. And if the young married women and girls, from the hypnotism produced on them by the ball, do not see it, they must not be condemned. They, poor things, are doing what their elders consider right; but can one explain the cruelty shown by those elders?

The elders always give one and the same explanation: 'I do not force anyone; I buy the things and hire people—the maids and the coachmen. There is nothing wrong in buying and hiring. I do not force anyone, I hire them; what is wrong in that?'

* A fashionable Moscow dressmaker.

The other day I called on an acquaintance of mine. Passing through the first room, I was surprised to see two women there at the table, for I knew my acquaintance was a bachelor. A lean, sallow, old-looking woman of about thirty, wearing a kerchief, was doing something very rapidly with her hands and fingers under the table, and was twitching nervously as if in a fit. Sideways to her sat a little girl who was doing something and twitching in just the same way. Both women seemed as if subject to St Vitus's dance. I went to them and looked at what they were doing. They glanced up at me and continued their work with the same concentration. Before them lay some loose tobacco and paper cartridges. They were making cigarettes. The woman rubbed the tobacco between her hands, placed it in a machine, drew on the cartridge, pressed it home, and threw it to the girl. The girl rolled up a piece of paper, pushing a wad into the cigarette, threw it aside, and started on another. This all was done with such rapidity and with such tension that it is impossible to describe it to a man who has not seen it. I expressed surprise at their rapidity.

'Have been doing nothing else for fourteen years,' said the woman.

'Is it hard?'

'Yes, one's chest hurts and it is hard to breathe.'

Indeed she need not have said so. One had only to look at her and at the little girl. The girl has been working for over two years, and anyone seeing her at it would say that she had a strong constitution but was already beginning to break up. My acquaintance, a kindly and liberal-minded man, had hired them to fill cigarettes at two rubles fifty kopeks a thousand. He has money and gives it them for their work—what harm is there in that? He gets up about noon; spends his evenings from six till two in the morning at cards or at the piano, and eats tasty and sweet food; other people do all his work for him. He devised a new pleasure—smoking. I remember when he began it.

Here are a woman and a girl who by making machines of themselves can barely manage to support themselves, and who spend their whole lives inhaling tobacco, and so ruin their health. He has money which he did not earn, and he prefers to play bridge* to making cigarettes for himself. He gives money to these women

* The game actually mentioned in the Russian is 'vint', which much resembles bridge.

only on condition that they continue to live as wretchedly as before, that is, that they make cigarettes for him.

I like cleanliness, and give my money only on condition that a laundress washes the shirt I change twice a day, and this work has drained her last strength and she has died.

'What is there bad in it? People buy and hire whether I do or not, and will go on compelling others to make velvet and sweets and will buy them, and will go on hiring people to make cigarettes and to wash shirts, even if I don't. So why should I deprive myself of velvet and sweets and cigarettes and clean shirts, if things are so arranged?' I often, almost always, hear this argument. It is the same that is used by a maddened crowd that is destroying something. It is the same that dogs are guided by when one of them flies at another and overthrows it, and the rest rush at it and tear it to pieces. Once it has been started and injury has been done, why should not I share in it? 'Well, what good will it do if I wear a dirty shirt and make my own cigarettes? Would anyone be the better for it?' ask those who wish to justify themselves. Were we not so far from the truth one would be ashamed to reply to such a question, but we are so entangled that this question seems natural to us, and, ashamed as one is to answer it, it must be met.

What difference will it make if I wear my shirt for a week instead of a day and make my cigarettes myself, or do not smoke at all?

This difference, that some washerwoman and some cigarette-maker will strain her strength less, and the money I should have paid for the washing and cigarette-making I shall be able to give to that washerwoman, or even to quite other washerwomen and workers who are weary of work, and who, instead of working beyond their strength, may then rest and drink tea. But to this I hear a reply (so reluctant are the rich, luxurious people to understand their position). They reply: 'Even if I wear dirty linen and stop smoking and give this money to the poor instead, all the same the poor will have everything taken from them, and my drop in the ocean will not help matters.'

One feels still more ashamed to reply to this retort, but it must be answered. It is such a common rejoinder and the answer is so simple.

If I visit savages and they treat me to tasty cutlets, and next day I learn (or perhaps see) that these tasty cutlets are made of a prisoner whom they have killed to make them; then if I do not think it right to eat people, however tasty the cutlets may be and however general the practice of eating men may be among those I am living with, and however little the prisoners who are kept to serve as food may gain by my refusal to eat the cutlets, still I shall not and cannot eat them again. Perhaps I might even eat human flesh if compelled by hunger, but I should not entertain others at, or take part in, feasts where human flesh was eaten, and should not seek such feasts or feel proud of taking part in them.

CHAPTER XXV

'Well, what must we do? We didn't make things so.' But if not we, who did? We say: we did not do it, it has just done itself, as children when they have broken something say it broke itself. We say that once the towns exist we, living in them, support people by buying their labour.

But it is not true, and we need only consider how we live in the country and support people there.

The winter is past in town, and Easter Week comes. In town that same orgy of the rich continues; on the boulevards, in the gardens, in the parks and on the river, are music, theatres, rides, promenades, all kinds of illuminations and fireworks, but in the country there are still better things—the air is better, the trees, the meadows, and the flowers are fresher. We must go where all this is budding and flowering. And so most rich people, utilizing the labour of others, go to the country to breathe this better air and to see these still better meadows and woods.

And so the rich people settle down in the country amid the rough peasants who live on ryebread and onion, work eighteen hours a day, do not get enough sleep at night, and wear tattered clothes. Here at least no one has tempted these people: there are no mills or factories here, and no idle hands of whom there are so many in town, and whom we are supposed to feed by giving them work. Here during the whole summer the people are unable to keep up with their work, and not only are there no unemployed hands but quantities of things perish for lack of labour, and many people, children, old men, and women with child, perish by overstraining themselves. How do the rich folk arrange their lives here?

Why . . . in this way. If there is an old house built in the days of serfdom, it is renovated and ornamented; or if there is none, a new one is built—two or three stories high, with from twelve to twenty or more rooms all about fourteen feet high.

Parquet floors are laid, the windows have large glass panes, there are costly carpets, expensive furniture, with a sideboard costing from two hundred to six hundred rubles.

The paths near the house are made of gravel, the ground is levelled, flower-beds are set out, a croquet-ground is arranged, a giant-stride is put up, reflecting globes are set up, and often conservatories, hot-houses, and high stables, always with ornamented ridge-pieces. It is all painted with oil-colours—made with the oil the old peasants and their children do not get in their porridge. If the rich man is able he settles down in such a house, or if he cannot afford that, he hires such a house; but however poor and liberal-minded a man of our circle may be, when he settles in the country he settles in a house for the building and cleaning of which dozens of working people have to be taken from the village where they are unable to cope with the work needed for growing grain for their own sustenance.

There at least one cannot say that factories exist and it will be all the same whether I do or do not make use of them; here it cannot be said that I feed idle hands; here we directly introduce the manufacture of things we want and directly exploit the needs of those around us, tearing them away from work necessary for them, for us, and for everybody, and we thus pervert some and ruin the life and the health of others.

An educated and honourable family let us say, of the gentry or official class, is living in the country.

All the members of the family and their guests gather there in the middle of June, for till then they have been studying and passing their examinations—that is, they arrive at the beginning of the mowing and stay there till September, that is, till the harvest and the sowing of the winter corn. The members of this family (like almost all people of that circle) remain in the country from the beginning of the busy season of urgent work—not to the end of it, for in September the sowing of the winter corn and the stacking of potatoes is still in progress, but—till the work is slackening.

All the time they are in the country the peasants' summer work goes on around them and beside them, of the intensity of which, however much we may have heard or read or witnessed it, we can form no conception unless we try it ourselves.

And the members of the family, some ten people, live just as they did in town or worse if possible than in town, for here in the country it is considered that the family are resting (from doing nothing), and so they have no longer any semblance of work or any excuse for their idleness.

During the Petróv fast* —the strict fast, when the peasants' food is kvas, rye-bread, and onions—mowing begins. The gentlefolk living in the country see this work, to some extent they give orders for it, to some extent admire it, are pleased by the odour of the wilting hay, the sound of the women's songs, the clanging of the scythes, and the sight of the rows of mowers and the women raking the hay.

They see this near the house, and then the young people and children, having done nothing all day, have to be driven half a verst for their bathe.

The work done at hay-making is one of the most important undertakings in the world. Almost every year, from lack of labourers and time, the meadows may be drenched with rain before the mowing is completed, and the greater or lesser intensity of the work decides whether twenty or more per cent of hay shall be added to the peoples' wealth or shall rot and perish on its roots. If more hay is gathered there will be more meat for the old men and more milk for the children. So it is in general; but for each of the mowers in particular the question of bread and of milk for himself and his children for the winter is here being decided. Each of the men and women knows this and even the children know that this work is important and that one must work to the limit of one's strength, carrying the jug of kvas to father in the field and, changing the heavy jug from hand to hand, running barefoot as fast as possible a mile and a half from the village to be in time for his dinner and that daddy may not scold. Everyone knows that from hay-time till harvest there will be no break in the work and no time for resting.

It is not the hay-making alone; everyone has work to do besides the mowing: there is land to turn up and harrow, the women have

* *The fast of St Peter and St Paul, from the ninth week after Easter till the 29th June, old style.*

to bleach the linen and attend to the bread and the washing, and the men have to drive to the mill and to town, look after the village communal affairs, attend the law courts, see the rural police-officer, and do the carting, and at night feed the horses; and all—old, young, and sick—work to the limit of their strength. The peasants work so that always, before the end of each turn of work the weak, the striplings, and the old men, tottering, hardly manage to do the last rows, and can scarcely rise again after the pause; and so do the women work, though they are often pregnant or nursing.

The work is intense and ceaseless. All work with their utmost strength and during this work eat up not only all their scanty supplies of food but also any reserves they may have had: never too stout, they grow leaner by the end of the harvest work.

Here is a small group engaged on mowing: three peasants—one an old man, another his nephew (a young married lad), and a boot-maker, a sinewy fellow who has been a domestic serf—this hay-harvest decides their fate for the coming winter for them all: whether they can keep a cow and pay the taxes. They have already worked unceasingly and continuously for two weeks. Rain has hindered the work. After the rain, when the wind has dried the grass, they decide to finish the work, and to get on more quickly they decide each to bring two women to it. With the old man comes his wife, a woman of fifty worn out by hard work and eleven childbirths, and deaf but still a good worker, and his thirteen-year-old daughter, a small girl but strong and quick. With the nephew comes his wife, a woman as strong and tall as a man, and his sister-in-law, the pregnant wife of a soldier. With the bootmaker comes his wife, a good worker, and her mother, an old woman finishing her eighth decade and who usually goes out begging. They all line up, and work from morning till evening in the sweltering blaze of the June sun. It is steaming and the rain threatens. Every hour of work is precious. They grudge the time to fetch water or kvas.

A tiny boy, the old woman's grandson, fetches some water for them. The old woman, evidently only anxious not to be driven away from the work, does not let the rake out of her hands, though she can hardly, with effort, move along. The lad, all bent up and taking short steps with his bare little feet, brings along the jug of water which is heavier than himself, changing it from hand to hand. The girl shoulders a load of hay which is also heavier than she; she takes a few steps, stops, and throws it down unable to carry it farther. The old woman of fifty rakes unceasingly and, with her kerchief brushed to one side, drags the hay along, breathing heavily and tottering in her walk; the woman of eighty does nothing but rake, but even that is beyond her strength: she slowly drags her feet in their bark shoes, and with wrinkled brows looks sombrely before her like one who is seriously ill or is dying. The old man purposely sends her farther away from the others to rake near the hay-cocks so that she should not have to keep up with them, but without pause and with the same death-like, sombre face she works on as long as the others do.

The sun is already setting behind the woods and the hay-cocks are not yet all cleared away and much remains to be done.

All feel it is time to knock off, but no one speaks, waiting for the others to do so. At last the bootmaker, feeling that he has no strength left, proposes to the old man to leave the cocks till tomorrow and the old man agrees, and the women at once run for their clothes, for the jugs, for the hay-forks, and the old woman sits down immediately where she stands, and then lies down still looking straight before her with the same deathlike face. But the women are going, and she gets up groaning and drags herself away after them.

But here is the proprietor's house. That same evening when from the village is heard the clang of the whetstones of the exhausted hay-makers returning from the fields, the sounds of the hammers straightening out the dents in the scythe blades, the shouts of women and girls who, having just had time to put down their rakes, are already running to drive in the cattle—from the proprietor's house other sounds are heard; drin, drin, drin! goes the piano, and an Hungarian song rings out, and amid those songs occasionally comes the sound of the knock of croquet-mallets on the balls. Near the stable stands a carriage to which four well-fed horses are harnessed. It is a smart hired carriage.

Guests have arrived who have paid ten rubles to be driven ten miles. The horses harnessed to the carriage are making their bells tinkle. There is hay in their trough and they trample it underfoot—the very hay that there in the hay-field is collected with such effort. At the proprietor's house there is movement—a healthy well-fed lad in a pink shirt (given him for his services as yardporter) is calling the coachmen to harness and saddle some horses. Two peasants who live here as coachmen come out of the coachmen's room and go leisurely to saddle the horses for the gentlefolk.

Still nearer to the proprietor's house one hears the sounds of another piano. This is a young lady student of the Conservatoire, who lives here to teach the children and is practising Schumann. The sounds of the one piano break in on those of the other. Close to the house two nurses are passing: one of them is young, the other old. They are taking and carrying children—of the same age as those who had run from the village with the jugs—to put them to bed. One of the nurses is English and cannot speak Russian. She was imported from England not for any known qualities, but only because she could not talk Russian. Farther off a peasant and two peasant women are watering flowers near the house, while another is cleaning a gun for the young master.

And here are two women carrying a basket with clean clothes; they have washed the linen for the gentry and for the English and French teachers. In that house two women hardly manage to wash up all the crockery for the gentlefolk who have just had a meal, and two peasants in dress coats are running up and down stairs serving coffee, tea, wine, and seltzer water. Upstairs a table is spread: they have just finished eating and will soon eat again till midnight, till three o'clock, often till cock-crow.

Some of them sit smoking and playing cards, others sit and smoke talking liberalism; others move about from place to place, eat, smoke, and not knowing what to do decide to go out for a drive. There are some fifteen healthy men and women there and some thirty able-bodied men and women servants working for them.

And this is happening where every hour and every boy is precious. And it will continue in July when the peasants, going short of sleep, will mow the oats by night not to let them shack, and the women will rise while it is still dark to thrash straw for sheaf-bands, and when that old woman by then quite worn out with the harvest work, and the woman with child, and the young lads, overstrain themselves and get ill from drinking too much water; and when there is a shortage of hands and horses and carts to carry to the stacks the corn which feeds everyone, and of which millions of puds* are needed every day in Russia that people may not die; and all this time the gentlefolk will continue the same way of life—there will be

* The 'pud' is about 36 lbs avoirdupois.

theatricals, picnics, hunts, drinking, eating, piano-playing, singing, dancing, in an unceasing orgy.

Here it is no longer possible to make the excuse that such is the order of things; none of it was prearranged. We ourselves carefully arrange this way of life, taking grain and labour away from the over-burdened peasant folk. We live as though we had no connection with the dying washerwoman, the fifteen-year-old prostitute, the woman fagged out by cigarette-making, and the strained, excessive labour of the old women and children around us who lack a sufficiency of food; we live—enjoying ourselves in luxury—as if there were no connection between those things and our life; we do not wish to see that were it not for our idle, luxurious and depraved way of life, there would also not be this excessive toil, and that without this excessive toil such lives as ours would be impossible.

We imagine that their sufferings are one thing and our life another, and that we, living as we do, are as innocent and pure as doves.

We read descriptions of the lives of the Romans and marvel at the inhumanity of the soulless Luculli glutting themselves on delicacies and costly drinks while people died of hunger; we shake our heads and marvel at the savagery of our grandfathers, the serf-owners who organized domestic orchestras and theatres and allotted whole villages for the upkeep of their gardens, and from the height of our humanitarianism we wonder at them.

We read the words of Isaiah, Chapter V:

(8) Woe unto them that join house to house, that lay field to field, till there be no place, that they may be placed alone in the midst of the earth.

(11) Woe unto them that rise up early in the morning, that they may follow strong drink; that continue until night, till wine inflame them!

(12) And the harp, and the viol, the tabret, and pipe, and wine, are in their feasts: but they regard not the work of the Lord, neither consider the operation of his hands.

(18) Woe unto them that draw iniquity with cords of vanity, and sin as it were with a cart rope:

(20) Woe unto them that call evil good and good evil; that put darkness for light, and light for darkness; that put bitter for sweet, and sweet for bitter!

(21) Woe unto them that are wise in their own eyes, and prudent in their own sight!

(22) Woe unto them that are mighty to drink wine, and men of strength to mingle strong drink:

(23) Which justify the wicked for reward, and take away the righteousness of the righteous from him!

We read these words, and it seems to us that it does not refer to us.

We read in the Gospels: Matthew III. 10:

And now also the axe is laid unto the root of the trees: therefore every tree that bringeth not forth good fruit is hewn down, and cast into the fire.

And we are fully convinced that we are just the good tree that brings forth fruit, and that these words are not addressed to us, but to some others, to bad people.

We read the words of Isaiah, VI:

(10) Make the heart of this people fat, and make their ears heavy, and shut their eyes; lest they see with their eyes, and hear with their ears, and understand with their hearts, and convert and be healed.

(11) Then said I, Lord, how long? And he answered, Until the cities be wasted without inhabitant, and the houses without man, and the land be utterly desolate.

We read this and are fully persuaded that this wonderful thing is not done to us, but to some other people. But the reason why we see nothing is just because this wonderful work is being done to us: we do not hear, nor see, nor understand with our hearts. How did this come about?

CHAPTER XXVI

How can one who considers himself, I will not say a Christian or even a cultured or humane man, but simply a man with some traces of reason and conscience, live in such a way so that, without taking part in the struggle of all humanity for life, he devours the labour of those who do struggle and increases by his demands the burden of the strugglers and the number of those who perish in that struggle? Yet our so-called Christian and cultured world is full of such people. Not only is our world full of such, but the ideal of people of our Christian and cultured world is to acquire the greatest possible fortune—that is, riches affording comfort and idleness: in other words, liberation from the struggle for life and opportunity to avail oneself fully of the labour of one's brethren, who are perishing in that struggle. How could people fall into such an amazing error?

How could they come to the pass of not seeing, nor hearing, nor understanding with their hearts, what is so clear, obvious, and indubitable?

One need but reflect for a moment, to be horrified at the amazing contradiction between our life and what we—I will not say Christian, but humane and cultured people—profess.

Whether well or ill arranged by the God, or the law of nature, by which the world and mankind exist—the position of man in the world from the time we first know it, has been and is, that men are naked, without wool on their bodies, without burrows in which to shelter, without food they can find in the fields like Robinson Crusoe on his island, and they are all so placed as to have constantly and ceaselessly to struggle with nature in order to cover their bodies, make themselves clothes, fence themselves in, have a roof over their heads, and produce their food, so as two or three times a day to satisfy their hunger and that of their children and old folk who cannot work.

Wherever, at whatever period and in whatever number, we observe the life of men, in Europe, China, America, or Russia, and whether we observe the whole of humanity or only some small part of it, in ancient times in the nomad state or in our times with steam-engines, sewing machines, electric lights, and improved agricultural methods, we see one and the same thing: that people, working incessantly and intensely, are unable to secure sufficient food, clothing, and shelter for themselves and their children and old people, and that a considerable number, now as in earlier ages, perish from lack of sufficient means of life and from excessive labour to obtain those means.

Live where we may, if we draw a circle around us of a hundred thousand, of a thousand, of ten miles, or of one mile, and observe the lives of those whom our circle encloses, we shall see in it starveling children, old men and old women, women in confinement, the sick and the weak; who have not sufficient food or rest and who therefore die prematurely, and we shall see men in their prime who are simply killed by dangerous and harmful work.

Since the world began we see that men have struggled with their common need and despite terrible efforts, deprivations, and sufferings, have not been able to vanquish it. We also know that each of us, wherever he may be and however he may live, every day and every hour, voluntarily or not, consumes part of the produce the labour of humanity has produced. Wherever and however he lives, the house and the roof over his head did not grow of their own accord. The wood in his stove did not walk in of itself, nor did the water; neither did the baked bread, the dinner, the clothes, and his boots, fall from the sky; but it has all been made not by men of the past alone, who are already dead, but has been, and is being, made for him now by people hundreds and thousands of whom wither up and die in unavailing efforts to obtain for themselves and their children the essentials of life—shelter, food, and clothing —the means to save themselves and their children from suffering and premature death. They all struggle against want: struggle with such tension that every moment their brethren perish around them: fathers, mothers, and children.

People in this world, like men on a waterlogged vessel with a small supply of food, are placed by God or by Nature so that they must spare the food and unceasingly exert themselves to avoid a calamity. Every stoppage of that work by any of us, every consumption by us of the work of others, that is not necessary for the common aim, is ruinous for ourselves and for our fellow-men.

How has it happened that the majority of the educated people of our time, without themselves labouring, calmly consume other people's labours which are necessary for the maintenance of life, and consider that to do so is quite natural and reasonable?

To free ourselves from the toil proper and natural to all and to lay it on others without considering ourselves traitors and thieves, only two assumptions are possible: first, that we—those who do not share in the common toil—are beings distinct from the working people and have a special function in society, like the drones or queen-bees that have a different function from working bees; and secondly, that what we, who are freed from the struggle for life, are doing for the others is so useful for all men that it certainly compensates for the harm we do by making their burden heavier.

In former times people who exploited the labour of others asserted, first that they were a special breed, and secondly that they were specially appointed by God to care for the welfare of the others, that is to govern them and teach them, and so they assured others, and often themselves believed, that what they were doing was more necessary and important for the people than was the labour they consumed. And that justification sufficed as long as people doubted neither the direct intervention of the Divinity in human affairs nor the distinction between different breeds. But with the coming of Christianity and the consciousness of the equality and unity of all men that flows from it, this justification could no longer be presented in that form. It was no longer possible to assert that people are born of different breeds and distinctions and with different functions, and the old justification, though still maintained by some people, was gradually abolished and now hardly exists.

The justification of the difference between various human breeds has disappeared, but the fact of the emancipation of self from toil and the consumption of the labour of others by those who have power to do so, remains as before, and new justifications for the existing fact have continually been devised, so that even without acknowledging a special breed of people it should seem right for those who can manage it to exempt themselves from labour. Very many such justifications have been devised. Strange as it may appear, the chief occupation of the activity that at a particular period was called science—the thing that constituted the ruling tendency of science—was, and still continues to be, the discovery of such justifications. That was the aim of the activity of the theological and of the juridical sciences, it was the aim of so-called philosophy, and it has latterly become (strange as this appears to contemporaries who employ this justification) the aim of present-day experimental science.

All the theological subtlety that tried to prove that a certain church is the only true successor of Christ and that therefore it alone has full and unlimited power over the people's souls and even over their bodies has that for its chief aim.

The juridical sciences: political, criminal, civil, and international law, all have that one purpose; most philosophic theories, especially the Hegelian theory that so long prevailed, with its assertion that whatever exists is reasonable and that the State is a form necessary for the perfecting of personality, have solely that aim.

A very inferior English publicist, whose other works have all been forgotten and acknowledged to be insignificant among the insignificant, writes a treatise on population in which he invents a pseudo-law about the increase of population disproportionately to the increase in means of subsistence. He sets out his pseudo-law in baseless mathematical formulae and publishes it to the world. From the levity and lack of talent of this work one would expect it not to attract anyone's attention and to be forgotten like all the same author's subsequent writings; but what happened was just the opposite. The publicist who wrote that treatise at once became a scientific authority, and remained so for nearly half a century. Malthus! Malthus's theory—the law of the increase of population in geometrical, and of the means of subsistence in arithmetical, progression, and of the natural and rational methods of limiting population, all became scientific, indubitable truths, which were not verified but were employed as axioms from which to deduce further conclusions. That was how learned, educated people behaved; and among the masses of idle people there was respectful faith in the great law discovered by Malthus.

Why did this happen? These seem to be scientific deductions which have nothing in common with the instincts of the herd.

But that only appears so to one who believes that science is something self-existent, like the Church, which is not subject to error; and not simply the thoughts of weak and erring men who just for importance's sake call their thoughts and words 'science'.

It was only necessary to make practical deductions from the theory of Malthus to see that that theory was a very human one with very definite aims.

The deductions that flowed directly from that theory were as follows: the wretched condition of the working people is not due to cruelty, egotism, or lack of understanding, on the part of the rich and powerful, but is what it is by an immutable law not dependent on man, and if anyone is to blame for it, it is the hungry workmen themselves: why have they been so stupid as to be born when they know they will have nothing to eat? And so the rich and powerful classes are not to blame for anything and may quietly continue to live as before.

And this deduction was so valuable for the crowd of idle people, that all the learned people overlooked the lack of proof, the incorrectness, and the completely arbitrary nature of this proposition, and the crowd of educated, that is to say idle, people, scenting what these propositions led to, enthusiastically acclaimed it, stamped it with the seal of truth, that is of science, and made much of it for half a century.

The positivist philosophy of Comte and the doctrine deduced from it that humanity is an organism, and Darwin's doctrine of a law of the struggle for existence that is supposed to govern life, with the differentiation of various breeds of people which follows from it, and the anthropology, biology, and sociology of which people are now so fond—all have the same aim. These have all become favourite sciences because they serve to justify the way in which people free themselves from the human obligation to labour, while consuming the fruits of other people's labour.

All these theories, as is always the case, are first formulated in the secret sanctuaries of the priests, and are diffused among the masses in indefinite, obscure expressions, and are so adopted by them. As in olden times all the theological subtleties justifying the violence committed by the Church and the State remained the special knowledge of the priests, while among the masses readymade conclusions circulated that were accepted on faith, to the effect that the power of the kings, the priests, and the nobles, was sacred; so later on the philosophic and juridical subtleties of so called science were the possession of the priests of science, while among the masses only conclusions accepted on faith were current, to the effect that the organization of society should be such as it is, and that it cannot be otherwise.

And so now, it is only in the sanctuaries of the priests of science that the laws of life and the evolution of organisms are analysed, while among the masses conclusions are accepted on faith, to the effect that the division of labour is a law confirmed by science and that things should be so: some should work and die of hunger, while others must everlastingly make holiday; and that just this very perdition of some and banqueting of others is an indubitable law of human life to which we ought to submit.

The current justification of this idleness among the mass of the so-called educated people, with their various activities, from railway officials to writers and artists, is now this:

We people who have emancipated ourselves from the duty common to humanity of taking part in the struggle for existence, are serving progress and thereby render service to the whole of society which compensates for all the harm we do to people by consuming their labour.

That reasoning appears to men of our time quite unlike that by which people who did not work used to justify themselves formerly; just as the reasoning of the Roman emperors and citizens that without them the cultured world would perish, seemed to them quite apart from the reasoning of the Egyptians and the Persians, and just as similar reasoning seemed to the medieval knights and clergy to be quite distinct from the reasoning of the Romans.

But that only seems so; it is only necessary to examine the essence of our present justification to become convinced that there is nothing new in it.

It is only a little disguised, but is the same, for it is founded on the same thing. Every justification of man for consuming the labour of others without himself working—the justification of Pharaoh and the priests, of the Roman and medieval emperors, and of the knights, priests, and clerics—was always constructed on two assumptions: (1) We take the labour of the common people because we are a special kind of people destined by God to rule the common folk and teach them divine truths; (2) members of the common people cannot be judges of the amount of labour we take from the common people, because, as was said already by the Pharisees (John VII. 49), *This multitude which knoweth not the law are accursed.* The people do not understand what is good for them, and cannot therefore be the judge of the benefits conferred on them.

The justification employed in our time, despite its apparent difference, is constructed essentially of those same two fundamental propositions: (1) We are special people, we educated people who serve progress and civilization and thereby confer great benefit on the common folk; (2) the common uneducated people do not understand the benefit we confer on them and therefore cannot be judges of it.

We free ourselves from toil, and use up the toil of others and thereby make their condition more burdensome, and we affirm that in exchange for this we render them great service of which, from their ignorance, they cannot be the judges.

Is not this the same? The difference is only in the fact that formerly the right to other people's work belonged to the Roman citizens, priests, knights, and nobles, but now to one caste of people who call themselves the educated classes. The falsehood is the same, for the false position of the people justifying themselves is the same. That falsehood lies in the fact that before reasoning about the advantage rendered to the people by those who free themselves from toil, certain people, the Pharaohs, the priests, or we educated people, occupy that position, maintain it, and then devise a justification for it.

That position of some people coercing others, both in former times and in the present, serves as the basis of it all.

The only difference between our justification and the most ancient one is that ours is more fallacious and has less basis than the former.

The ancient emperors and popes if they themselves and the people believed in their divine appointment, could explain simply why they were the people who should have the use of other people's labour: they said they were appointed thereto by God himself, and that God destined them to transmit to the people the divine truths which had been revealed to them, and to govern the people.

But educated people of our times who do not work with their hands, acknowledging the equality of man, can no longer explain why just they and their children (for education also is only obtained by money, that is by power) are the chosen, fortunate people ordained to confer a certain easy benefit, and not others from among the millions who perish by hundreds and thousands while rendering education for the few possible.

Their only justification is that they—those who are there now —in exchange for the evil they do to people by avoiding work and consuming the labour of others, confer on the people a benefit the people do not understand, but which compensates for all the harm they do.

CHAPTER XXVII

THE PROPOSITION by which people who have emancipated them-selves from labour justify their emancipation, in its simplest and at the same time its most exact expression is this: We, people who, having emancipated ourselves from labour, are able by violence to make use of other people's work, as a result of this position of ours confer benefits on those other people; or in other words, certain people in exchange for palpable and comprehensible harm they inflict on the masses by forcibly taking their labour and thus augmenting the hardship of their struggle with nature, confer a benefit on the masses which is impalpable and incomprehensible to them. This proposition is a very strange one, but like the people of former times those of the present who sit on the backs of the working folk believe in it and relieve their consciences by it.

Let us see how this proposition is in our times justified among the various classes that have emancipated themselves from labour.

I serve people by my official or ecclesiastical activity, as a king, a minister of state, or a prelate; I serve people by my commercial or industrial activity; I serve people by my scientific or artistic activity. All our activities are as necessary to the people as their work is to us.

So say the various kinds of people of our day who have exempted themselves from labour.

Let us examine in succession each of the grounds on which they affirm the utility of their activities.

There can only be two tests of the utility of one man's activity for another: the external, consisting in the recognition of this utility by him who is benefited, and the internal, a desire to benefit another which lies at the root of the activity of him who confers the benefit.

The government people (I include among them the ecclesiastics of the Church established by the State) confer benefit on those whom they rule.

An emperor, king, president of a republic, prime minister, minister of justice, minister of war, of education, a bishop, and all their subordinates who serve the State, live exempting themselves from the struggle of humanity for life and leaving the whole burden of that struggle to other people, on the ground that their activity compensates for this.

Let us apply the first test: is the benefit conferred by this activity recognized by the working men upon whom the activity of the governing class is directly exerted?

Yes, it is acknowledged: the majority of men consider the governmental activity to be necessary for them—the majority acknowledges the usefulness of this activity in principle; but in all its known manifestations, in all particular cases known to us, each of the institutions and acts of that activity encounters in the circle of those for whose benefit it is done not merely a denial of benefit received, but assertion that this activity is harmful and disastrous.

There is no State or social activity which is not considered to be harmful by very many people; there is no institution which is not considered harmful: the courts, banks, county councils, district councils, the police, the clergy, every State activity from the highest authorities down to the town and rural police, from the bishops to the sextons, is by some people considered to be beneficial and by others harmful. And this is so not in Russia only, but in the whole world also—in France, and in America.

The whole activity of the Republican party is considered harmful by the Democratic party, and vice versa; the whole activity of the Democratic party, if it is in power, is considered harmful by the Republican party and by others.

But not only is the activity of the government people in general never considered useful by all men—that activity has also this characteristic, that it always has to be enforced by violence, and that to attain its benefit, murders, executions, jails, forcibly collected taxes and so forth, are necessary.

It turns out, therefore, that besides the fact that the advantage of government activity is not acknowledged by all men and is always denied by part of the people, this benefit is characterized by always manifesting itself by means of violence. And so the benefit of political activity cannot be confirmed on the ground that it is acknowledged by those people for whom it is carried on.

Let us apply the second test. Let us question the government people themselves, from king to policeman, from president to office-clerk, and from patriarch to sexton, asking them to reply sincerely: Have they all of them in view, when occupying their positions, the benefit they wish to confer on the people, or some other aim? Are they prompted in their wish to occupy the post of king, president, minister, rural policeman, sexton, or schoolmaster, by a striving for other people's benefit or for their own personal advantage?

And the reply of conscientious men will be, that their chief impulse is their own personal advantage.

And so it appears that one class of people availing themselves of the work of others, who perish at their labour, redeem the indubitable harm they cause, by an activity which is always considered by very many people to be not a benefit but an injury, and is not accepted voluntarily but must always be enforced by violence, and the aim of which is not the benefit of others but the personal advantage of those who exert it.

What then confirms the supposition that governmental activity is beneficial to the people?

Only this, that those who carry it on are firmly convinced that it is useful, and that this activity has always existed. But institutions have always existed which were not merely useless but even harmful, such as slavery, prostitution, and wars. Industrialists—including under that heading traders, manufacturers, railroad men, bankers, and landowners—believe that they confer benefits which redeem the unquestionable harm they do.

On what grounds do they think so?

To the question, who and what sort of people acknowledge the usefulness of their activity, the participants in government, including the ecclesiastics, could point to thousands and millions of working people who in principle acknowledge the utility of governmental and clerical activity; but to whom will the bankers and the manufacturers of vodka, velvet, bronzes, and mirrors, to say nothing of cannon, refer us? To whom will the traders and land-owners refer us when we ask them whether the benefits which they confer are admitted by public opinion? If some people are found who consider the production of chintz, rails, beer, and similar articles, to be useful, others in greater numbers can be found who consider the production of these articles harmful. No one will defend the activity of landowners and of traders who raise the price of commodities. Besides this, such activity is always connected with harm to the labourers and violence, which though less direct than the violence of government is equally cruel in its consequences, since industrial and commercial activities are all founded on taking advantage of want in every form: taking advantage of it to compel the workers to do hard and undesirable labour; taking advantage of it again to purchase materials at cheap prices and to sell things the people need at the highest possible prices; and taking advantage of it to exact interest for money lent. From whatever side we view their activity, we see that the benefit rendered by the industrialists is not acknowledged by those for whom it is exerted, either in principle or in particular cases, and for the most part is considered simply harmful.

If we apply the second test and ask what is the impelling motive of the activity of the industrialists, we receive a yet more definite answer than on the activity of those who govern.

If a man employed by government says that besides his personal advantage he has the public welfare in view, one has to believe him, and we all know such men; but an industrialist by the very *raison d'être* of his business cannot have the public welfare for his aim, but will appear ridiculous to his fellows if in his business he pursues any other aim than the increase or maintenance of his wealth.

So the working people do not consider the activity of the industrialists useful to them.

That activity is accompanied by violence employed against the workers, and its aim is not to benefit the working people but is always personal advantage; and yet—strange to say—these industrialists are so convinced of the benefit they confer on people by their activity, that for the sake of that imaginary benefit they inflict undoubted and obvious harm on the workers by exempting themselves from labour and consuming what the workers produce by labour.

The scientists and artists have exempted themselves from labour and have imposed that labour on others, and live with calm consciences, firmly convinced that they confer on others benefits compensating for all that.

On what is their conviction based?

Let us ask them as we asked the government men and the industrialists: do all or even a majority of working folk acknowledge the benefit science and art confers on them?

The reply will be a most lamentable one.

The activity of the rulers and the Church people is, in principle, considered useful by nearly everybody and in its application is so considered by more than half the working people on whom it is directed; the activity of the industrialists is considered useful by a small number of working people; but the activity of the men of science and art is not recognized as useful by any working people. The utility of that activity is recognized only by those who carry it on or wish to carry it on. The working people—those who bear on their shoulders the whole labour of life, and feed and clothe the scientists and artists—cannot recognize the activity of those men as being of use to them, for they cannot even have any conception of this activity which is so useful to them. That activity appears to the working folk to be useless and even corrupting.

That is how all working folk regard the universities, libraries, conservatories, picture and sculpture-galleries, and the theatres, which are built at their expense. A labouring man so definitely regards this activity as an evil that he does not send his children to school, and to compel the masses to accept this activity it has everywhere been necessary to pass laws to compel school attendance. A labouring man always regards this activity with hostility, and will only cease so to regard it when he himself ceases to be a labourer and, by gain and afterwards by what is called education, passes from the ranks of labour into the ranks of those who live on the backs of others. Yet despite the fact that the activity of the scientists and artists is not recognized and cannot be recognized by any of the workers, the latter are nevertheless compelled to make sacrifices for the benefit of that activity.

A man of the executive sends another directly to the guillotine or to jail; a trader exploiting the labour of another takes all he possesses from him, leaving him to choose between starvation or pernicious work; but a scientist or artist does not seem to compel others, he only offers his wares to those who wish to take them; but to produce his wares, which the working man does not want, he takes from them by force, through government agents, a large part of their labour for the erection and maintenance of academies, universities, high schools, primary schools, museums, libraries, conservatories, and for the support of the scientists and artists.

If we ask the scientists and artists about the aim they pursue in their activities, we get most remarkable replies. A man belonging to the government can reply that his aim is the common good, and in such a reply there is a measure of truth confirmed by public opinion.

In the reply of an industrialist that his aim is the common good there would be less probability, but even that might be affirmed.

But the reply made by the scientists and artists is startlingly unproven and audacious.

The scientists and artists, without offering any proofs of it, say just what the priests of old said, that their activity is most important and necessary for all men and that without this activity all humanity would perish. They affirm this although no one but they understands or recognizes their activity and despite the fact that true science and true art, by their own definition, ought not to aim at utility. And scientists and artists devote themselves to their favourite occupation regardless of what benefit people may derive from it, and are always convinced that they are doing most important and necessary work for humanity. So that while a sincere man engaged in the government, acknowledging the chief motive of his activity to be a personal impulse, tries as far as possible to be useful to the working people, and an industrialist, admitting the selfishness of his activity, tries to give it a character of public utility, scientists and artists do not even consider it necessary to appear to try to be useful, and even reject the aim of utility, so confident are they not merely of the utility but even of the sanctity of their avocations.

And so it turns out that a third division of people, having exempted themselves from labour and imposed it on others, are busying themselves with things quite incomprehensible to the workers, which the latter regard as rubbish and often as harmful rubbish; and they busy themselves with these things without any thought of being useful to the people, merely for their own pleasure, being for some reason fully convinced that their activity will always be such as is essential for the life of the working folk.

Men have exempted themselves from labour for life and have thrown that work onto others who perish in their toil. They exploit such labour, and assert that their own occupations, incomprehensible to the people and not directed towards the service of others, redeem all the harm they inflict by exempting themselves from labour for the maintenance of life and by consuming the labour of others.

The men engaged in the government, to compensate for the undoubted and evident evil they inflict by exploiting other people's work and exempting themselves from the struggle with nature, add another evident and undoubted evil—that of inflicting all sorts of violence.

The industrialists, to redeem the undoubted and evident evil they cause by using up the fruits of their toil, strive to obtain for themselves and consequently to take from others as much wealth as possible, that is, as much of people's labour as possible.

Scientists and artists, in return for the unquestionable and obvious harm they do to the labouring people, occupy themselves with things that are incomprehensible to the labourers and which, on their own assertion, to be real must not aim at utility—but to which they feel drawn. And so all these people are quite convinced that their right to consume other people's labour is impregnable.

It would seem obvious that all these people who have exempted themselves from labour to maintain life, have no ground for this. But amazing to say, they firmly believe in their own integrity and live as they do with a calm conscience.

There must be some ground—there must be some false doctrine—underlying such a terrible delusion!

CHAPTER XXVIII

AND INDEED, UNDERLYING THE POSITION of people who live on work done by others there lies not only a belief but a whole doctrine, and not one doctrine but three, which during ages have grown up one on the other and solidified into one monstrous deception—or humbug, as the English expression has it—which hides their injustice.

The most ancient doctrine in our world justifying people's neglect of the fundamental duty of working for their living was the Church-Christian doctrine, according to which men are differentiated one from another by God's will, as the sun differs from the moon and stars, and the stars from one another: some men being appointed by God to rule over all the rest, others over many, others again over a few, and the rest being appointed to obey.

That doctrine, though now shaken to its foundations, still continues by inertia to act on people, so that many without accepting the teaching and often without being acquainted with it are still guided by it.

The second justificatory doctrine in our world is one I do not know how to describe otherwise than as the State-philosophic. According to that doctrine, fully expressed by Hegel, all that exists is reasonable, and the order of life people have set up and are maintaining is not established and maintained by men but is the only possible form for the manifestation of the spirit, or in general for the life of humanity. This doctrine, too, is no longer held by those who guide public opinion in our day, but only maintains itself by force of inertia.

The third and now dominant doctrine—on which is based the justification now adopted alike by scientific and artistic people—is not a scientific doctrine in the simple meaning of that word as indicating knowledge in general, but in the sense of one kind of knowledge special both in form and in matter.

This new doctrine, called scientific, is what in our day chiefly supports the justification that hides from idle people their neglect of their duty.

This doctrine made its appearance in Europe contemporaneously with a large class of rich and idle people who served neither Church nor State and were in want of a justification corresponding to their position.

Not very long ago, up to the time of the French revolution, all in Europe who were not workers, in order to have a right to appropriate other people's work had to have some very definite occupation in the service of the Church, the Government, or the Army. The men who served the Government ruled the people, those who served the Church taught people divine truths, while those who served in the Army defended the people.

Only three classes—the clergy, the rulers, and the military—considered themselves to have a right to appropriate the labour of the workers, and they could always adduce the services they rendered to the people: other rich men who had not that justification were despised and, conscious of their fault, felt ashamed of their wealth and idleness.

But a time came when this class of rich people not belonging to the clergy, the government, or the army, multiplied and became powerful thanks to the defects of those three classes, and these new people needed a justification. And the justification was produced.

Not a century passed before all these people, not serving State or Church and taking no part in their affairs, had not only obtained the same right to appropriate other people's labour as the former classes, and ceased to be ashamed of their wealth and idleness, but had come to consider their position fully justified. And an enormous number of such people have arisen in our times and their number continually increases. And what is surprising is that these new people, the very ones the justice of whose exemption from toil was so recently not acknowledged, now consider that they alone are fully justified, and attack the three earlier classes—the servants of the Church, the State, and the Army—considering their exemption from toil to be unjust and even considering their activity harmful.

And what is still more surprising is that the former servants of the State, the Church, and the Army, no longer rely on their divine vocation, nor even on the philosophic importance of the State as necessary for the manifestation of individuality, but they abandon these supports which so long maintained them, and now seek the support on which the new dominant class stands—headed by scientists and artists—which has now found a fresh justification. If a man of the government now sometimes by old habit defends his position on the ground that he was set in it by God, or that the State is a form of the development of personality, this indicates that he lags behind the age, and he feels that no one believes him. To defend himself effectively he must now no longer produce theological or philosophic supports, but other, new, scientific ones. He has to put forward the principle of national or organic development, and has to curry favour with the dominant order, as in the Middle Ages it was necessary to curry favour with the churchmen, and at the end of the eighteenth century with the philosophers, as was done by Frederick and Catherine the Great.

If now a rich man sometimes, by old habit, speaks of the divine will that chose him to be rich, or of the importance of an aristocracy for the nation's good, he does so because he lags behind the times. To justify himself effectively he ought to put forward the assistance he renders to the progress of civilization by improvement in methods of production, cheapening articles of consumption, or promoting international intercourse. A rich man should talk the language of science and should offer sacrifices to the dominant order, as was formerly done to ecclesiastics; he should publish newspapers and books, arrange a picture gallery, musical societies, a kindergarten, or technical schools.

The dominant order consists of the scientists and artists of a certain tendency: they possess a complete justification of their avoidance of toil, and on their justification, as formerly on the theological and afterwards on the philosophic, all justification now rests, and it is these men who now issue diplomas of exemption to other classes.

The class that now has a complete justification for its avoidance of toil is that of scientists, and especially experimental, positive, critical, evolutionary scientists, and the class of artists who follow the same tendency.

If a scientist or artist, by old association, now speaks about prophecy, revelation, or the manifestation of the spirit, he does so because he lags behind the age, and he fails to justify himself: to stand firmly he must somehow associate his activity with experimental, positive, critical science, and must put that science at the base of his activity.

Only then will the science or art he is occupied with be real, and only then will he, in our day, stand on unshakable foundations and be certain of the benefit he confers on humanity.

On experimental, critical, positive science the justification of all who have exempted themselves from labour now rests.

The theological and philosophic justifications are obsolete, announce themselves timidly and shamefacedly, and try to transform themselves into the scientific justification; while the scientific justification boldly upsets and destroys the remains of the former justifications, ousts them everywhere, and lifts its head high, assured of its own invincibility.

The theological justification said that people by their vocation were called—some to command, others to obey, some to live sumptuously, others to live in want; and therefore those who believed in the revelation of God could not doubt the justice of the position of those who by the will of God were called to command and be rich.

The State-philosophic justification said that the State, with all its institutions and grades differing in property and rights, is that historic form which is essential for the due manifestation of the spirit in mankind, and that therefore the position each one occupies in the State and in society in respect of property and rights, should be what it is for the due life of mankind.

The scientific theory says that the others are all nonsense and superstition: the one the fruit of thought of the theological period, the other of the metaphysical period. For the study of the laws of the life of human societies there is only one sure method—that of positive, experimental, critical science. Only sociology, based on biology, based on all the other positive sciences, can give us the laws of the life of humanity. Humanity, or human society, is an organism, formed or still in process of formation and subject to all the laws of the evolution of organisms. One of the chief of these laws is division of labour among the parts of the organism. If some people command and others obey, if some live in opulence and others in want, this occurs, not by the will of God, and not because the State is a form of the manifestation of personality, but because in societies as in organisms a division of labour occurs which is necessary for the life of the whole: some people in society perform the muscular work, others the brain work.

On that doctrine in our times the dominant excuse is built.

CHAPTER XXIX

A NEW TEACHING is preached by Christ and recorded in the Gospels. This teaching is persecuted and not accepted, and a story is invented of the fall of the first man and of the first angel and this invention is accepted as being the teaching of Christ. This invention is absurd and quite unfounded, but from it the deduction naturally flows that man may live badly and yet consider himself justified by Christ, and this deduction is so convenient for the crowd of weak people who dislike moral exertion that it is at once accepted as the truth, and even as divine revealed truth, though nowhere in what is called revelation is there even a hint of it—and for a thousand years this invention is made the basis of the labours of the learned theologians on which they construct their theories.

The learned theologians split up into sects, begin to deny each other's constructions, and themselves begin to feel that they are confused and no longer understand what they are saying; but the crowd demands of them confirmation of the favourite doctrine and they pretend that they understand and believe what they say, and continue to preach it. But a time comes when the deductions prove unnecessary, the crowd peeps into the sanctuaries of the priests, and to its astonishment, instead of the solemn undoubted truths the mysteries of theology had appeared to it to be, sees that there is and has been nothing there except the grossest deception, and it marvels at its own blindness.

The same thing happened with philosophy, not philosophy in the sense of the wisdom of a Confucius, a Socrates, or an Epictetus, but with professorial philosophy, when it pandered to the instincts of the idle rich.

Not long ago in the learned educated world the philosophy of the spirit reigned, according to which it appeared that all that exists is reasonable, that there is no evil and no good, and that man need not struggle with evil but need only manifest the spirit: one man in military service, another in the law-courts, and a third on a fiddle.

There have been many different expressions of human wisdom and those expressions were known to the men of the nineteenth century. Rousseau and Pascal and Lessing and Spinoza were known, as well as all the wisdom of antiquity, but no one else's wisdom captured the crowd. Nor can it be said that Hegel's success depended on the symmetry of his theories. There were other equally symmetrical theories: Fichte's, and Schopenhauer's. There was only one cause of that theory having become, for a short time, the belief of the whole world; the cause was the same as that of the success of the theory of the fall and redemption of man, namely that the deductions flowing from this philosophic theory pandered to men's weaknesses. They said: everything is reasonable, everything is good, no one is to blame for anything. And just as the theologians had built on the theory of redemption, so the philosophers built their tower of Babel on Hegelian foundations (and some backward people still sit in it even now) and their tongues became similarly confused, and similarly they felt that they did not themselves know what they were saying, and in the same way, without sweeping the rubbish out of their house, they laboriously strove to maintain their authority with the crowd and, as before, the crowd demanded confirmation of what suited it and believed that what to it seemed obscure and contradictory was all clear as day there, on the philosophic heights. And again, in the same way, a time came when that theory was worn out and a new one appeared in its place; the old one became useless, the crowd peeped into the secret sanctuaries of the priests and saw that there was nothing there and never had been anything but very obscure and senseless words. That happened within my own recollection.

When I started life Hegelianism was the basis of everything: it was in the air, found expression in magazine and newspaper articles, in novels and essays, in art, in histories, in sermons, and in conversation. A man unacquainted with Hegel had no right to speak: he who wished to know the truth studied Hegel. Everything rested on him; and suddenly forty years have gone by and there is nothing left of him, he is not even mentioned—as though he had never existed. And what is most remarkable is that, like pseudo-Christianity, Hegelianism fell not because anyone refuted it, but because it suddenly became evident that neither the one nor the other was needed by our learned, educated world.

If we now speak to a modern educated man about the fall of the angel and of Adam, or about redemption, he will not attempt to argue or to prove the falsity of it, but will ask with perplexity: What angel? Why Adam? What redemption? What use is it to me? Similarly with Hegelianism, a man of our time will not argue about it but will only be surprised. What spirit? Where does it come from? Why does it manifest itself? What use is it to me?

'Yes, that came about'—say the present-day scientists—'because of the ravings of the theological and the metaphysical periods; now we have critical, positive science which does not deceive because it is based on induction and experiment. Now our knowledge is not shaky, as that was, and only along our path lie the answers to all the questions of mankind.'

But then that is just what the theologians said, and they were certainly not fools, for we know that among them were men of immense intellect; and within my own recollection the Hegelians spoke with no less confidence, and were not less accepted by the crowd of so-called educated people. And they—our Herzens, Stankéviches, and Belínskis, for instance—were not fools either. Why then did this surprising phenomenon occur that clever people should preach with the greatest confidence, and the crowd should reverently accept, such unfounded and empty doctrines? The reason is the same, namely—that the doctrines justify people in their bad lives.

Is not the reason of the confidence of the positive, critical, experimental scientists, and of the reverent attitude of the crowd towards their doctrines, still the same? At first it seems strange how the theory of evolution (which, like the redemption in theology, serves the majority as a popular expression of the whole new creed) can justify people in their injustice, and it seems as if the scientific theory dealt only with facts and did nothing but observe facts.

But that only seems so. It seemed just the same in the case of theological doctrine: theology, it seemed, was only occupied with dogmas and had no relation to people's lives, and it seemed the same with regard to philosophy, which appeared to be occupied solely with transcendental reasonings.

But that only seemed so. It was just the same with the Hegelian doctrine on a large scale and with the particular case of the Malthusian teaching.

Hegelianism seemed to be concerned only with its logical constructions and to have no relation to people's lives; and this seemed to be the case with the Malthusian theory also—it seemed solely occupied with statistical facts. But that only seemed to be so.

Contemporary science investigates facts.

But what facts? Why those particular facts and not others?

Scientists of to-day are very fond of saying solemnly and confidently: 'We only investigate facts,' imagining these words to have some meaning.

One cannot possibly only investigate facts for the number of facts available for investigation is *innumerable* (in the exact sense of that word). Before investigating the facts one must have a theory on the basis of which such or such facts are selected from among the innumerable quantity. And such a theory exists and is even very definitely expressed, though many of those engaged on contemporary science either ignore it, that is, do not wish to know it, or actually do not know it, or pretend not to. So it has always been with all reigning, guiding creeds—both theological and philosophic.

The foundations of every creed are always contained in the theory, and the so-called learned people only devise further deductions from the given data, sometimes without knowing them. But there always is a fundamental theory. So now, contemporary science chooses its facts on the basis of a very definite theory which it sometimes knows, sometimes does not wish to know, and sometimes really does not know, though that theory exists.

The theory is this: all mankind is an undying organism, men are the particles of this organism and each of them has his special vocation in the service of the whole.

Just as the cells composing an organism divide among themselves the labour needed for the struggle for the existence of the whole organism—strengthen one quality and weaken another, and coalesce with one organ the better to satisfy the needs of the whole organism: and just as among social animals—ants and bees—separate individuals divide the work among themselves: the queen lays eggs, the drone fertilizes her, and the workers labour for the life of the whole—so in humanity and human societies the same differentiation and integration of parts occurs.

And therefore to discover the law of man's life it is necessary to study the laws of the life and development of organisms; in the life and development of organisms we find the following laws: a law that every phenomenon is accompanied by other consequences besides its immediate one, another law of the frailty of the undifferentiated, and a third law of heterogeneity and homogeneity, and so forth. All this seems very innocent, but it is only necessary to draw deductions from all these observed facts in order to see at once whither they tend. They all tend to one thing, namely, to the recognition of humanity or human society as an organism, and so to a recognition of the division of activities that exists in human societies as organic, that is to say, as necessary; and as in human societies very many cruelties and abominations are perceptible, these phenomena must not be regarded as cruel or abominable but must be regarded as indubitable facts confirming a general law—namely, the law of the division of labour.

The philosophy of the spirit also justified every cruelty and abomination, but there it was philosophic and is therefore considered questionable; but in science it all turns out to be scientific and therefore indubitable.

How can one help accepting so admirable a theory! One has only to regard human society as an object of observation and one can calmly devour the labour of others who are perishing, comforting oneself with the reflection that one's activity as a dancer, lawyer, doctor, philosopher, actor, investigator of mediumism, or of the forms of atoms, is a functional activity of the human organism, so that there can be no question of whether it is just that I should make use of the labour of others, (I only do what pleases me) as there can be no question of the justice of the activity of a brain-cell which avails itself of the work of the cells in the muscles.

How can we help accepting such a practical theory enabling us to pocket our conscience for ever and quietly live an unrestrained animal life, feeling under our feet the unshakable support of modern science? And it is on this new creed that the justification of the idleness and cruelty of men is now built.

CHAPTER XXX

THIS CREED BEGAN but recently—some fifty years ago. Its chief founder was the French savant, A. Comte. Under the influence of Bichat's physiological researches, which were then new, he, a systematizer and a religious man, was struck by the old idea expressed long ago by Menenius Agrippa, that human societies and even all humanity may be regarded as one whole, as an organism, and men may be regarded as the living cells of separate organs each having its definite function in the service of the whole organism. This thought so pleased Comte that he began to construct a philosophic theory on it, and he was so carried away by this theory that he quite forgot that his starting-point was merely a nice little analogy, suitable in a fable but quite unsuitable for the foundation of a science. As often happens, he regarded his favourite supposition as an axiom and imagined that his whole theory was based on the firmest experimental foundations. According to his theory it appeared that as humanity is an organism, the knowledge of what man is and what his relations to the universe should be can be attained only by studying the properties of this organism. In order to learn these properties man can make observations on other—lower—organisms and draw inferences from the facts of their life.

In the first place, the only true and scientific method according to Comte is therefore the inductive method and science is only such as is based on experiment. Secondly, the aim and apex of science is the new science of the imaginary organism of humanity or of the super-organic being—humanity: this new imaginary science being sociology. From this view of science in general it appeared that all former knowledge was false, and the whole history of humanity's knowledge of itself fell into three, or really two, periods:

(1) The theological and metaphysical periods, lasting from the commencement of the world until Comte, and (2) the present period of true science—positivism—which began with Comte.

This was all very nice; there was only one error, namely, that the whole edifice was built on the sand—on the arbitrary assertion that humanity is an organism.

That assertion was arbitrary because we have no more right to acknowledge the existence of an organism of humanity not subject to observation than we have to acknowledge the existence of a triune God, and similar theological propositions.

That assertion was fallacious because to the conception of humanity, that is, of men, the definition of an organism was incorrectly affixed despite the fact that humanity lacks the essential sign of an organism, namely a centre of sensation and consciousness. We only call an elephant or a bacterium an 'organism' because, by analogy, we attribute to those beings a similar unification of sensation and of consciousness to that we are conscious of in ourselves; but in human societies and in humanity this essential indication is lacking, and therefore, however many other indications we may detect that are common to humanity and to an organism, in the absence of that essential indication, the acknowledgement of humanity as an organism is incorrect.

But despite the arbitrariness and incorrectness of its fundamental basis the positive philosophy was accepted most cordially by the so-called educated world, so important for that world was the justification this philosophy afforded to the existing order of things by regarding the present rule of violence among men as just. What is remarkable in this connection is that of Comte's works, which consist of two parts—the positive philosophy and the positive politics—the learned world only accepted the first: the part which on the new experimental basis, offered a justification for the existing evil of human societies; but the second part, dealing with the moral obligations of altruism resulting from acknowledging humanity as an organism, was considered not merely unimportant but even insignificant and unscientific.

What had occurred with the two parts of Kant's philosophy was repeated. The criticism of pure reason was accepted by the learned crowd, but the criticism of practical reason—the part which contained the essence of his moral teaching—was rejected. In Comte's teaching they accepted as scientific what pandered to the prevailing evil. But the positive philosophy accepted by the crowd, being based on an arbitrary and unsound proposition, was itself so unfounded and therefore so unstable that it could not be maintained by itself. And then among the many idle speculations of so-called science there appears an assertion—lacking equally in novelty and in truth—to the effect that living creatures, that is organisms, have been derived from one another—not only one organism from another but one organism from many: that is, that in a very long period of time, in a million years, a fish and a duck, for instance, may not merely have come from one and the same ancestor but that one organism may have come from many separate organisms, so that, for instance, a single animal might be produced from a swarm of bees. And this arbitrary and incorrect assertion was accepted by the learned world with yet greater sympathy. This assertion was arbitrary because no one has ever seen how some organisms are produced from others, and so the assumption about the origin of species always remains an assumption and not a fact of experience. And the assumption was incorrect because the solution of the question of the origin of species by the assertion that they were produced in accordance with a law of heredity and adaptation during an infinitely long period of time is not at all a solution, but only the repetition of the question in a new form.

According to the solution of the question by Moses (in a polemic with whom lies the whole importance of the theory) it appears that the diversity of the species of living beings is due to God's will and infinite power, but according to the theory of evolution it turns out that the diversity of living beings came about of itself in consequence of endlessly varied conditions of heredity and environment during an infinite period of time. The theory of evolution, put into plain words, only asserts that in infinite time anything you please may originate from anything you please.

There is no reply to the question but the same statement is differently put: instead of a will, accident is predicated, and the coefficient of infinity is transferred from power to time. But this new assertion (made still more arbitrary and incorrect by Darwin's followers) supported the former assertion of Comte, and so became the revelation of our age and the basis of all the sciences, even of history, philology, and religion, and more than that, according to the naïve confession of the founder of the theory—Darwin – his idea was suggested by Malthus's law and therefore put forward the theory of the struggle of living beings and of men for existence as a fundamental law of all life. And one sees that that was just what the crowd of idle people needed for their justification.

Two unstable theories which did not stand firmly on their own feet, supported one another and obtained a semblance of stability. Both theories contained within them the meaning—so precious to the crowd—that men are not to blame for the existing evil in human societies but that the existing order is just the one that ought to exist; and the new theory was accepted by the crowd, in the sense in which it was needed, with full faith and unheard-of enthusiasm. And on these two arbitrary and incorrect propositions, accepted as articles of faith, the new scientific creed was consolidated.

Both in subject and in form this new creed is extraordinarily like the Church-Christian creed.

As to the subject, the resemblance consists in the fact that in both of them an unreal fantastic meaning is ascribed to something real and this unreal meaning is made the subject of investigation.

In the Church-Christian creed to Christ who really existed is attached the fantastic meaning of God Himself, while in the positivist creed, to mankind which really exists is attached the fantastic meaning of an organism.

In form, the resemblance of the two creeds is striking, for both in the one and in the other a certain conception held by some people is accepted as the one infallibly true conception.

In Church-Christianity the conception of a divine revelation to men who call themselves the Church is accepted as being sacred and exclusively true; according to the Positivist creed the comprehension of science by the men who call themselves scientific is accepted as indubitable and true. Just as the Church-Christians acknowledged a beginning of true knowledge of God only from the institution of their Church, and merely as it were out of civility said that earlier believers were also a Church; so also positivist science, according to its assertion, began only with Comte, and these scientists, again merely out of civility, admit a previous existence of science, and that only in certain representatives such as Aristotle. Just like the Church, positivist science excludes the knowledge possessed by all the rest of humanity, treating all knowledge outside its own as *an error*.

The resemblance goes farther: just as to aid the fundamental dogma of theology—the divinity of Christ and the Trinity—there came the old dogma, which received a new meaning, of the fall of man and his redemption by Christ's death, and out of these two dogmas the popular Church doctrine was composed—so in our time, to the aid of Comte's fundamental dogma about the organism of humanity, came the old dogma of evolution but with a new meaning, and out of them both the popular scientific creed was composed.

In both creeds the new dogma was necessary for the support of the old one and is intelligible only in connection with the fundamental dogma. If to a believer in the divinity of Christ it is not clear or intelligible why God came down to earth, the dogma of the redemption supplies an explanation.

If to a believer in the organism of humanity it is not clear why an aggregate of individuals should be considered an organism, the dogma of evolution furnishes this explanation.

The dogma of the redemption is needed to reconcile the contradiction between the first dogma and reality.

God came to earth to save men but men have not been saved—how reconcile this contradiction? The dogma of the redemption says: 'He has saved those who believe in the redemption: if you believe in it you are saved.'

Similarly the dogma of evolution is needed to solve the contradiction between reality and the previous dogma: humanity is an organism yet we see that it does not respond to the chief sign of an organism—how is this to be harmonized? Then the dogma of evolution says: 'Humanity is an organism in process of formation. If you believe this you can regard humanity as an organism.'

And as it is impossible for a man free from superstitious belief in a Trinity and the divinity of Christ even to understand wherein the interest and meaning of the doctrine of the redemption lies, and that meaning is explained only by recognizing the fundamental dogma about Christ being God Himself—so also to humanity free from the positivist superstition it is impossible even to understand wherein lies the interest of the teaching about the origin of species, and this interest is explained only when one knows the fundamental dogma that humanity is an organism.

And just as all the refinements of theology are intelligible only to him who believes in the basic dogmas, so also all the refinements of sociology, which now occupy the minds of all the very latest and profoundest scientists, are intelligible only to believers.

The resemblance of the two creeds lies also in this, that propositions once accepted on faith and no longer subject to investigation serve as basis for the strangest theories, and the preachers of these theories, having adopted a method of asserting their right to consider themselves holy in theology and scientific in knowledge—that is to say, infallible—arrive at most arbitrary, improbable, and quite unfounded assertions, which they express most solemnly and seriously, and the details of which are disputed with similar seriousness and solemnity by those who disagree on particular points but equally accept the basic dogmas.

The Basil the Great of this creed, Herbert Spencer, for example, in one of his first works expresses it thus: Society and organisms resemble one another in the following:

(1) That beginning as small aggregates, they imperceptibly grow in mass till they sometimes reach dimensions ten thousand times greater than their original size;

(2) That whereas at first they are of such simple structure that they may be regarded as deprived of all structure, during their growth they acquire a continually increasing complexity;

(3) That though in their early, undeveloped period there hardly exists any interdependence of parts, their parts gradually acquire a mutual interdependence, which at last becomes so strong that the activity and life of each part is only made possible by the activity and life of the rest;

(4) That the life and development of society are independent of, and more prolonged than, the life and development of any of its component units, which are born, grow, act, reproduce, and die, while the body politic they form continues to live generation after generation and increases in size owing to the perfection of its structure and functional activity.

After that follow points of difference between organisms and societies, and it is shown that these differences are only apparently so, but that organisms and societies are completely alike.

To a new observer the question plainly presents itself: 'What are you talking about? Why is humanity an organism? Or how does it resemble one?'

'You say that societies according to these four indications resemble organisms, but nothing of the kind is true. You only take a few signs of an organism and place human societies under those signs.

'You adduce four signs of resemblance, then take signs of differences, but these (in your opinion) are so only in appearance, and you conclude that human societies may be regarded as organisms. But that is nothing but an idle play of dialectics. On such a basis anything you please can be brought under the signs of an organism.'

I take the first thing that occurs to me, say, for instance, a wood as it is sown in the field and grows up:

(1) 'Beginning as small aggregates,' etc., just the same occurs in the fields when the seeds gradually take root in them and the fields become overgrown with trees.

(2) 'At first the structure is simple, afterwards the complexity increases,' etc.; just the same occurs with the wood: first there are only birch trees, then willows and hazel bushes; at first they all grow straight, afterwards their branches intertwine.

(3) 'The interdependence of the parts increases so that the life of each part depends on the life and activity of the rest'; it is just the same with the trees: the hazel bushes warm the trunks (cut them out and the other trees will freeze), the outskirts of the wood protect it from the wind, the seed trees continue the species, tall and leafy trees give shade, and the life of one tree depends on another.

(4) 'The separate parts may die, but the whole lives'; the same is true of a wood. As the proverb says: 'The wood does not weep for a tree.'

It is just the same with the example usually adduced by defenders of the theory: that if you cut off an arm the arm perishes. Transplant a tree beyond the shade and the forest-soil, and it dies.

There is also a remarkable resemblance between this creed and the Church-Christian creed and all other creeds founded on dogmas that are accepted on faith, in its imperviousness to logical arguments. Having shown that on their theory you have a right to consider a wood to be an organism, you think you have shown them the incorrectness of their definition—but not at all!

The definition they give to an organism is so inexact and elastic that they can bring anything they please in under it.

'Yes,' they will say, 'a wood may also be regarded as an organism. A wood is a peaceful interaction of individual parts which do not destroy one another—an aggregate—whose parts can come into closer connection and like a swarm of bees may become an organism.'

Then you remark that, if so, then the birds and insects and grasses of that wood, which interact and do not destroy one another, together with the trees may also be regarded as an organism.

They will agree even to that. Every aggregate of living things interacting and not destroying one another may, according to their theory, be regarded as an organism. You may assert a connection and co-operation between any things you please, and you may say that by evolution from anything you please may be produced anything you please in a very great length of time.

To believers in the triune nature of God it is impossible to prove that it is not so, but it is possible to show them that their assertion is an assertion not of knowledge but of belief, and that if they assert that there are three Gods, I with equal right may assert that there are seventeen and a half Gods, and the adherents of positive and evolutionary science may be met similarly and yet more indubitably. On the basis of that science I will undertake to prove anything you please. And what is most remarkable is that this same positive science recognizes the scientific method as a sign of true knowledge and has itself defined what it calls 'the scientific method'. What it calls 'the scientific method' is common sense. And just this common sense exposes it at every step.

As soon as those who occupied the seats of the Saints felt that there was nothing saintly left in them and that they were all accursed, they immediately (like the Pope and our Synod) called themselves not merely Holy but Most Holy. And as soon as science felt that nothing reasonable was left in it, it called itself reasonable, that is, 'scientific' science.

CHAPTER XXXI

DIVISION OF LABOUR is the law of all that exists, and so it must exist in human societies. Very likely that is so, but the question still remains: Is the division of labour now existing in human societies quite the division which should exist? For if a certain division of labour appears to men unreasonable and unjust, no science can prove to them that what they consider unreasonable and unjust ought to prevail.

Theological theory proved that power is ordained by God and very likely it is so, but the question remained: Whose power is from God—Catherine's or Pugachëv's?* And no finesse of theology has been able to solve that doubt.

The philosophy of the Spirit showed the State to be a form of the development of personality, but the question remained: Should the State of a Nero or Genghis Khan be considered a form of the development of personality? And no transcendental words could solve that problem.

The same applies to the science of the scientists.

Division of labour is a condition of the life of organisms and of human societies; but what are we to consider an organic division of labour in human societies? However much science may study the division of labour among the cells of the tapeworm, such observations will fail to induce a man to consider a division of labour just which his reason and conscience repudiate.

However convincing may be the proofs of the division of labour among the cells of the organisms we investigate, man, as long as he is not deprived of reason, will still say that no one ought to have to weave cotton cloth all his life long, and that such an employment is not a division of labour but an oppression of men.

Spencer and others say there are whole populations of weavers and that therefore the weaver's activity is an organic division of labour—but in saying this they are in fact saying precisely what the theologians said.

There is a power and therefore it is from God no matter what it may be like. There are weavers, so such is the proper division of labour. It would be all right to say so if the power and the population of weavers had resulted of themselves, but we know that they do not come of themselves but that we produced them. So we have to know whether we produced that power by God's will or by our own, and whether we made these weavers by an organic law or by something else.

* Catherine II (the Great) of Russia reigned from 1761 to 1796. Pugachëv was leader of a very serious peasant revolt from 1773 to 1775; he captured several towns and overran several provinces.

Men live and support themselves by agriculture as is proper for all men: one man puts up a forge and mends his plough, and his neighbour comes and asks him to mend his and promises to pay him with work or with money. A third and a fourth come and among these people there is a division of labour: a blacksmith is set up. Another man teaches his children well and his neighbour brings his children to him and asks him to teach them—a teacher has been set up. But both the smith and the teacher became and remain such because they were asked, and they remain such only so long as they are asked to be smith or teacher. But should it happen that many smiths or teachers appear or that their work is not wanted, they would, as common sense demands and as always happens where there are no causes infringing the proper division of labour—at once give up those occupations and return to agriculture.

People who act so are guided by their reason and their conscience, and therefore we, men endowed with reason and conscience, declare such division of labour to be proper. But if it happened that black-smiths were able to compel others to work for them and continued to make horseshoes when these were not wanted, and that teachers taught when there was no one to teach, it would be plain to every new-comer endowed with reason and conscience that this was not a division but an exploitation of other men's labour, for such activity would infringe the only standard by which a fair division of labour can be known—a demand made for such labour by others, and a voluntary offer of remuneration for it. And yet it is just such an exploitation that the scientists' science calls 'the division of labour'.

People make things that others do not think of asking for, and demand to be fed for doing so and say that this is proper because it is a division of labour.

What constitutes the chief public evil the people suffer from—not in our country alone—is the Government, the innumerable quantity of officials; and the cause of the economic distress of our time is what the English call over-production: the making of a quantity of goods no one wants or knows what to do with, and all this results from the strange conception people have of the division of labour.

It would be strange to find a shoemaker who considered that people were bound to feed him because he unceasingly made boots that had long since ceased to be wanted by any one; but what are we to say of those occupied with Government, the Church, science, and art, who produce nothing palpable or useful to the people, and whose goods find no demand, but who yet (pleading the division of labour) boldly demand to be well fed and well dressed?

There may be wizards whose activity meets a demand and to whom cakes and ale are given, but it is difficult to imagine that there can be wizards whose witchery nobody wants but who yet boldly demand to be well fed for their performances.

Yet that is just what is happening in our world among those employed in Government, and in the Church, and on science and art.

And all this results from a false understanding of the division of labour, defined not by man's conscience but by the investigations that are announced with such unanimity by the men of science.

A division of labour always has existed and does exist, but it is only justified when man's conscience and reason decide what it should be, and not when man merely observes that it does exist. And the conscience and reason of all men decide this question very simply, indubitably, and unanimously.

They decide that the division of labour is fair only when a man's special activity is so needed by others that they, asking him to serve them, willingly offer him support in return for what he does for them.

But when a man can live on the backs of others from childhood till he is thirty, promising when he has finished his education to do something useful, that no one asks him to do, and when from the age of thirty till death he can go on living in the same way, still promising to do something no one asks him to do, this cannot be, and in our society is not, a division of labour, but simply a seizure by the strong of the fruits of the labour of others: it is the very robbery theologians used to speak of as a 'divine dispensation', and philosophers afterwards declared to be 'a necessary form of life', and the scientists'science now calls 'the organic division of labour'.

The whole significance of the reigning science lies simply in that.

It has now become the granter of diplomas for idleness, for it alone in its sanctuaries examines and decides what is a parasitic and what an organic activity in the social organism—as if every man cannot recognize that much more truly and quickly by consulting his reason and conscience.

And as formerly for the priesthood and afterwards for the government, there could be no doubt as to who were the people others most needed, so now to the scientists' science it seems there can be no doubt that its activity is unquestionably organic: they, the scientists and artists, are the most precious brain-cells of the organism. But God be with them! Let them reign, eat and drink well, and live idly, as the priests and the sophists of old lived and reigned, if only they did not, like those priests and sophists, pervert people.

Since men, rational beings, existed they have discriminated between good and evil and have made use of the distinctions those who went before them had made in this respect. They have striven against evil, sought the true and best path, and slowly but steadily advanced along it. And, obstructing that path, various deceptions have always been set in their way in order to show that this should not be done, but that men should go on living as of old. The terrible old deceptions of the Church arose, with fearful struggles and labour men gradually freed themselves from these, but before they were completely free there arose a new — State-philosophic — fraud to replace the old one. Men broke through that also. And now a new and yet worse fraud has grown up obstructing man's path: the scientific fraud.

This new fraud is just like the old ones: its essence lies in substituting something external for the use of our own reason and conscience and that of our predecessors: in the Church teaching this external thing was revelation, in the scientific teaching it is observation.

The trick played by this science is to destroy man's faith in reason and conscience by directing attention to the grossest deviations from the use of human reason and conscience, and having clothed the deception in a scientific theory, to assure them that by acquiring knowledge of external phenomena they will get to know indubitable facts which will reveal to them the law of man's life. And the mental demoralization consists in this, that coming to believe that things which should be decided by conscience and reason are decided by observation, these people lose their consciousness of good and evil and become incapable of understanding the expression and definitions of good and evil that have been formed by the whole preceding life of humanity. All this, in their jargon, is conditional and subjective. It must all be abandoned—they say—the truth cannot be understood by one's reason, for one may err, but there is another path which is infallible and almost mechanical: one must study facts. And facts must be studied on the basis of the scientists' science, that is, on the basis of two unfounded propositions: positivism and evolution—which are put forward as indubitable truths.

And the reigning science, with not less misleading solemnity than the Church, announces that the solution of all questions of life is only possible by the study of the facts of nature, and especially of organisms.

A frivolous crowd of youths mastered by the novelty of this authority, which is as yet not merely not destroyed but not even touched by criticism, throws itself into the study of these facts of natural science as the sole path which, according to the assertions of the prevailing doctrine, can lead to the elucidation of the questions of life.

But the further these disciples advance in this study the further and further are they removed not only from the possibility but even from the very thought of solving life's problems, and the more they become accustomed not so much to observe as to take on trust what they are told of the observations of others (to believe in cells, in protoplasm, in the fourth state of matter,* etc.), the more and more does the form hide the contents from them; the more and more do they lose consciousness of good and evil and capacity to understand the expressions and definitions of good and evil worked out by the whole preceding life of humanity; the more and more do they adopt the specialized scientific jargon of conventional expressions which have no general human significance; the farther and farther do they wander among the débris of quite unilluminated observations; the more and more do they lose capacity not only to think independently but even to understand another man's fresh human thought lying outside their Talmud; and, what is most important, they pass their best years in growing unaccustomed to life, that is, to labour, and grow accustomed to consider their condition justified, while they become physically good-for-nothing parasites. And just like the theologians and the Talmudists they completely castrate their brains and become eunuchs of thought. And just like them, to the degree to which they become stupefied, they acquire a self-confidence which deprives them for ever of the possibility of returning to a simple clear and human way of thinking.

* A reference to Sir William Crookes' theory of the 'fourth state of matter', a novelty at the time Tolstoy wrote this work.

CHAPTER XXXII

DIVISION OF LABOUR has always existed in human society, and probably always will; but the question for us is not whether it exists and will exist, but what we must be guided by to see that the division shall be a fair one. If we take observation for our standard we thereby renounce all standards, and any division of labour we see existing that seems to us suitable, we shall accept as right, and this is what the reigning science leads us to.

Division of labour! Some are occupied with mental and spiritual, others with muscular physical work. With what assurance people say that! They wish to believe so, and it seems to them that in fact a perfectly correct exchange of services occurs, whereas what exists is really only a simple and very old form of coercion.

'Thou, or rather you' (for it always takes many to feed one), 'feed me, clothe me, and do all that rough work for me which I demand and to your performance of which I have been accustomed from childhood, and I will do for you the mental work of which I am capable and to which I am accustomed. You give me bodily food and I will give you spiritual food.' (The account seems quite correct, and would be correct if this exchange of services were voluntary; if those who supply the bodily food were not obliged to furnish it before they receive the spiritual food.)

The producer of spiritual food says: 'In order that I may give you spiritual food, feed me, clothe me, and clean up all the dirt I make.' But the producer of bodily food has to do all this without presenting any demands, and must deliver the bodily food even if he does not receive any spiritual food. If the exchange were voluntary the conditions of the two would be alike.

We agree that spiritual food is as necessary for man as bodily food. The savant and the artist say: 'Before we can begin to serve men with spiritual food we require them to supply us with bodily food.' But why does not the producer of bodily food say that before he serves them with bodily food he needs spiritual food, and unless he receives it he cannot work?

You say: 'I need the work of a ploughman, blacksmith, boot-maker, carpenter, bricklayer, privy-cleaner, and others, in order that

I may prepare my spiritual food.' Every labourer ought equally to say: 'Before I go to work to prepare bodily food for you, I must first have the fruits of your spiritual work. To have strength for my work I need religious teaching, good order in social life, applications of science to my work, and the enjoyments and consolations afforded by art. I have not time to work out my own explanation of the meaning of life—furnish me with it. I have not time to devise regulations for social life which would prevent infringements of justice—furnish me with them. I have not time to busy myself with mechanics, physics, chemistry, and technology—give me books which show how to improve my tools, my methods of work, my dwelling, my heating, and my lighting. I have not time to busy myself with poetry, plastic art, and music—furnish me with the stimulations and consolations that life requires; supply me with the products of art. You say you cannot occupy yourself with your important and necessary affairs if you are deprived of the work done for you by the labouring people, but I say,' the labourer remarks, 'that I cannot occupy myself with my not less important and necessary labours—ploughing, carting manure, and cleaning up your dirt—if I am deprived of religious guidance adapted to the demands of my reason and conscience, of wise government to make my labour secure, of indications supplied by knowledge to facilitate my work, and of the joys of art to ennoble my toil. All that you have as yet offered me as spiritual food does not suit me, I cannot even understand what good it can be to anyone. And till I receive food suitable for me, as for every man, I cannot feed you with the bodily food that I produce.' What will happen if the labourer says that?

If he should, you know it will not be a joke but the simplest justice.

If a labourer should say that, justice will be far more on his side than on that of the mental worker. Justice will be more on his side because the work supplied by the labourer is more important, more indispensable, than the work of the mental worker, and because nothing prevents the mental worker from giving the labourer the spiritual food promised him; while the labourer is hindered from supplying bodily food by the fact that he himself has not enough of it.

What shall we, mental workers, reply if such simple and legitimate demands are presented to us? How shall we satisfy them? With Filarét's *Catechism*, Sokolóv's *Sacred Stories*, and with leaflets issued by various monasteries and from St Isaac's Cathedral—to satisfy his religious needs; with the Code of Laws, decisions of the various Departments of the Court of Appeal and the statutes of various Committees and Commissions—to satisfy his demands for social justice; with spectral analysis, measurements of the Milky Way, abstract geometry, microscopic investigations, disputes about spiritualism and mediumism, the proceedings of the Academy of Science—to satisfy his demands for knowledge? With what shall we satisfy his artistic demands? With Púshkin, Dostoévski, Turgénev, L. Tolstóy, with pictures from the French Salon and by our own artists, representing naked women, satin, velvet, landscapes, and genre pictures, with Wagner's music and that of our own composers? None of these things suits him or can suit him, for we with our right to make use of the labour of the people and the absence of any obligation as to our production of spiritual food have entirely lost sight of the one purpose our activity should have. We do not even know what the working-folk need, we have forgotten their manner of life, their view of things, and their way of speaking; we have even forgotten the labouring man himself, and study him as an ethnographic rarity or as a newly discovered America.

So we, demanding bodily food for ourselves, have undertaken to supply spiritual food, but as a result of an imaginary division of labour allowing us not only to dine first and then work, but allowing whole generations to eat well without producing anything—we have prepared as payment to the people for our sustenance something that is only suitable, or it appears to us suitable, for science and art—but unsuitable and (like Limburg cheese) quite incomprehensible and repulsive to the very people whose labour we have devoured on the pretext that we would supply them with spiritual food.

We in our blindness have to such an extent lost sight of the obligation we had taken upon ourselves, that we have even forgotten the purpose for which our work is done and have made the very people we had undertaken to serve a subject for our scientific and artistic activity.

We study and depict them for our own amusement and distraction, and have quite forgotten that we should not study and depict them—but should serve them.

To such an extent have we lost sight of the obligation we took upon ourselves, that we do not even notice that what we had undertaken to do in the sphere of science and art has been done not by us but by others, and that our place has been occupied. It turns out that while we were disputing—as the theologians disputed about the Immaculate Conception—now about the spontaneous generation of organisms, now about spiritualism, now about the form of atoms, now about pangenesis, and now about what there is in protoplasm, and so on—the people all the same required spiritual food, and men who were the failures and outcasts of science and art began, at the order of businessmen anxious solely for profit, to supply the masses with spiritual food, and have supplied it. For some forty years elsewhere in Europe, and for some ten years past in Russia, millions of books and pictures and song-books have been circulated, and shows have been opened, and the people look on, and sing, and receive their spiritual food, but not from us who had undertaken to supply it—while we who justify our idleness by the spiritual food we are supposed to supply, sit and gape. But we must not gape, for our last justification is slipping from under our feet.

We have specialized. We have our special functional activity. We are the brain of the people. They feed us, and we have undertaken to instruct them. Only on that account have we emancipated ourselves from labour. What have we taught the labourers and what are we teaching them? They have waited one year, ten years, hundreds of years. And still we discuss and teach and entertain one another, but have forgotten them. To such an extent have we forgotten them that others have started to teach and entertain them and we did not even notice it, so little was our talk of the division of labour serious, and so evident is it that what we say of the benefit we confer on the masses is merely a shameless pretence.

CHAPTER XXXIII

THERE WAS A TIME when the Church guided the spiritual life of the people of our world; the Church promised people welfare and on that score excused itself from participation in humanity's struggle for life. And as soon as it did that it went astray from its vocation and the people turned away from it. It was not the errors of the Church that ruined it but the abandonment of the law of labour by its servants, secured by the aid of the government in the time of

Constantine; their privilege of idleness and luxury begot the errors of the Church. With that privilege began the Church's care for the Church and not for the people whom it had undertaken to serve. And the servants of the Church abandoned themselves to idleness and depravity.

The State undertook to guide the lives of men. The State promised men justice, tranquillity, security, order, the satisfaction of their general spiritual and material needs, and on this account the men who served the State emancipated themselves from participation in humanity's struggle for life. And the servants of the State, as soon as ever it was possible for them to exploit the labour of others, did what the servants of the Church had done. Their aim became not the people but the State, and the servants of the State—from kings down to the lowest officials and employees—in Rome, France, England, Russia, and America, abandoned themselves to idleness and depravity.

And people ceased to believe in the State, and anarchy is already consciously presented as an ideal.

The State lost its fascination for people only because its servants considered that they had a right to exploit the people's labour.

The same thing has been done by science and art with the help of the State authorities whom they have undertaken to support. They too stipulated for the right to idleness and to the use of other people's labour, and have similarly been false to their vocation.

And they too ran into error only because the servants of science, having adopted the wrongly understood principle of division of labour, allowed themselves the right to appropriate other people's labour and lost the meaning of their own vocation, taking for their aim not the benefit of the people but the mystic benefit of science and art; like their predecessors they yielded to idleness and depravity, not so much sensuous as intellectual.

It is said that science and art have given much to humanity. That is perfectly true.

The Church and the State gave much to humanity, not because they misused their power and their servants neglected the eternal obligation of man to labour for his livelihood—which applies to all men—but in spite of it.

So also science and art have given much to humanity, not because the scientists and artists on the plea of a division of labour live on the back of the working class but despite that fact. The Roman republic was strong not because its citizens were able to lead depraved lives, but because there were among them some worthy citizens. And it is the same with science and art.

Science and art have given much to humanity not because their servants sometimes formerly had, and now always have, opportunity to emancipate themselves from labour, but because there were men of genius who, not availing themselves of that opportunity, moved humanity forward.

The class of the learned and of artists who on the ground of a false division of labour demand the right to exploit the labour of others cannot contribute to the success of true science and true art, for falsehood cannot produce truth.

We are so accustomed to our pampered, fat, or enfeebled representatives of mental work, that it seems to us barbarous that a learned man or an artist should plough or cart manure. It seems to us as if all his wisdom would perish or be shaken to pieces on the cart, and the manure would soil the grand artistic images he carries in his breast; but we are so accustomed to it that it does not seem strange when a servant of science, that is a servant and teacher of truth, compelling others to do for him what he could do for himself, spends half his time in eating tasty food, in smoking, gossip, or liberal tittle-tattle, reading the papers and novels, and visiting the theatres. It does not surprise us to see our philosopher at a restaurant, a theatre, or a ball; nor does it seem strange to us to learn that those artists who delight and ennoble our souls spend their lives in drunkenness, card-playing, or with wenches—if not doing something worse . . . .

Science and art are beautiful things, but just because they are beautiful they should not be spoilt by joining depravity to them, that is, by freeing oneself from a man's obligation to support his own and other people's lives by labour.

Science and art have advanced humanity, yes! but not because the men of science and art, on the plea of a division of labour, by word and above all by deed have taught people to avail themselves of violence, and of the poverty and suffering of others, to free themselves from the first and most unquestionable human obligation of working with their own hands in the struggle with nature that is common to all humanity.

CHAPTER XXXIV

'BUT IT IS only the division of labour, and the emancipation of the men of science and art from the necessity of producing their own food, that has made possible the extraordinary progress of science that we see in our time,' is what people say to this.

'If everyone had to plough, those enormous results could not have been attained that have been attained in our time; there would not have been the striking progress which has so increased man's power over nature, nor those astronomical discoveries which have so impressed man's mind and made navigation safer, nor those steamers, railroads, marvellous bridges, tunnels, steam engines, telegraphs, photographs, telephones, sewing-machines, phonographs, electricity, telescopes, spectroscopes, microscopes, chloroform, antiseptics, and carbolic acid.'

I cannot enumerate all the things our age so prides itself on. That enumeration, and the raptures over ourselves and over our achievements, can be found in almost any newspaper or popular book. Those raptures over ourselves are so often repeated, we are so overjoyed at ourselves, that we are seriously convinced, with Jules Verne, that science and art never made such progress as in our time.

And we owe all this wonderful success to the division of labour, so how can we fail to acknowledge it?

Let us grant that the successes achieved in our age are really striking, wonderful, and extraordinary. Let us admit that we are such peculiarly fortunate people as to live in such an extraordinary time. But let us try to value these successes not by our self-satisfaction but by that same principle of division of labour in defence of which they are quoted: that is by the mental work of the men of science for the benefit of the people, which is to pay for the scientists' and artists' emancipation from labour. All these successes are very wonderful, but by some unfortunate accident—admitted by scientists themselves—up to now these successes have not improved the condition of the labourer but rather have made it worse.

If a workman instead of walking can go by train, on the other hand the railroad has consumed his forest, carried away the grain from under his nose, and brought him to a condition not far removed from slavery to those who own the railroad.

If, thanks to the steam-engines and machines, the labourer can buy wretched cotton prints, those steam-engines and machines have deprived him on the other hand of earnings at home, and have reduced him to a condition of complete slavery to the manufacturer.

If there are telegraph stations which he is not forbidden to use but which his means do not allow him to use, on the other hand his produce, as soon as the price is rising, thanks to the telegraph system gets bought up from under his nose by capitalists before the labourer hears of the demand there is for it.

If there are telephones and telescopes, verses, novels, theatres, ballets, symphonies, operas, picture galleries, and so forth, the workman's life is not improved by all this, for by the same unfortunate accident it is beyond his reach. So that in general up to now—as men of science admit—all these extraordinary inventions and productions of art, if they have not injured have quite failed to improve the labourer's life.

So that if the question of the reality of the successes achieved by science and art is measured not by our raptures over ourselves, but by the same standard by which the division of labour is defended—namely that of advantage to the labouring people, we shall see that we have as yet no firm basis for the self-satisfaction to which we so willingly yield.

A peasant goes by rail, his wife buys cotton prints, they have a lamp in their hut instead of a wooden torch, and the man lights his pipe with a match—that is convenient; but what right have I to say that the railroad and factories have benefited the people?

If the peasant travels on the railroad and buys a lamp, cotton prints, and matches, this is only because it is impossible to forbid him to do so, but we all know that the railroads and the factories were not built for the benefit of the labouring people, so why bring forward accidental conveniences, of which the peasants chance to be able to avail themselves, as proofs of the utility of those institutions to the people?

For we all know that if the technicians and capitalists who built the railroads and the factories thought about the workers, it was only of how to squeeze the last bit of work out of them. And as we have seen, both among ourselves and in Europe and America, they have fully succeeded in doing this.

In all harmful things there is some good. After a conflagration we can warm ourselves and light our pipes with the glowing charcoal; but why say that the conflagration is useful?

Let us at least not deceive ourselves. We all know the motives which prompt the building of railroads and factories and the production of kerosene and matches.

The engineer builds the railroad either for the government for military purposes or for capitalists for financial purposes. He makes machinery for the factory-owner for his own profit and for that of the capitalist. All that he makes and devises he makes and devises for the purposes of the government or of the capitalist and the rich people. The most cunning of his inventions are directly aimed either at injuring the people—as with cannon, torpedoes, solitary confinement cells, apparatus for the spirit-monopoly, telegraphs, and so forth, or for producing things that not only are not useful but are quite beyond the reach of the people, such as electric light, telephones, and all the innumerable appliances for the increase of comfort—or, finally, for things by which people can be corrupted and induced to part with the last of their money—that is, their last labour—such as, first of all vodka, spirits, beer, opium, and tobacco, then cotton prints, kerchiefs, and all sorts of trifles.

If it happens that the inventions of men of science and the work of engineers sometimes are of use to the people, as with railroads, cotton prints, iron pots, and scythes, that only proves that everything in the world is connected, and from any harmful activity some chance advantage may accrue even to those for whom the activity is generally harmful.

The scientists and artists could only say that their activity was useful to the people if they made it their aim to serve the labourers as they now make it their aim to serve the governments and the capitalists.

We could say it if scientists and artists set themselves the aim of serving the people's needs, but there are none who do so.

All the learned people are absorbed with their priestly occupations, from which result the investigations of protoplasm, spectral analyses of the stars, and so forth. But with what kind of axe and what kind of axe-handle it is best to chop, what sort of saw works best, how best to knead bread, what flour to use, how to set it, how to make a fire, and how to build the stove, what food, what drink, and what dishes, to use, which mushrooms should be eaten and how best to prepare them—about these things science never reflects. Yet it is all matter for science to deal with,

I know that by its definition science should be useless, but that is an obvious and too impudent excuse. The business of science is to serve men. We have invented telegraphs, telephones, and phonographs; but in real life, in the people's work, what progress have we made? We have enumerated two million insects! But have we domesticated a single new animal since Biblical times when the animals we now have, had already long been domesticated? The elk, the stag, the partridge, the quail, and the grouse, are all still wild. Our botanists have discovered the cell, and in the cell protoplasm, and in protoplasm something else, and in that again something else. These occupations will evidently not end for a long time—because there can be no end to them; and so they have no time to occupy themselves with what people need. And then again, since Egyptian and Jewish antiquity, when wheat and lentil were already cultivated, down to our own time, not a single plant has been added to the food of the people except potatoes, and it was not science that gave us them.

They have invented torpedoes, appliances for the use of the spirit-monopoly, and for privies, but our spinning-wheel, peasant-woman's loom, village plough, hatchet, flail, rake, and the yoke and bucket, are still the same that they were in the times of Rúrik,* or if they have been altered it has not been done by scientists.

The same is true in regard to art. We have raised a multitude of men to the rank of great writers, have analysed them minutely, and written mountains of criticisms, and criticisms of those criticisms, and criticisms of the criticisms of the criticisms, and have collected galleries of pictures, and have studied all the schools of art acutely, and we have such symphonies and operas that it becomes hard for us ourselves to listen to them. But what have we added to the folk-tales and legends and stories and songs? What pictures have we given to the people and what music? In Nikówski-street† books and pictures

* The first Russian Prince (830 to 879 A.D.).   † A street in the centre of Moscow, where cheap chapbooks for the peasants were sold.

for the people are produced, and in Túla concertinas are made, but in neither have we taken any part.

Most striking and obvious is the false direction of our science and art in the very branches which, one would think, should by their very purpose be of use to the people, but which in consequence of the false direction appear harmful rather than useful.

The engineer, doctor, teacher, artist, author, by the very purpose of their calling, one would imagine, should serve the people—and what happens? Under the present tendency they can bring nothing but harm to the people.

An engineer, a mechanic, must work with capital. Without capital he is useless. All his knowledge is such that, to apply it, he needs capital and the exploitation of labour on a large scale, and not to mention that he is himself accustomed to spend at least fifteen hundred to two thousand rubles a year, and therefore cannot live in a village, where no one could give him such a remuneration, his occupation itself prevents his serving the people. He can by higher mathematics reckon the span of a bridge, calculate the power and efficiency of a motor, and so forth, but faced by the simple problems of peasant-toil he sticks fast. How to improve the village plough or cart, how to make the streams fordable—of all this, in the conditions in which the peasants live, he knows and understands less than the meanest peasant. Give him workshops, all the various kinds of people he needs, import machines for him from abroad, and then he will arrange matters. But in the existing conditions of labour of millions of people, he is quite unable to find ways of lightening their toil, and his own occupations, habits, and needs, render him unsuited for such an affair.

The doctor is in a still worse position. His pseudo-science is all so arranged that he can only cure those who do nothing and can command the labour of others. He needs an endless number of expensive appliances, instruments, medicaments, and hygienically arranged rooms, food, and water-closets, to enable him to act scientifically; besides his own salary he needs such expenses that to cure one patient he has to starve hundreds of others who bear those expenses. He has studied in the capitals under celebrities who only take patients who can be treated in hospitals, or who while being treated can purchase the apparatus needed for the treatment, and can even travel immediately from the north to the south, or to such and such watering-places.

Their science is of such a kind that every Zémstvo* doctor complains of not having the means to treat the labourers—that they are so poor that it is impossible to place the patients in hygienic conditions; and at the same time that doctor complains that there are no hospitals, that he cannot manage all the work, and that he needs more assistants, doctors, and trained helpers. What does this mean? It means that the chief calamity of the people, causing illnesses to arise and spread and remain untreated, is the insufficiency of their means of livelihood.

And science, under the banner of a division of labour, calls its combatants to help these people. Science has adapted itself entirely to the wealthy classes and accordingly has set itself to heal those who can afford everything, and it prescribes the same methods for those who have nothing to spare.

But the means are lacking, and therefore they must be taken from the peasants who fall ill and become infected and are not cured from lack of means.

The defenders of medicine for the people are always saying that, as yet, this business is but little developed.

Evidently it is little developed, for if—which God forbid—it should be developed, and on the people's backs instead of two doctors, midwives and trained female assistants to a District, there were twenty such—as is proposed—there would soon be no one left to heal. Scientific assistance for the people, of which the defenders of science talk, should be of quite a different kind. And the kind of assistance that should be given has not yet been begun. It will begin when the man of science, the technician, or the doctor, will not consider permissible the division—which is to say, the seizure—of the labour of other people which now exists; will not consider himself to have a right to take from people, I will not say hundreds of thousands, but even a modest one thousand or five hundred rubles for the aid he renders them, but will live among the labouring people under the same conditions as they do and as they do, and will then apply his knowledge to the labouring people's problems of mechanics, engineering, hygiene, and medicine. But now science, fed by the labour of the working folk, has completely forgotten the conditions of those people's lives, ignores those conditions,

* The Zémstvos resembled our County Councils, and had charge of the medical service in country districts.

and is seriously offended because its pseudo-knowledge finds no application among them.

The sphere of medicine, like that of engineering, lies as yet untouched. All the questions of how best to divide the worktime, how best to nourish oneself, on what and in what form, when and how it is best to clothe oneself, to cover one's feet, to resist dampness and cold, how best to wash and feed the children, swaddle them, and so forth, in the actual circumstances in which the working people live—all these questions have not yet been put. So it is, too, with the scientific, pedagogic, teachers' activity. Science has, in just the same way, so managed that, in accord with pedagogic science, only rich people can be taught, and the teachers, like the engineers and doctors, involuntarily pay court to money and among us especially to the government.

And this cannot be otherwise, for a school with model arrangements (as a general rule the more scientifically arranged a school the more expensive it is), with adjustable benches, globes and maps, and libraries, and methodics for teachers and for pupils, is such as would involve the doubling of the rates in each village. Such is the demand of science.

The people need their children for work, and the poorer the people the more they need them. The defenders of science say: pedagogy even now benefits the people, but when it is developed things will be still better. But if it develops and instead of twenty schools to a district there are a hundred and all of them scientific, and the people have to pay for those schools, they will be more and more impoverished and will be yet more in need of their children's work.

What, then, is to be done? say people in reply to this.

The government will establish schools and make education compulsory as is done in Europe; but the money will again be taken from the people, who will be worked yet harder and will have yet less leisure, and compulsory education will not act. Again the only salvation is for the teacher to live the life of a labourer and teach for such remuneration as may be freely and willingly given him.

Such is the false tendency of science, which deprives it of the possibility of fulfilling its duty, which is to serve the people. But this false tendency of our intellectuals is yet more evident in the activity of art, which by its very nature should be accessible to the people.

Science may fall back on its stupid excuse that science works for science, and that when it has been developed by the scientists it will become accessible to the people also; but art, if it be art, should be accessible to all, and particularly to those for whom it is produced. And the position of our art strikingly arraigns the producers of art for not wishing, not knowing how, and being unable, to serve the people.

For the preparation of his great works, an artist who is a painter must have a studio in which an association of at least forty carpenters or boot- makers could work who now freeze or stifle in a slum. Nor is that enough; he needs nature, costumes, travel. The Academy of Arts has expended millions of rubles, collected from the people, on the encouragement of art, and the productions of this art are to be found in palaces and are not understood or wanted by the masses.

To express their great ideas musicians have to collect some two hundred men in white neckties or in costumes, and to expend hundreds of thousands of rubles on producing an opera. And the productions of this art could produce nothing but perplexity and weariness among the people, were they ever able to hear them.

Authors and writers of stories, one would think, do not need special surroundings, studios, nature, orchestras, and actors; but here, too, it appears that for the preparation of his great works a writer besides comfortable lodgings and all the pleasures of life, needs travel, palaces, studies, the pleasures of art, and visits to theatres, concerts, watering places, etc. If he does not himself earn money he is given a pension to enable him to write better. And again these writings, so much esteemed by us, remain rubbish for the people, who do not want them at all.

What if, as the men engaged on science and art desire, yet more of these producers of spiritual food are reared and it becomes necessary in each village to build a studio and introduce an orchestra and maintain an author in such conditions as artists consider essential?

I imagine that the working people would sooner pledge themselves never to see a picture, or hear a symphony, or read any poem or story, than be obliged to feed all those drones.

But why, one would ask, should artists not serve the people? In every hut there are icons and pictures; every peasant and every peasant woman sings; many of them have musical instruments, and they all tell stories and recite verses, while many of them read.

How is it that these two things—made for one another like lock and key—have gone so far apart that there seems no possibility of bringing them together?

Tell a painter that without studios, nude models, and costumes, he should paint penny pictures, and he will tell you that this would be to abandon art as he understands it: tell a musician that he should play on a *balaláyka*, a concertina, or a guitar, and should teach the peasant women to sing songs: tell a poet or an author that he should abandon his poems, his novels, his satires, and should compose songs, books, stories and fairy tales, which unlettered folk could understand—and they will tell you that you are mad. But is it not a worse madness that people who have emancipated themselves from labour on the plea that they would provide spiritual food for those who have reared them and who feed and clothe them, should afterwards have so forgotten this obligation that they do not know how to prepare food fit for the people, and should consider this abandonment of their duty a merit?

'But it is so everywhere,' is what is said in reply.

It is very irrational everywhere; and it will remain irrational as long as people, under the pretext of a division of labour and a promise to serve the people with spiritual food, continue merely to devour the people's labour. Service of the people by sciences and arts will only exist when men live with the people and as the people live, and without presenting any claims will offer their scientific and artistic services, which the people will be free to accept or decline as they please.

CHAPTER XXXV

TO SAY THAT the activity of science and art helps humanity's progress, if by that activity we mean the activity which now calls itself by those names, is as though one said that the clumsy, obstructive splashing of oars in a boat moving down stream assists the boat's progress. It only hinders it.

The so-called division of labour, that is, the seizure of the labour of others which in our time has become a usual condition of the activity of men of science and art, has been and still remains the chief cause of the slowness of humanity's forward movement. The proof of this is seen in the confession made by men of science that the achievements of the arts and sciences are inaccessible to the labouring masses on account of the unequal distribution of wealth.

And the unfairness of this distribution is not diminished in proportion to the successes achieved by the sciences and arts, but is only increased. Nor is it surprising that this is so, for this unjust distribution of wealth results simply from the theory of the division of labour which is preached by the men of science and art for their personal selfish ends. Science defends the division of labour as an immutable law, sees that the division of wealth based on the division of labour is unjust and pernicious, and asserts that its activity, which accepts the division of labour, will result in benefit to mankind. It appears that some men make use of the labours of others, but that if they go on for a very long time and to a still greater extent making use of the labour of others, then this unjust distribution of wealth—that is, this exploitation of other people's work—will come to an end.

Men are standing at an ever-increasing spring of water and are busy diverting it from thirsty people, but assert that it is they who produce the water and that very soon so much of it will be collected that there will be enough for everybody. But this water, which has flowed and flows unceasingly and supplies drink to all humanity, is not only not the result of the activity of these men who standing round the spring turn the water aside, but on the contrary, flows and spreads despite their efforts to prevent its flowing.

There always was a true church, in the sense of people united in the highest truth accessible to man at any given period, and this has always been other than the church which called itself so; and there have always been science and art, but they have not been the activities that called themselves by those names.

To those who regard themselves as the representatives of the science and art of a particular period, it always seems as though they had done and were doing, and above all were just about to do, wonderful miracles; and that apart from them no real science or art has existed or does exist. So it seemed to the Sophists, the Schoolmen, the Alchemists, the Cabalists, the Talmudists, and so it seems to our scientific scientists and art-for-art's-sake-ists.

CHAPTER XXXVI

'BUT SCIENCE AND ART! You are denying science and art: that is you are denying that by which humanity lives.' People constantly make this rejoinder to me, and they employ this method in order to reject my arguments without examination.

'He rejects science and art, he wishes man to revert to a state of savagery—why listen to him or discuss with him?'

But this is unjust. Not only do I not repudiate science, that is, the reasonable activity of humanity, and art—the expression of that reasonable activity—but it is just on behalf of that reasonable activity and its expression that I speak, only that it may be possible for mankind to escape from the savage state into which it is rapidly lapsing thanks to the false teaching of our time. It is only on that account that I speak as I do.

Science and art are as necessary to man as food and drink and clothing—even more necessary—but they become so not because we decide that what we call science and art are essential, but only because science and art really are essential to humanity.

If people prepared hay for man's bodily food, no conviction of mine that hay is human food would cause it to become so. I must not say: 'Why do you not eat hay when it is your necessary food?' Food is necessary, but perhaps what I am offering is not food.

And this is just what has happened with our science and art. It seems to us that if we add the termination *logy* to some Greek word and call it a science, it will be a science; and if some nastiness, such as the dancing of naked women, is called by a Greek word, and we say it is an art, it will be art. But however much we may say this, the things we occupy ourselves with—counting up the beetles, investigating the chemical constituents of the Milky Way, painting water-nymphs and historical pictures, or composing stories and symphonies—will not become either science or art till it is willingly accepted by those for whom it is being done. And up to the present it is not so accepted.

If certain people had the exclusive right to produce food and all others were forbidden to do so, or it were made impossible for them to do so, I imagine that the quality of our food would deteriorate. If the people who had the monopoly of food production were Russian peasants, there would be no other food than rye-bread, kvas, potatoes, and onions—the food they are fond of, the food which pleases them. And this would happen to the highest human activity—science and art—if a single caste were to monopolize it—but with this difference, that in bodily food there can be no great deviation from what is natural: both rye-bread and onion, though not very tasty foods are nevertheless wholesome; but in mental food there may be very great deviations and some men may feed for a long time on mental food that is quite unnecessary for them, or is even harmful and poisonous. They may slowly kill themselves with opium and spirits and may offer this same food to the masses.

That is what has happened among us. And it has happened because scientists and artists occupy a privileged position, and because science and art in our world are not the whole reasonable activity of the whole of mankind without exception, devoting its best strength to the service of science and art, but are the activity of a small circle of people having a monopoly of these occupations and calling themselves scientists and artists, and who, therefore, having perverted the very conception of science and art, have lost the very meaning of their calling and are merely occupied in amusing a small circle of idle consumers and saving them from the ennui that oppresses them.

Since men first existed they have always had science in the plainest and widest sense of the word. Science, in the sense of all man's knowledge, always has existed and does exist and life is inconceivable without it: it calls neither for attack nor for defence. But the point is that the domain of knowledge is so various, so much information of all kinds is included in it—from the knowledge of how to obtain iron, to the knowledge of the movements of the celestial bodies—that man loses himself amid these various kinds of knowledge unless he has a clue to enable him to decide which of them all is most important for him, and which is less so.

And therefore the highest aim of human wisdom has always been to find that clue, and to show the sequence in which our knowledge should rank: what of it is of the first and what is of lesser importance.

And just this knowledge, that guides all other knowledge, is what men have always spoken of as science in the strict sense. And right down to our own times such science has always existed in human societies after they have emerged from the primeval, savage conditions.

Since humanity existed always among all peoples teachers have appeared who have produced science in that strict sense—the knowledge of what it is most necessary for man to know. That science has always dealt with the knowledge of what is the destiny, and therefore the true welfare, of each man and of mankind. And *that* science has served as the clue in determining the importance of all other knowledge, and of the activity which gives it expression, namely, art.

Those kinds of knowledge which aided and came nearest to the fundamental science of the destiny and welfare of all men, stood highest in general esteem, and those least useful stood lowest. Such was the science of Confucius, Buddha, Moses, Socrates, Christ, Mohammed: such is science, and so it has been and is understood by everybody, except by our circle of so-called educated people.

Such science has always not merely occupied the first place, but has alone determined the importance of all the other sciences.

And this occurred not at all, as is supposed by the so-called learned men of to-day, because deceivers—the priests and teachers of that science—gave it that importance, but because indeed, as every one can learn by his inner experience, without a science of man's destiny and welfare there can be no evaluation or choice of any science or art, and therefore there can be no study of science: for the subjects for science to deal with are *innumerable*; I emphasize the word 'innumerable', because I use it in its literal meaning.

Without knowledge of what constitutes the destiny and welfare of all men, all other science and art becomes, as they have become among us, an idle and pernicious amusement. Mankind has lived long, but never without a science to show wherein its destiny and welfare lie. It is true that the science of the welfare of man appears on superficial observation to differ among the Buddhists, Brahminists, Jews, Christians, Confucians, and the followers of Lao-Tsze (though it is only necessary to consider these teachings, to find one and the same essence), but wherever we know of men who have emerged from the state of savagery, we find this science, and now suddenly it seems that people to-day have decided that it is just this very science—which has hitherto guided all human knowledge—which hinders everything.

People build an edifice, and one architect draws up one set of plans, another—another, and a third—a third. The plans vary somewhat, but are correct in that everyone sees that if all is carried out according to the plan the edifice will get built.

Such architects were Confucius, Buddha, Moses, and Christ.

Suddenly people come and assure us that the chief thing is not to have any plans at all, but to build anyhow, by the look of the thing. And this 'anyhow' these people call the most exact scientific science, as the Pope terms himself the 'Most Holy'. People deny every science, the very essence of science—the ascertaining of the destiny and welfare of man, and this denial of science they call 'science'. Since men first appeared, great intellects have arisen among them who in struggle with the demands of their reason and conscience have asked themselves what our destiny and welfare consist in—not mine only but every man's.

What does that Power which produced and guides us demand of me and of every man? What must I do to satisfy the craving implanted in me for my personal welfare and that of the world in general?

They have said to themselves: 'I am a whole, and I am a particle of something immeasurable and unending. What are my relations to other particles similar to myself—to individuals and to that whole?'

And from the voice of conscience and reason, and from consideration of what has been said by predecessors and contemporaries who set themselves those same questions, these great teachers have deduced a doctrine—plain, clear, and intelligible to all men, and always such as could be practised.

There have been such men of first-rate, second-rate, third-rate, and of quite minor greatness. The world is full of them.

All living men put to themselves the question: How reconcile our desires for personal welfare with the general welfare of mankind demanded by conscience and reason? And from this general travail, new forms of life nearer to the demands of reason and conscience are slowly but unceasingly evolved.

Suddenly a new caste of men appear who say: This is all rubbish, it must all be abandoned. This is the deductive method of thought (though what the difference is between the deductive and the inductive methods, nobody has ever been able to understand), it is the method of the theological and metaphysical periods. All that men have discovered by inner experience, and communicate to one another, concerning consciousness of the law of their life (functional activity, in the new jargon), all that from the commencement of the world has been accomplished in that direction by the greatest intellects of mankind, is rubbish and of no importance.

According to this new teaching it seems that you are a cell of an organism, and the aim of your reasonable activity is to ascertain your functional activity; and in order to do that you need only observe things outside yourself. That you are a cell that thinks, suffers, speaks, understands, and that you can therefore ask another similar speaking cell whether, like you, it suffers, rejoices, and feels, and so can verify your own experience; that you can avail yourself of what cells that lived, suffered, thought, and spoke, before you did have written about the matter; that millions of other cells confirm your observations by their agreement with those who have recorded their thoughts; and above all, that you yourselves are living cells always by direct experience recognizing the justice or injustice of your functional activities—all this means nothing at all, it is all a bad, false method. The true scientific method is this: if you wish to know what your functional activity consists in, that is to say, what is your vocation and welfare and those of humanity and of the whole world, you must first of all cease to listen to the voice and demands of the conscience and reason that manifest themselves within you and in your fellow-men; you must cease to believe what the great teachers of mankind have said about their reason and conscience, and must consider all these to be trifles, and begin all over again. And to begin from the beginning you must look through a microscope at the movements of amoebas and at the cells of tapeworms, or easier still, must believe everything that may be told you about them by people who have the diploma of infallibility. And observing the movements of these amoebas and cells, or reading what others have seen, you must attribute to these cells your own human feelings and calculations as to what they desire, what they strive for, their reflections and calculations, and what they are accustomed to; and from these observations (in which every word is an error in thought or expression) you must by analogy decide what you are, what your vocation is, and wherein lies your own welfare and that of other cells similar to yourself. To understand yourself you must not only study tapeworms which you can see, but also microscopic beings you can hardly see, and the transformations from one being into another which no one has ever seen and which you will certainly never see.

It is the same with art. Wherever there has been a true science, art has always been an expression of the knowledge of man's vocation and welfare.

Since the time that men first existed, from amid the whole activity which presents various kinds of knowledge they have selected the principal kind, that which presented man's vocation and welfare, and the expression of the results of that knowledge has been art in the restricted sense of the word. Since men first existed there have been persons specially sensitive and responsive to the teaching of man's welfare and vocation, who on psaltery and cymbals, by imagery and by words, have expressed their human struggle against deceptions which drew them from their vocation, expressed their sufferings in this struggle, their hopes for the triumph of goodness, their despair at the triumph of evil, and their rapture at the expectation of approaching blessedness.

Since man existed, true art which was highly esteemed has had no other purpose than to express man's vocation and welfare. Always till recent times, art has served the teaching of life—which was afterwards called 'religion'—and only such art has been held in high esteem. But simultaneously with the appearance, in place of a science of man's vocation and welfare, of the science of whatever comes to hand—since science has lost its meaning and purpose, and true science has come to be contemptuously called 'religion'—from that very time art as an important human activity has disappeared.

As long as the church existed as a teaching of our vocation and welfare, art served the church and was true art, but since art left the church and began to serve science, while science served anything that came to hand, art has lost its importance and, in spite of its traditional claims and the absurd assertion that 'art serves art' (which only shows that it has lost its purpose), it has become a trade supplying people with what is agreeable, and has inevitably mingled with the choreographic, culinary, tonsorial, and cosmetic arts, whose producers call themselves artists with the same right as do the poets, painters, and musicians of our day.

We look back and see that during thousands of years, out of milliards of people a few dozen stand out, such as Confucius, Buddha, Solon, Socrates, Solomon, Homer, Isaiah, and David. Evidently such men were seldom to be met with, though in those days they were drawn not from a single caste but from among the whole people; evidently such true scientific and artistic producers of spiritual food were rare. And it is not for nothing that humanity so highly esteemed and esteems them. But now it turns out that all these great moving spirits in science and art are no longer of any use to us. To-day producers of science and art can by the law of division of labour be produced on the factory system, and in a single decade we can turn out more great scientists and artists than had appeared among mankind from the commencement of the world.

There is now a guild of scientists and artists, and by a perfect method they prepare all the spiritual food needed by mankind.

And they have prepared so much of it that the old, the former, geniuses, both the ancients and those nearer to ourselves, need no longer be held in remembrance—that was all an activity of the theological and metaphysical period, it all has to be wiped out; but real reasonable activity began about fifty years ago. And in these fifty years we have produced so many great men that in a single German university there are now more of them than there had been in the whole world; and we have produced so many sciences—fortunately they are easy to produce (one has only to add *logy* to a Greek noun and classify it among the ready-made tables, and a science is ready)—that not only can no man know them all, but no one man can even remember the names of them all—their names alone fill a stout dictionary, and new sciences are coming into existence every day.

They have made many that remind one of the story of the Finnish tutor who taught a landowner's children Finnish instead of French. They have taught it all beautifully; the only pity is that nobody, except themselves, understands any of it, everyone else regards it as worthless rubbish.

But of this too there is an explanation: people do not understand all the utility of scientific science because they are still under the influence of the theological period of knowledge—that stupid period when the whole people, both among the Hebrews, the Chinese, the Hindus, and the Greeks, understood all that their great teachers said to them.

But however it happened, the fact is that both science and art have always existed among men, and when they were real they were wanted by and were comprehensible to the whole people.

We are busy with something we call science and art, but it turns out that what we are doing has no right to be called either science or art.

CHAPTER XXXVII

'BUT YOU ARE merely giving another, narrower, definition of science and art – which science does not agree with,' people say to me in reply. 'But this does not exclude the rest, and there still remains the scientific and artistic activity of the Galileos, Brunos, Homers, Michelangelos, Beethovens, Wagners, and all the scientists and artists of lesser magnitude who have devoted their whole lives to the service of science and art.' This they usually say in order to establish a succession (which at other times they disavow) between the former scientists and artists and the present ones, trying also to forget that special new principle of the division of labour on the basis of which science and art now occupy their privileged position.

But first of all it is impossible to establish such a succession between the former workers and the present ones—as the holy life of the first Christians has nothing in common with the lives of the Popes, so the activity of men like Galileo, Shakespeare, and Beethoven has nothing in common with the activities of men like Tyndall, Victor Hugo, and Wagner. As the holy Fathers would have repudiated connection with the Popes, so the former leaders in science would have repudiated connection with those of today.

And secondly, thanks to the importance science and art now attribute to themselves, we have a very clear standard set by science itself, by which to determine whether or not they fulfil their purpose, and so to decide not arbitrarily but according to an accepted standard, whether the activity calling itself science and art has a right to do so.

When Egyptian and Grecian priests performed mysteries which were concealed from everybody, and said that these mysteries contained all science and all art—we could not on the score of benefits conferred by them on the people verify the validity of their science, for they alleged it to be super natural; but now we all have a very clear and simple standard excluding everything supernatural: science and art undertake to perform the brain-work of humanity for the benefit of society or of mankind. And therefore we have a right to call only such activity 'science and art' as has that aim in view and attains it.

And therefore, however those learned men and artists call themselves who excogitate the theory of penal, civil, and international law, who invent new guns and explosives, who compose obscene operas and operettas or similarly obscene novels, we have no right to call such activity science and art; for that activity has not the welfare of society or of mankind in view, but is on the contrary directed to the injury of man. All this therefore is not science or art. In the same way, however learned men may call themselves who in their simplicity devote their whole lives to the study of microscopic animalculae and of telescopic and spectral phenomena, or those artists who after a laborious study of the memorials of antiquity are busy writing historical novels, painting pictures, or composing symphonies and beautiful verses—all these men, despite their zeal, cannot, on the basis of the scientific definition itself, be called men of science and art: first, because their activity of science for science's sake and art for art's sake has not human welfare in view and secondly, because we do not see the results of their activity in the welfare of society and of humanity. The fact that from their activity something pleasant and profitable for certain people sometimes results, by no means allows us, according to their own scientific definition, to consider them scientists and artists.

Just in the same way, however people may call themselves who devise applications of electricity to lighting or heating or the transmission of power, or new chemical combinations yielding dynamite or fine colours, or play Beethoven's symphonies correctly, or perform in theatres and paint good portraits, genre paintings, landscapes or other pictures, or write interesting novels—the aim of which is merely to relieve the dullness of the wealthy classes—these people's activity cannot be called science and art, because it is not directed, like the brain-activity of an organism, to the welfare of the whole, but is guided merely by personal profit, privileges, and money, received for the inventions and productions of so-called art; and therefore this activity can in no way be separated from every other kind of interested personal activity adding to the pleasure of life, like the activity of restaurant-keepers, jockeys, milliners, prostitutes, and so forth; for the activity of the first, the second, and the third, of these does not come under the definition of science and art which promise on the basis of a division of labour to serve the welfare of mankind or of society.

The definition of science and art given by science is quite correct, but unfortunately the activity of present-day science and art does not come under it. Some of its representatives are doing what is directly harmful, others what is useless, and again others what is insignificant and available only for rich people.

They are all perhaps very good people, but they do not do what by their own definition they have undertaken to do, and therefore they have as little right to consider themselves scientists and artists as the clergy of to-day, who do not fulfil the duties they have undertaken, have a right to claim to be the bearers and teachers of divine truth.

And it is not difficult to understand why those who are active in science and art to-day do not fulfil, and cannot fulfil, their calling. They do not fulfil it because they have converted their duties into rights.

Scientific and artistic activity in its real sense is only fruitful when it ignores rights and knows only duties. Only because it is always of that kind and its nature is to be self-sacrificing, does humanity value this activity so highly.

Men who are really called to serve others by mental labour will always suffer in performing that service, for only by sufferings as by birthpangs, is the spiritual world brought to birth.

Self-sacrifice and suffering will be the lot of a thinker and an artist because their aim is the welfare of man. People are unhappy, they suffer and perish. There is no time to wait and refresh oneself.

The thinker and artist will never sit on Olympian heights as we are apt to imagine; he will always be in a state of anxiety and agitation; he might discover and utter what would bring blessings to people, might save them from sufferings, but he has not discovered it and has not uttered it, and to-morrow it may be too late—he may have died.

Not *that* man will be a thinker and artist who is educated in an institution where they profess to produce learned men and artists (but really produce destroyers of science and art) and who obtains a diploma and a competence, but he who would be glad not to think and not to express what is implanted in his soul, but cannot help doing what he is impelled to by two irresistible forces—an inner necessity and the demands of men.

Plump self-satisfied thinkers and artists, enjoying themselves, do not exist.

Mental activity and its expression, of a kind really needed by others, is the hardest and most painful calling for a man—his cross, as the Gospel expresses it. And the sole and indubitable indication of a man's vocation for it is self-denial, a sacrifice of himself for the manifestation of the power implanted in him for the benefit of others.

One can teach how many insects there are in the world and examine the spots on the sun and write novels and operas, without suffering; but to teach men their welfare, which lies in denying oneself and serving others, and to express this teaching powerfully, is impossible without suffering.

The church existed as long as its teachers endured and suffered, but as soon as they became fat their teaching activity ended.

'There used to be golden priests and wooden chalices; but now the chalices are golden and priests wooden,' as the peasants say.

There was reason for Christ to die on the cross: the sacrifice of suffering conquers all.

Our science and art are provided for and diplomaed and people are only concerned how to provide for them still better, that is, make it impossible for them to serve mankind.

True science and true art have two indubitable indications: the first internal—that a minister of science or art fulfils his calling not for gain but with self-sacrifice; and the second external—that his productions are intelligible to all men whose welfare he has in view.

Whatever it may be that men regard as representing their vocation and welfare, science will teach that vocation and welfare, and art will express that teaching. The laws of Solon and Confucius are science; the teachings of Moses and of Christ are science; buildings in Athens, the psalms of David, the church service, are art; but studying the fourth dimension of matter and tabulating chemical compounds and so forth—never has been and never will be science. The place of real science is occupied in our time by theology and jurisprudence, and the place of real art is occupied by church and state ceremonies, in neither of which do people believe and which no one regards seriously; but what among us is called science and art is a production of idle thought and feeling which aims at tickling similarly idle minds and feelings, and it is unintelligible and inarticulate to the people because it has not their welfare in view.

From the time we know anything of the life of man we everywhere and always find a dominant teaching falsely calling itself science, and not revealing to people, but concealing from them, the meaning of life. So it was among the Egyptians, the Hindus, the Chinese, and to some extent among the Greeks (the sophists), and later among the mystics, gnostics, and cabalists, and in the Middle Ages among the schoolmen and alchemists, and so on, everywhere, down to our own day.

What peculiar luck is ours that we live just at the particular time when the mental activity calling itself science not only does not err, but is (as we are constantly assured) extraordinarily successful! Does not this peculiarly good fortune result from the fact that man cannot and will not recognize his own deformity? How is it that of those other sciences, theological and cabalistic, nothing but words remain, while we are so peculiarly lucky?

Notice that the indications are exactly the same: the same self-satisfaction and blind assurance that we, just we and only we, are on the real path and are the first to tread it: the self-same expectation that there—directly—we shall discover something extraordinary; and above all the same sign exposing us, namely, that all our wisdom remains with us while the mass of the people neither understand, nor accept, nor need it. Our position is a very sad one, but why not face it as it is?

It is time to come to our senses and look around us.

For we are indeed nothing but scribes and Pharisees who have seated ourselves in Moses' seat and taken the keys of the kingdom of heaven, neither entering in ourselves nor allowing others to enter. We priests of science and art are the most worthless frauds, with far less right to our position than the most cunning and depraved Church priests. For we have absolutely no right to our privileged position, we obtained it by guile and keep it by fraud.

The pagan priests and the clergy of our own and of the Catholic Church, however depraved they may be, or have been, had this right to their position—that they at least proposed to teach life and salvation to the people. We have undermined them and proved that they deceived, and have taken their place, but we do not teach people how to live: we even admit that it is no use trying to learn this. Yet we suck the juice out of the people, and in return teach our children our Talmud of Greek and Latin grammar, that they in their turn may continue to lead the same parasitic life as we do.

We say, there used to be castes but we have none. But how is it that some people and their children work while other people and their children do not? Bring a Hindu who does not know our language and show him our life as it has gone on for generations, and he will recognize the same two chief, distinct castes of workers and nonworkers as exist among his people. As with them so with us, the right not to work is given by a special initiation, which we call science and art and in general—education.

It is this education, and the whole perversion of reason attached to it, that has brought us to the amazing state of insanity which causes us not to see what is so clear and indubitable.

We consume the lives of our brother men, and continue to consider ourselves Christian, humane, educated, and perfectly justified.

CHAPTER XXXVIII

'WHAT THEN MUST WE DO? What must we do?'

This question—including an admission that our way of life is wrong and bad, together with a suggestion that all the same it is impossible to change it—this question I hear from all sides, and for that reason I chose it as the title of my work.

I have described my sufferings, my search, and my solution of this question. I am a man like everybody else, or if I am at all different from an ordinary man of our circle it is chiefly that I have served and connived at the false teaching of our world more than he, have been more praised by the men of the dominant school and have therefore been perverted and gone astray more than others.

And therefore I think the solution I have found for myself will be valid for all sincere men who set themselves the same question. First of all, to the question: What must we do? I replied to myself: I must not lie either to myself or to others, nor fear the truth wherever it may lead me. We all know what lying to other people means, and yet we lie unceasingly from morning to night: 'Not at home,' when I am at home; 'Very pleased,' when I am not at all pleased; 'My respects,'when I do not respect; 'I have no money,' when I have some, and so on. We consider lies to other people, especially certain kinds of lies, to be bad, but are not afraid of lying to ourselves; yet the very worst, most downright and deceptive lie to others, is as nothing in its consequences compared with that lie to ourselves on which we have built our whole life.

That is the lie we must not be guilty of, in order to be able to answer the question: *What must we do?*

How can the question be answered when all I do, my whole life, is based on a lie and I carefully give out this lie as truth to others and to myself? Not to lie, in that sense, means not to fear the truth, not to invent excuses to hide from myself the conclusions of reason and conscience, and not to accept such excuses when they are invented by others: not to fear to differ from all those around me or to be left alone with reason and conscience, and not to fear the position to which truth will lead me, believing firmly that what truth and conscience will lead me to, however strange it may be, cannot be worse than what is based on falsehood. Not to lie, in our position as privileged mental workers, means not to fear to make up one's accounts. Perhaps we already owe so much that we cannot meet our obligations, but however that may be it is better to face the facts than not to know how we stand. However far we may have gone along a false path, it is better to return than to continue to go along it. Falsehood to others is simply disadvantageous. Every affair is settled more directly and more quickly by truth than by falsehood. Falsehood to others only confuses the matter and hinders its solution, but falsehood to oneself presented as truth, entirely ruins man's life.

If a man having started on a wrong road accepts it as the right one, every step he takes along that road takes him farther from his aim. If a man who has been going for a long time along a false road guesses, or is told, that that road is wrong, but being frightened at the thought that he has gone so far astray tries to assure himself that by following this road he may still come out on the right one, he will never reach the right road. If a man is frightened of the truth, and on seeing it does not acknowledge it but accepts falsehood for truth, he will never know what he should do.

We, not only rich men but men in a privileged position, so-called educated men, have gone so far along a false road that we need either great resolution, or the experience of great suffering on our false path, to enable us to come to ourselves and acknowledge the lie in which we are living.

Thanks to the sufferings to which the false path led me, I saw the falsehood of our life, and having acknowledged it I had the courage (at first only in thought) to follow reason and conscience without considering what they would lead me to. And I was rewarded for that courage. All the complex, disjointed,confused, unmeaning phenomena of life around me became at once clear, and my position amid those phenomena, which had been a strange and burdensome one, suddenly became natural and easy. And in that new situation my activity determined itself quite exactly, and was nothing like what I had previously imagined it would be, but was a new activity much more tranquil, agreeable, and joyous. The very things that formerly frightened me now became attractive.

And therefore I think that a man who sincerely sets himself the question, *What to do?* and in answering it does not lie to himself but goes the way his reason leads him, will have already answered the question. If only he does not lie to himself he will find out what to do, where to go, and how to act. The one thing which may hinder his finding the way is a false and too high estimate of himself and his position. So it was with me, and therefore a second reply—which flows from the first—to the question: *What to do?* consisted for me in repenting, in the full significance of that word, that is, completely changing my estimate of my own position and activity. Instead of considering our position useful and important, we must acknowledge its harmfulness and triviality; instead of priding ourselves on our education we must admit our ignorance; in place of pride in our kindness and morality we must acknowledge our immorality and cruelty, and instead of our importance admit our insignificance.

I say that apart from not lying to myself I had also to repent, because, though the one flows from the other, a false impression of my high importance had so grown upon me that until I sincerely repented and put aside that false estimate of myself, I did not see the greater part of the lie I had told myself. Only when I repented, that is, ceased to consider myself a special kind of man and began to look on myself as a man like all others—only then did my path become plain to me.

Before that, I could not answer the question: *What to do?* because I put the very question wrongly. Till I repented I put the question thus: What activity shall I—a man with the education I have acquired and the talents I possess—what activity shall I choose?

How am I—by means of this education and these talents—to repay what I have taken and still take from the peasants? That question was incorrect because it contained in itself a false conception that I was not like other men but was a special kind of man called to serve people by the talents and education I had acquired by forty years' exercise. I put the question to myself, but in reality I had answered it in advance by fixing beforehand the kind of activity agreeable to myself by which I was called upon to serve men. I really asked myself: How am I, such an admirable writer, who have acquired so much knowledge and possess such talents, to utilize them in the service of mankind? The question should have been put as it should be put to a learned Rabbi who has studied the whole Talmud and learned the number of letters in all the sacred books and all the subtleties of his science. The question, both for the Rabbi and for me, should have been this: What am I, who owing to my unfortunate position, during the best years for study have been learning the French language, the piano, grammar, geography, the science of jurisprudence, verses, stories and novels, philosophic theories, and military exercises, instead of learning to labour, what am I, who have passed the best years of my life in idle occupations depraving to the soul—what am I to do despite those unfortunate conditions of the past, in order to requite those who have all this time fed me and clothed me and who still continue to feed and clothe me? If the question had presented itself as it does to me now after I have repented: What must I do, who am such a perverted man?—the answer would have been easy: try, first of all, to feed yourself honestly, that is to say, learn not to live on the backs of others; and while learning that, and after learning it, take every opportunity to serve others with hands, feet, brain, heart, and all the powers you possess and on which people make demands.

And therefore I say that for a man of our circle—besides not lying to himself or to others—it is also necessary to repent, to scrape off the pride that has grown upon us; pride of education, of refinement, and of talents, and to acknowledge oneself to be not a benefactor of others and an advanced man who is willing to share his useful acquisitions with the people, but to acknowledge oneself guilty all round, a spoilt, quite good-for-nothing man, who wishes not to be a benefactor to the people but to reform himself and cease to offend and wrong them.

I often hear questions from good young people who sympathize with the negative part of my writings, and ask: 'Then what must I do? What am I to do, who have taken my degree at the university, or some other establishment—What am I to do to be of use?'

These young people ask that, but in the depth of their souls have already decided that in the education they have received they possess a great advantage, and that they wish to serve the people just by means of that advantage. And therefore the one thing they will on no account do is to examine what they call their education honestly and critically and ask themselves whether it is a good or bad thing. If they do that, they will inevitably be led to repudiate their education and be obliged to begin to learn afresh; and that is just what is necessary.

They are quite unable to decide the question, *What to do?* because they do not see the question in its true light.

The question should be put thus: How can I, a helpless, useless man, who owing to unfortunate circumstances have wasted the best years for learning or studying a scientific Talmud pernicious to soul and to body, how can I rectify this mistake and learn to be of service to men? But it presents itself to them thus: How am I, who have acquired such admirable knowledge, to be of use to people by means of my admirable knowledge? And therefore the man will never answer the question: *What to do ?* until he ceases to deceive himself, and repents. And repentance is not dreadful, just as the truth is not dreadful, but is equally joyous and fruitful. We need only accept the truth completely and repent fully, to understand that no one possesses any rights or privileges or can possess them, but has only endless and unlimited duties and obligations; and man's first and most unquestionable duty is to participate in the struggle with nature to support his own life and that of others.

And this acknowledgement of a man's duty forms the essence of the third answer to the question: *What to do?*

I tried not to lie to myself. I tried to extirpate the false conception of the importance of my education and talents, and to repent; but on the road to the solution of the question, *What to do?* a new difficulty presented itself: there were so many things to be done that one needed an indication just what should be done in particular. And the reply to this question was given by sincere repentance of the evil in which I was living. What to do? Just what to do?—everyone asks, and I, too, asked it as long as, under the influence of a high opinion of my vocation, I did not see that my first and unquestionable business was to procure my own food, clothing, heating, and dwelling, and in doing this to serve others, because since the beginning of the world that has been the first and surest obligation of every man.

Only in that occupation does a man, if he participates in it, obtain full satisfaction for the physical and spiritual demands of his nature: to feed, clothe, and take care of himself and of those near to him, satisfies his physical needs, while to do the same for others satisfies his spiritual needs.

All man's other activities become legitimate only when this prime demand is satisfied.

No matter wherein a man may see his vocation: whether in ruling men, in defending his compatriots, in performing Church services, in teaching, in devising means to increase the pleasures of life, in discovering the laws of nature, in embodying eternal truths in artistic images—for a rational man the duty of taking part in the struggle with nature for the maintenance of his own life and the lives of other people, will always be the first and most indubitable. This duty will always rank first, because what people most need is life, and therefore to defend people and to teach them and to make their lives more agreeable it is necessary to preserve life itself, and my neglect to take part in that struggle and my consumption of other people's labour destroys people's lives.

And therefore it is impossible and insane to try to serve men while destroying their lives.

Man's duty to struggle with nature for the means of livelihood will always be the very first and most certain of all duties, because it is the law of life, neglect of which involves inevitable punishment by the destruction either of man's physical or rational life. If a man living in solitude avoids the struggle with nature he is at once punished by the fact that his body perishes. And if in a community a man frees himself from his duty by making others do his work for him to the detriment of their lives, he is at once punished by the fact that his life becomes unreasonable and unjustifiable.

So perverted had I been by my past life, and so concealed in our society is that primary and unquestionable law of God or of nature, that it seemed to me strange, terrible, and even shameful, to obey that law, as though the fulfilment of an eternal and unquestionable law, and not its neglect, could be strange, terrible, or shameful.

At first it seemed to me that in order to do rough manual work some special arrangement or organization was necessary: a circle of like minded men, the consent of my family, or residence in the country. Then I felt ashamed to appear to wish to show off by doing something so unusual in our circle as physical work, and I did not know how to set about it.

But I had only to understand that it was not some exceptional activity that had to be devised and arranged, but that it was merely returning to a natural position from the false one in which I had been—merely rectifying the falsehood in which I had been living—I had only to admit this for all difficulties to vanish.

It was not at all necessary to arrange, to adapt, or to await the consent of others, because in whatever condition I might be there were always people who fed, clothed, and attended to the heating, not only for themselves but also for me, and I could do this for myself and for them everywhere, under any conditions, if I had sufficient time and strength.

Nor could I feel false shame in the unaccustomed work that seemed to surprise people, for while not doing it I already felt not false but real shame. And on arriving at this consciousness and at the practical deductions from it, I was fully rewarded for not having feared the conclusions of reason and for having gone where they led me.

On reaching that practical deduction I was surprised at the ease and simplicity with which all these questions which had seemed to me so difficult and complex solved themselves.

In reply to the question: What must I do? I saw that the most indubitable answer was: First, do all the things I myself most need—

attend to my own room, heat my own stove, fetch my water, attend to my clothes, and do all I can for myself. I thought this would seem strange to the servants, but it turned out that the strangeness only lasted for a week and afterwards it would have seemed strange had I resumed my former habits.

To the question whether this physical work had to be organized, and whether one should arrange a village community on the land—it turned out that all that was unnecessary, and that work—if its aim is to satisfy one's needs, rather than to make idleness possible and utilize other people's toil as is the case with people who are making money—draws one naturally from the town to the country, where such labour is most productive and most joyful.

It was unnecessary to arrange any community, because a man who works himself naturally joins up with the existing community of working people.

To the question: Would not this work absorb all my time and prevent my doing the mental work I love, to which I am accustomed, and which I sometimes consider useful? I received a most unexpected reply. The energy of my mental work increased—and increased in proportion to my bodily exertion and to my emancipation from all superfluity.

It turned out that after devoting eight hours to physical toil (the half of the day I had formerly passed in arduous efforts to avoid dullness) I still had eight hours left, of which I only needed five for mental work.

It turned out that if I—a very prolific writer who for forty years have done nothing but write, and have written some 5,000 pages,—if I had worked all those forty years at a peasant's usual work, then, not reckoning winter evenings and workless days, if I had read and studied for five hours every day and had written only on holidays two pages a day (and I have sometimes written as much as sixteen pages a day) I should have produced those 5,000 pages in fourteen years.

I came upon a wonderful fact—a very simple arithmetical calculation a seven-year-old boy could have made, but which I had never made before. There are twenty-four hours in the day; we sleep eight, so sixteen remain. If a brainworker devotes five hours a day to his work he will get through an immense amount. What becomes of the remaining eleven hours?

It turned out that physical labour, far from rendering mental work impossible, improved and aided it.

To the question whether this physical work would not deprive me of many harmless pleasures natural to man, such as enjoyment of the arts, acquisition of knowledge, intercourse with people, and the happiness of life in general, the answer is that the opposite turned out to be true: the more intensive the labour and the nearer it approached to rough work on the land, the more enjoyment and information I obtained and the closer and more amiable was the intercourse I had with men, and the more happiness life brought me.

To the question (so often heard by me from people who are not quite sincere)—what result could come from such an insignificant drop in the ocean as my own physical work in the ocean of labour I consumed, again a very surprising and unexpected reply was obtained.

It turned out that I only needed to make physical labour the customary condition of my life, for most of the bad expensive habits and requirements that had accompanied a state of physical idleness to drop away of themselves without the least effort on my part. Not to speak of the habit of turning night into day and vice versa, and the kind of bedding, clothes, and conventional cleanliness, which are simply impossible and irksome when one is engaged on physical labour, the quality of food I wanted changed completely.

Instead of the sweet, rich, delicate, refined, and spicy foods that formerly attracted me, the simplest food: cabbage-soup, buckwheat porridge, black bread, and tea, now seemed pleasantest.

So that, not to mention the simple example of the plain peasants with whom I came in touch, who satisfied themselves with little, my needs themselves imperceptibly changed in consequence of my life of labour, so that in proportion as I accustomed myself to and assimilated habits of work, my drop of physical labour became more noticeable; and in proportion as my own work became more productive my demands on the labour of others became less and less, and my life naturally, without effort or deprivation, approximated to a simplicity of which I could not have dreamed had I not fulfilled the law of labour. It turned out that my most expensive demands on life, the demands of vanity and for distraction from ennui, were directly due to an idle life.

With physical labour there was no room for vanity and no need for diversions, as my time was pleasantly occupied, and after becoming fatigued a simple rest at tea over a book, or in conversation with those near to me, was incomparably more agreeable than a theatre, cards, a concert, or grand society—all of them things that cost a great deal.

As to whether this unaccustomed labour would not injure the health necessary to enable me to be of use to men, it turned out that (despite the positive assertions of leading physicians that hard physical exertion, especially at my age, might injure my health, and that Swedish gymnastics, massage, and so forth—arrangements to replace the natural conditions of man's life—would be preferable)—the harder I worked the stronger, fitter, happier, and kindlier did I feel. So that it appeared indubitable that just as all those cunning devices: newspapers, theatres, concerts, visits, balls, cards, periodicals, and novels, are nothing but means of maintaining man's mental life without the natural condition of labour for others, so also are all the ingenious hygienic and medical devices for the preparation of food, drink, housing, ventilation, heating, clothing, medicines, mineral waters, massage, gymnastics, electrical and other cures—it turned out that all these cunning devices are nothing but means of supporting man's physical life when cut off from its natural conditions of labour—that it all was like an arrangement by means of chemical apparatus in an hermetically closed chamber, to evaporate water and provide plants with the kind of air best suited to their breathing—when it is only necessary to open the window: only necessary to do what is natural not only for man but for animals, namely, to discharge and expend by muscular labour the supply of energy produced by swallowing food.

The profound complexities of medicine and hygiene for people of our class are such as a mechanician might devise in order, when he has heated a boiler and screwed down all the valves, to prevent the boiler from bursting.

And when I clearly understood all this, it seemed to me ludicrous. By a long series of doubts, searchings, and reflection, I have reached the extraordinary truth that man has eyes in order to see with them, ears in order to hear with them, legs in order to walk with them, and hands and a back to work with, and that if he does not use them for their natural purpose it will be the worse for him.

I came to the conclusion that with us privileged people the same thing happens as occurred with the stallions of an acquaintance of mine.

His steward, who did not care for horses and did not understand them, having received his master's orders to take the best stallions to the horse-market, chose them out of the herd and put them in the stalls; he fed them on oats and watered them, but wishing to be careful with such expensive horses, he did not allow anyone to ride them or drive them or even exercise them. The horses all went wrong in the legs and became worthless.

The same has happened with us, only with this difference, that it is impossible in any way to cheat the horses, and in order that they should not get out they had to be kept tied up, whereas we are kept in a similarly unnatural and ruinous condition by the temptations which enmesh us and bind us as with chains. We have arranged for ourselves a life contrary both to man's moral and physical nature, and we direct all the strength of our minds to persuading men that this is just what life should be. All that we call 'culture', our sciences and arts and the improvements of life's comforts, are attempts to cheat man's moral and natural demands; all that we call hygiene and medicine is an attempt to cheat the natural physical demands of human nature. But these deceptions have their limits and we have nearly reached them.

If such is man's true life it is better not to live at all, says the prevalent most fashionable philosophy of Schopenhauer and Hartmann. If such is life it is better not to live, say an increasing number of suicides among the privileged classes. If life is such, it is better for the coming generation not to live, says medical practice in collusion with science and the devices invented by it for the destruction of woman's fecundity.

In the Bible it is said that it is a law for human beings to eat bread in the sweat of their brow, and in sorrow to bring forth children.

A peasant, Bóndarev, who wrote an article about this, lit up for me the wisdom of that saying. (In my whole life two Russian thinkers have had a great moral influence on me, enriched my thought, and cleared up my outlook on life. These men were not Russian poets, or learned men, or preachers—they were two remarkable men who are still living, both of them peasants: Sutáev and Bóndarev.)

But *nous avons changé tout ça*, as a character in Molière said after having blundered on medical matters and said that the liver was on the left side. *Nous avons changé tout ça*: men need not work to feed themselves, it will all be done by machines, and women need not bear children. Science will teach us various methods and there are too many people as it is.

In the Krapívenski district* there is a ragged peasant who wanders about. During the war† he was employed by a commissariat officer in the purchase of grain. Having attached himself to this official, the peasant, it seems, went out of his mind with the idea that he, like the gentlefolk, need not work but would receive the maintenance due to him from his Majesty the Emperor. He now calls himself the Most-Serene-Military-Prince Blokhín, Contractor for military provisions of all ranks. He says he has 'completed all grades of the service', and having 'finished the military profession' he is to receive from the Emperor 'an open Bank, clothes, uniforms, horses, carriages, tea, peas, servants, and all supplies'.

To the question: Does he not want some work? he always proudly replies: 'Much obliged—that will all be performed by the peasants.'

If one tells him that the peasants also may not want to work, he replies: 'For the peasants the performance of labour presents no difficulty' (he always prefers grandiloquent language). 'There is now the invention of machinery for the facilitation of the peasants,' he says. 'For them it is not irksome.' When one asks him what he lives for, he replies: 'To pass the time.'

I always look at this man as into a mirror. In him I see myself and our whole class.

To finish with a rank enabling one to live 'to pass the time', and to receive an 'open Bank', while the peasants, as the invention of machinery makes work no longer irksome for them, do all the labour, is a complete formulation of the insensate creed of our circle.

When we ask: What then must we do?—we do not really ask anything, but merely affirm—only not with the frankness of the

* *The district in which Yásnaya Polyána is situated.*
† *The Russo-Turkish war of 1887-8.*

Most-Serene-Military-Prince Blokhín, who has completed all the grades and has lost his reason—that we do not want to do anything.

He who comes to his senses cannot put the question, because on the one side all that he uses has been made and is made by man's hands, and on the other side, as soon as a healthy man wakes up and eats something he feels a need to work with his legs, hands, and brain. To find work and to do it he needs only not to hold himself back; only he who considers it a shame to work—like a lady who asks her guests not to trouble to open the door, but to wait till she calls a servant to do so—only he can put to himself the question, what he is to do.

What is necessary is, not to invent work to do—you can't overtake all the work needed for yourself and for others—but what is needed is to get rid of the criminal view of life, that I eat and sleep for my pleasure, and to acquire the simple and true view which the peasants grow up with and hold, that man is primarily a machine which has to be stoked with food, and that it is therefore shameful and uncomfortable and impossible to go on eating and not to work; that to eat and not to work is a most dangerous condition, resembling a conflagration. If one only has that consciousness, plenty of work will always be at hand and it will be joyous and satisfying for the needs of one's body and soul. The case presented itself to me like this: our food divides our day into four 'spells', as the peasants term it: (1) till breakfast, (2) from breakfast till dinner, (3) from dinner till evening meal, (4) and the evening. Man's natural activity is also divided into four kinds: (1) muscular activity—work of hands, feet, shoulders, and back—heavy work which makes one sweat; (2) the activity of the fingers and wrists—that of craftsmanship; (3) activity of the mind and imagination; (4) and the activity of social intercourse. And the blessings men make use of can also be divided into four classes. First, the products of heavy labour—grain, cattle, buildings, wells, etc.; secondly, the products of craftsmanship—clothes, boots, utensils, and so forth; thirdly, the products of mental activity—the sciences and arts; and fourthly, the arrangements for intercourse with people—acquaintanceships, etc. And it seemed to me that best of all would be so to vary the day's occupations as to exercise all four human faculties and re-create all four kinds of produce we consume, in such a way that the four spells should be devoted: the first, to heavy labour; the second, to mental labour; the third, to craftsmanship; and the fourth, to intercourse with one's fellows. It would be well if one could arrange one's work so, but if not, the one important thing is to retain consciousness of one's duty to work—of the duty of employing each spell usefully.

It seemed to me that only then would the false division of labour that exists in our society be abolished, and a just division established which would not infringe man's happiness.

I, for instance, have occupied myself all my life long with mental work. I said to myself that I have so divided labour that writing, that is, mental work, was my special occupation, and the other necessary occupations I allowed (or compelled) others to do for me. That arrangement, apparently the most advantageous for mental labour, to say nothing of its injustice, was after all disadvantageous for mental labour.

All my life long I had arranged my food, sleep, and amusements with regard to those hours of specialized work, and besides that work I had done nothing.

The result was: first that I limited my circle of observation and knowledge and often lacked a subject of study, and often when setting myself the task of describing the lives of men (and the lives of men are the perpetual problem of all mental activity) I felt my ignorance and had to learn and inquire about things known to every man who is not occupied with specialized work; secondly, it happened that I sat down to write without any inner compulsion to write, and no one demanded of me writing for its own sake, that is to say for my thoughts, but only wanted my name for journalistic purposes. I tried to squeeze what I could out of myself: sometimes nothing could be squeezed out, sometimes only something very poor, and I felt dissatisfied and dull. So that very often days and weeks passed when I ate and drank, slept and warmed myself, without doing anything, or doing only what nobody needed; that is to say, I committed an unquestionable and nasty crime of a kind hardly ever committed by a man of the labouring classes. But now after having recognized the necessity of physical work, both rough work and handicraft, something quite different happened: my time was occupied, however humbly, in a way that was certainly useful and joyous and instructive for me. And so I tore myself away from that unquestionably useful and joyous occupation to my speciality only when I felt an inner need and saw a demand directly addressed to me for my work as a writer.

And just these demands conditioned the quality, and therefore the value and joyousness, of my specialized work.

So it turned out that occupation with the physical work necessary for me as for every man, not only did not hinder my specialized activity but was a necessary condition of the utility, quality, and pleasurability of that activity.

A bird is so made that it is necessary for it to fly, walk, peck, and consider, and when it does all that it is satisfied and happy, in a word, it is then really a bird. Just so is it with man: when he walks, turns about, lifts, draws things along, works with his fingers, eyes, ears, tongue, and brain—then and only then is he satisfied and really a man.

A man conscious that it is his vocation to labour will naturally aim at such a rotation of work as is natural for the satisfaction of his internal and external needs, and he will change this order only if he feels within him an irresistible vocation for some exceptional work and if other people require that work of him.

The nature of work is such that the satisfaction of all man's needs requires just the change to different kinds of work that makes it not burdensome but gladsome. Only a false belief that work is a curse could bring people to such an emancipation of themselves from certain kinds of work—that is, to such a seizure of the work of others—as requires the compulsory engagement of others in special occupations, which is called 'the division of labour'.

We are so accustomed to our false conception of the arrangement of work, that it seems to us that it will be better for a bootmaker, a mechanic, a writer, or a musician, if he exempts himself from the labour natural to all men.

Where there is no violence exercised to seize other people's work and no false faith in the pleasure of idleness, no one will free himself from the physical work necessary for the satisfaction of his needs, in order to occupy himself with specialized work; for specialized work is not an advantage, but a sacrifice a man makes to his special bent and to his fellow men.

A bootmaker in a village tearing himself from his customary and joyous field labour and taking to that of mending or making boots for his neighbours, deprives himself of the very joyous and useful field-work only because he likes sewing, and knows that no one can do it as well as he and that people will be grateful to him for it. But he cannot desire to deprive himself for life of joyous change of work. And so it is with a village Elder, a mechanic, a writer, or a scholar. It is only we, with our perverted notions, who suppose that if a master dismisses a clerk from the counting-house and sends him back to work as a peasant, or if a minister is dismissed and deported, that he has been punished and placed in a worse position. In truth he has been benefited, that is to say his special oppressive and difficult work has been changed for a joyous alteration of labour.

In a natural society this is quite different. I know of a Commune in which the people grew their own food. One of the members of this Commune* was more educated than the others, and he was required to give lectures, which he had to prepare during the day and deliver in the evening. He did this willingly, feeling that he was being of use to others and doing good work. But he grew tired of doing exclusively mental work and his health suffered, and the members of the Commune took pity on him and invited him to work on the land.

For people who look on labour as the essence and joy of life, the background and basis of life will always be the struggle with nature—work on the land, handicraft, mental work, and the establishment of intercourse among men.

A withdrawal from one or several of these kinds of work and a specialization of work will only occur when the specialist, loving such work and knowing that he does it better than other people, sacrifices his own advantage to satisfy direct demands made on him. Only by such an opinion about work and by the natural division of labour that results from it, is the curse lifted which in our imagination is laid on work; and all labour becomes joyful, because either a man does unquestionably useful and joyful work that is not burdensome, or he will be conscious of sacrificing himself in the performance of a more difficult and exceptional task done for the good of others.

'But the subdivision of labour is more advantageous!' For whom is it more advantageous?

* The Commune in question was the one founded by N. Chaikóvsky, in Kansas State, in the eighteen seventies; and the man referred to in this passage was V. K. Heins, who changed his name to William Frey. He visited Tolstoy at Yásnaya Polyána.

It is advantageous for the production of more boots and cotton-prints. But who will have to make those boots and prints?

People such as those who for generations have made pin-heads and nothing else. Then how can it be more profitable for them?

If the chief thing were to make as many prints and pins as possible, it would be all right; but men and their welfare are the chief consideration. And the welfare of men lies in life, and their life is in their work. Then how can compulsion to do tormenting and degrading work be advantageous?

If the aim were the advantage of some men regardless of the welfare of all, then the most advantageous thing might be for some men to eat others; it is said that they taste nice. But what is most profitable for all is what I desire for myself: the greatest possible welfare and satisfaction of all the needs of body and soul and conscience and reason implanted within me. And personally I found that for my welfare and the satisfaction of these needs, I only had to be cured of the madness in which I—like the Krapívenski madman—lived, believing that gentlefolk ought not to work and that all should be done by others—and, without any subtleties, that I had to do only what is natural for a man to do when satisfying his needs. And when I found this out, I became convinced that this work for the satisfaction of one's needs naturally divides itself into different kinds of work, each of which has its charm and not only is not burdensome but serves as a rest from the other kinds of labour.

Roughly (without at all insisting on the correctness of such a division) I divided that work, according to the demands I make on life, into four parts corresponding to the four spells of work which make up the day, and I endeavour to satisfy those demands.

So these are the replies I found to my question: What must we do?

First: not to lie to myself; and—however far my path of life may be from the true path disclosed by my reason—not to fear the truth.

Secondly: to reject the belief in my own righteousness and in privileges and peculiarities distinguishing me from others, and to acknowledge myself as being to blame.

Thirdly: to fulfil the eternal, indubitable law of man, and with the labour of my whole being to struggle with nature for the maintenance of my own and other people's lives.

CHAPTER XXXIX

I HAVE FINISHED, having said all that relates to myself; but I cannot refrain from a desire to say what relates to everyone, and to verify the conclusions I have come to, by general considerations.

I wish to say why it seems to me that very many people of our circle must reach the same conclusion that I arrived at; and also what will come of it if even a few people do so.

I think many will come to the conclusion I came to, because if only men of our circle, of our caste, look seriously about them, the young people seeking personal happiness will be horrified at the ever-increasing misery of their lives, clearly drawing them towards perdition; the conscientious people will be horrified at the cruelty and injustice of their lives, and the timid people will be horrified at the danger of their lives.

The unhappiness of our life; patch up our false way of life as we will, propping it up by the aid of the sciences and arts—that life becomes feebler, sicklier, and more tormenting every year; every year the number of suicides and the avoidance of motherhood increases; every year the people of that class become feebler; every year we feel the increasing gloom of our lives.

Evidently salvation is not to be found by increasing the comforts and pleasures of life, medical treatments, artificial teeth and hair, breathing exercises, massage, and so forth; this truth has become so evident that in the newspapers advertisements of stomach-powders for the rich are printed under the heading, 'Blessings for the poor', in which it is said that only the poor have good digestions but that the rich need aids, among which are these powders.

It is impossible to remedy this by any amusements, comforts, or powders—it can only be remedied by a change of life.

Discord of our life and our conscience; try as we may to justify to ourselves our betrayal of humanity, all our excuses crumble to dust in face of the obvious facts: people around us die from excessive work and from want, while we use up food, clothes, and human labour, merely to find distraction and change. And therefore the conscience of a man of our circle, if he retains but a scrap of it, cannot rest, and poisons all the comforts and enjoyments of life supplied to us by the labour of our brothers, who suffer and perish at that labour.

And not only does every conscientious man feel this himself (he would be glad to forget it, but cannot do so in our age) but all the best part of science and art—that part which has not forgotten the purpose of its vocation—continually reminds us of our cruelty and of our unjustifiable position. The old firm justifications are all destroyed; the new ephemeral justifications of the progress of science for science's sake and art for art's sake do not stand the light of simple common sense.

Men's consciences cannot be set at rest by new excuses, but only by a change of life which will make any justification of oneself unnecessary as there will be nothing needing justification.

The danger of our way of life: try as we may to hide from ourselves the simple, most obvious, danger that the patience of those whom we are stifling may be exhausted; try as we may to counteract that danger by all sorts of deception, violence, and cajolery—that danger is growing every day and every hour and has long threatened us, but now has matured so that we hardly maintain ourselves in our little boat above the roaring sea which already washes over us and threatens angrily to swallow and devour us. The workers' revolution with horrors of destruction and murder not merely threatens us, but we have been living over it for some thirty years already, and only for a while have somehow managed by various temporary devices to postpone its eruption. Such is the condition of Europe; such is the condition with us, and it is yet worse with us because it has no safety-valves. Except the Tsar, the classes that oppress the masses have now no justification in the people's eyes; those masses are all held down in their position merely by violence, cunning, and opportunism, that is, by agility, but hatred among the worst representatives of the people and contempt for us among the best of them, increases hour by hour.

During the last three or four years a new significant word has come into general use among our people, which I never heard formerly; it is used opprobriously in the street, and defines us as 'drones'.*

* Not finding a new English word with which to translate 'darmoédy', I have to use 'drones', which is an old one. Literally 'darmoédy' means 'people who eat giving nothing in return'. [Translator]

The hatred and contempt of the oppressed masses are growing and the physical and moral forces of the wealthy classes are weakening; the deception on which everything depends is wearing out, and the wealthy classes have nothing to console themselves with in this deadly peril.

To return to the old ways is impossible, to restore the ruined prestige is impossible; only one thing is left for those who do not wish to change their way of life, and that is to hope that 'things will last my time'—after that let happen what may.

That is what the blind crowd of the rich are doing, but the danger is ever growing and the terrible catastrophe draws nearer.

Three reasons indicate to people of the wealthy classes the necessity of altering their way of life: the need of well-being for themselves and for those near to them, which is not met on the path they are following; the need of satisfying the voice of conscience, to do which is evidently impossible on the present path; and the menace and ever-growing danger of their life, which is not to be avoided by any external means. All three reasons together should move men of the wealthy classes to change their lives—to a change satisfying their welfare and their conscience, and averting the danger.

And there is only one such change: to cease to deceive, to repent, and to recognize toil to be not a curse but the joyful business of life.

But of what avail will it be that I do ten, eight, or five hours' physical work which thousands of peasants would gladly do for the money I have?—people say in reply to this.

In the first place the simplest and most certain result will be that you will be merrier, healthier, fitter, and kindlier, and will learn what real life is, from which you have been hiding yourself or which has been hidden from you.

In the second place, if you have a conscience, it not only will not suffer as it does now, seeing people's labour (the hardship of which from ignorance we always either exaggerate or underrate), but you will experience all the time the joyous consciousness that every day you satisfy the demands of your conscience more and more, and get away from the terrible position of having such an accumulation of evil in your life as makes it impossible to do good to people; you will feel the joy of living freely, with the possibility of doing good; you will pierce a window, letting in a chink of light from the sphere of the moral world which has hitherto been closed to you. Instead of the constant fear of revenge for the evil you do, you will feel that you are saving others from that revenge, and above all that you are saving the oppressed from the grievous sensation of hatred and vengeance.

'But really it is ridiculous', people usually say, 'for us, people of our society, with the profound problems that confront us—philosophic, scientific, political, artistic, ecclesiastical, and social—for us, ministers, senators, academicians, professors, artists, and singers; for us, a quarter of an hour of whose time is so highly valued—for us to spend our time on what? On cleaning our boots, washing our shirts, digging, planting potatoes, or feeding our chickens, our cows, and so forth, on affairs which are gladly done for us not only by our own porters and cooks but by thousands of people who appreciate the value of our time. But why do we dress ourselves, wash ourselves, scratch ourselves (excuse the details), hold the po for ourselves, why do we walk, hand chairs to ladies and to guests, open and shut doors, help people into carriages, and do hundreds of similar things that used to be done for us by slaves?

Because we consider that so it ought to be, that it accords with human dignity, that it is a man's duty and obligation.

So it is with physical labour. It is man's dignity, his sacred duty and obligation, to use the hands and feet given him for the purpose for which they were given, and to expend the food he consumes on labour to produce food, and not to let them atrophy, nor to wash them and clean them and use them only to put food, drink, and cigarettes into his own mouth.

That is a significance physical labour has for every man in any society, but in our society where the evasion of this law of nature has become the misfortune of a whole circle of people, occupation with physical labour acquires yet another significance—that of a sermon and an activity preventing terrible calamities that threaten humanity. To say that for an educated man physical labour is an insignificant occupation is the same as to ask, when a temple is being built: what importance is there in setting one stone evenly in its place?

All the most important things are done unnoticed, modestly, simply; neither ploughing, nor building, nor grazing cattle, nor even thinking, can be done in uniforms amid illuminations and the roar of cannon. The illuminations, the roar of cannon, music, uniforms, cleanliness, and glitter, with which we are accustomed to connect the idea of the importance of an occupation, always serve on the contrary as signs that the matter lacks importance.

Great and real affairs are always simple and modest.

And so it is with the most important affair before us: the solution of the terrible contradictions amid which we live.

And the things that solve those contradictions are these modest, imperceptible, apparently ridiculous acts: serving oneself, doing physical labour for ourselves and if possible for others—which we rich people have to do if we understand the misfortune, wrongfulness, and danger of the position into which we have fallen.

What will result if I, and a dozen or two others, do not despise physical work but consider it essential for our happiness, tranquillity of conscience, and security? The result will be, that one or two or three dozen people, without conflict with anyone and without governmental or revolutionary violence, will solve for themselves the apparently insoluble question that presents itself to the whole world, and will solve it in such a way that they will live better, their consciences will be more at ease, and the evil of oppression will no longer terrify them: the result will be that other people will see that the good they seek everywhere is close at hand, that the apparently insoluble contradictions between their conscience and the arrangements of the world solve themselves in the easiest and most joyous manner, and that instead of being afraid of the people around us we should draw near to them and love them.

The apparently insoluble economic and social question is the question of Krylóv's box.* It opens simply. But it will not open until people do the first and simplest thing, and just open it.

The apparently insoluble question is the old one of the exploitation by some men of the labour of others, and in our time that question is expressed by property.

Formerly men took the labour of others simply by violence—slavery. To-day we do it by property.

Property to-day is the root of all evils: of the sufferings of those who possess it or are deprived of it, the reproaches of conscience of those who misuse it, and the danger of collision between those who have a superfluity and those who are in need. Property is the root of the evil, and at the same time is the very thing to gain which all the

* Krylóv's fable tells of a box which several people failed to unlock. It turned out that it was not locked at all; one had only to raise the lid.

activity of our society to-day is directed. It guides the activity of our whole world.

States and Governments intrigue and go to war for property: for the banks of the Rhine and territories in Africa, China, or the Balkan Peninsula. Bankers, traders, manufacturers, and landowners work, scheme, and torment themselves and others for property; officials and artisans struggle, cheat, oppress and suffer for the sake of property; our Law Courts and police defend property; our penal settlements and prisons and all the horrors of our so-called repression of crime, exist on account of property.

Property is the root of all evil, and the division and safeguarding of property occupies the whole world.

What then is property?

People are accustomed to think that property is something really belonging to a man. That is why they call it 'property'. We say of a house and of one's hand alike, that it is 'my own' hand, 'my own' house.

But evidently this is an error and a superstition.

We know, or if we do not know it is easy to perceive, that property is merely a means of appropriating other men's work. And the work of others can certainly not be my own. It has even nothing in common with the conception of property (that which is one's own)—a conception which is very exact and definite. Man always has called, and always will call, 'his own' that which is subject to his will and attached to his consciousness, namely, his own body. As soon as a man calls something his 'property' that is not his own body but something that he wishes to make subject to his will as his body is—he makes a mistake, acquires for himself disillusionment and suffering, and finds himself obliged to cause others to suffer.

A man speaks of his wife, his children, his slaves, and his things, as being his own; but reality always shows him his mistake, and he has to renounce that superstition or to suffer and make others suffer.

In our days, nominally renouncing ownership of men, thanks to money and its collection by Government, we proclaim our right to the ownership of money, that is to say, to the ownership of other people's labour.

But as the right of ownership in a wife, a son, a slave, or a horse, is a fiction which is upset by reality and only causes him who believes in it to suffer—since my wife or son will never submit to my will as my body does, and only my own body will still be my real property—in the same way monetary property will never be my own, but only a deceiving of myself and a source of suffering, while my real property will still be only my own body—that which always submits to me and is bound up with my consciousness.

Only to us who are so accustomed to call other things than our own body our 'property', can it seem that such a wild superstition may be useful, and can remain without consequences harmful to us; but it is only necessary to reflect on the reality of the matter to see that this superstition, like every other, entails terrible consequences.

Let us take the most simple example.

I consider myself to be my own property and another man to be my property also.

I want to be able to prepare a dinner. If I did not suffer from a superstitious belief in my ownership of the other man, I should teach that art, like any other that I needed, to my own property, that is to my own body; but as it is, I teach it to my imaginary property, and the result is that when my cook does not obey me or wish to please me, or even runs away from me or dies, I am left with the unsatisfied necessity of providing for myself, but unaccustomed to learning, and with a consciousness that I have spent as much time worrying over that cook as would have sufficed me to learn cooking myself. So it is with property in buildings, clothes, utensils, landed property, and property in money. All imaginary property evokes in me unsuitable requirements that cannot always be satisfied, and deprives me of the possibility of acquiring for my true and unquestionabie property—my own body—that knowledge, that skill, those habits, and that perfection, which I might acquire.

The result always is that with no benefit to myself—to my true property—I have expended strength, sometimes my whole life, on what was not and could not be my property.

I arrange what I imagine to be my own library, my own picture-gallery, my own apartments and clothes, and acquire my 'own' money in order to buy what I want, and it ends with this, that busy with this imaginary property, as though it were really mine, I quite lose consciousness of the difference between what is my property, on which I really can labour, which can serve me and will always remain under my control, and that which is not and cannot be my own, whatever I may call it, and cannot be the object of my activity.

Words always have a clear meaning until we intentionally give them a false one.

What then does property mean? Property is that which belongs to me alone and exclusively, that with which I can always do just what I like, that which no one can take from me, which remains mine to the end of my life and which I must use, increase, and improve.

Each man can own only himself as such property.

And yet it is just in this very sense that people's imaginary property is understood—the very property for the sake of which (in a vain effort to do the impossible: to try to possess things external to oneself, which cannot be one's own) all the terrible evil of the world takes place: wars, executions, courts of law, prisons, luxury, vice, murder, and people's ruin.

So what will come of it if a dozen people plough, split logs, and make boots, not from necessity but because they recognize that man must work and that the more he works the better it will be for him? The result will be that a dozen men, or were it but one man, both by his consciousness and by actions will show men that the terrible evil from which they suffer is not a law of fate, the will of God, or some historic necessity, but is a superstition, neither strong nor terrible but weak and insignificant, which need only be no longer believed in (as people believe in idols) for us to be free from it and destroy it like a flimsy cobweb.

Men who work to fulfil the joyous law of their life, that is, who work to fulfil the law of labour, will free themselves from the superstition of personal property so pregnant with calamities, and all the world's institutions which exist to maintain that supposed property outside one's own body will become for them not merely unnecessary but irksome; and it will become clear to all that these institutions are not indispensable, but are harmful, artificial, and false conditions of life.

For a man who regards work not as a curse but as a joy, property outside his own body, that is, the right or power to use another man's labour, will be not merely useless but irksome.

If I like to prepare my dinner and am accustomed to doing so, the fact of another man doing it for me deprives me of an accustomed occupation and does not give me the satisfaction I gave myself: besides which the acquisition of imaginary property will be useless to a man who regards labour as life itself, fills his life with it, and so is less and less in need of the labour of others, that is, less and less in need of property to fill his idle time—for pleasure and for the adornment of his life.

If a man's life is filled with labour he does not need apartments, furniture, and a variety of handsome clothes: he needs less expensive food and does not need conveyances and distractions.

Above all, a man who regards labour as the business and joy of his life will not seek to lessen his labour at the cost of other people's work.

A man who regards his life as work, will make it his aim, in proportion as he acquires skill and endurance, to accomplish more and more work and so fill his life ever more and more completely.

For such a man, placing the meaning of his life in labour and not in its results, not in acquiring property, that is, the labour of others, there can never be any question about implements of labour.

Though such a man will always choose the most productive implement, he will get the same satisfaction from work even if he has to use the least productive.

If there is a steam-plough he will plough with it, if there is none he will plough with a horseplough, and if that also is lacking he will use a wooden peasant-plough, or for lack of that will dig with a spade, and under all conditions equally he will attain his aim of spending his life in work useful for others, and so will obtain full satisfaction.

And the condition of such a man, both in external and internal respects, will be happier than that of one who makes the acquisition of property the aim of his life.

Externally such a man will never be in want, for people seeing his desire to work will always try to make his work as productive as possible—as they do with the water power that turns a mill-wheel—and that it should be as productive as possible they will make his material existence secure, which they do not do for one who strives after property. And security of material conditions is all that a man needs.

Inwardly such a man will always be happier than one who seeks property, because the latter will never obtain what he strives for, while the former will always do so to the measure of his strength: feeble, old, dying as the proverb has it 'with a tool in his hand', he will obtain full satisfaction, and the love and sympathy of other people.

So that is what will come of it if a few mad cranks plough, make boots and so forth, instead of smoking cigarettes, playing bridge, and driving about everywhere carrying their ennui with them during the ten hours a day that all mental workers have to spare.

The result will be that these crazy people will show in practice that the imaginary property on account of which people suffer and make others suffer, is not necessary for happiness, but is hampering and nothing more than a superstition; that property, real property, exists only in one's own head, hands, and feet, and that actually to exploit that real property usefully and joyfully, it is necessary to reject the false conception of property outside one's own body, in the service of which we expend the best forces of our life. It will result that these people will show that a man will only cease to believe in imaginary property when he has developed his real property—his capacities, his body—so that it yields him fruit a hundredfold, and happiness of which we have no conception, and becomes such a useful, strong, kindly man that wherever he may be thrown he will always fall on his feet, will everywhere be brother to everyone, and will be understood and needed and prized by all. And people, seeing this one or that dozen lunatics, will understand what they all should do to untie the terrible knot in which the superstition of property has involved them, and to free themselves from the unfortunate position about which they now all groan, not knowing how to escape from it.

But what can one man do amid a crowd who do not agree with him?

No reflection shows the insincerity of those who employ it more obviously than this.

Bargees tow a barge up-stream. Can one find a single bargee stupid enough to refuse to haul at his tow-rope because by himself he is not strong enough to pull the barge up-stream?

He who recognizes that beside his rights to an animal life, to food and sleep, he has some human duties, knows very well wherein his duty lies, just as the bargee does who shoulders the tow-rope. The bargee knows very well that he has only to haul and pull up-stream. He will only look for something to do and ask how to do it when he has dropped the tow-rope. And as with the bargees and with all men engaged on a common task, so with all humanity: each man has not to unhitch the tow-rope but to haul at it in the direction up-stream shown by the master. And that the direction may always be the same we have been endowed with reason.

And that direction has been given so clearly and indubitably in the life of all men about us and in the conscience of each man, and in all the expressions of human wisdom, that only he who does not wish to work can say that he does not see it.

So what will come of this?

This, that one or two men will haul, and seeing them a third, and so the best people will join up until the matter moves and goes along as of itself, pushing and inviting even those to join up who do not understand *what* is done or why.

At first those who consciously work to fulfil the law of God will be joined by others who accept it semi-consciously and half on trust; afterwards a large number will join them merely from faith in those advanced men who acknowledge it, and finally the majority will acknowledge it, and then men will cease to destroy themselves and will find happiness. That would happen very soon if the people of our circle, and following them the whole great majority of the workers, no longer considered it shameful to clean out privies and cart away the contents, but not shameful to fill them for others, their brothers, to cleanse; no longer considered it shameful to call on their neighbours in boots they have made themselves, while not considering it shameful to walk in boots and goloshes past people who have nothing to put on their feet; no longer felt it shameful not to know French or the latest news, but not shameful to eat bread without knowing how to make it; or shameful not to wear a starched shirt and clean clothes, but not shameful to go about in clean clothes which show one's idleness, and shameful to have dirty hands, but not shameful to have hands unhardened by toil.

All this will happen when public opinion demands it. And public opinion will demand it when those delusions in people's minds have been destroyed which hide the truth from them. Within my own recollection great changes have been accomplished in this sense. And those changes were only accomplished because public opinion changed. I can remember the time when rich people were ashamed to drive out with less than four horses and two lackeys; were ashamed not to have a lackey or a chambermaid to dress them, put their boots on for them, wash them, hold the pot for them, and so on; and now people have suddenly become ashamed not to dress themselves, not to put on their own boots, and to drive out with lackeys. All these changes were caused by public opinion.

Are not the changes obvious that are now being prepared in public consciousness? It was only necessary twenty-five years ago to destroy the sophistry which justified serfdom, and public opinion as to what was praiseworthy and what was shameful changed, and life changed. It is now only necessary to destroy the sophistry which justifies the power money has over men, and public opinion as to what is praiseworthy and what is shameful will change and life will change with it.

And the destruction of the sophistry justifying the monetary power, and the change of public opinion in that respect, is already rapidly taking place. That sophistry is already becoming transparent and barely hides the truth. It is only necessary to look closely in order to see clearly that change in public opinion which not only ought to take place but has already taken place, and is merely unacknowledged and not yet put into words. It is only necessary for a man of our time of some little education to reflect on what flows from the views of the world he professes, to convince himself that the valuation of what is good and what is bad, what is praiseworthy and what is shameful, which by inertia still guides him in life, is in direct contradiction to his whole world-conception.

It is only necessary for a man of our time to detach himself for a moment from life as he lives it by inertia, and to regard it from aside and weigh it in accordance with his whole world-conception, and he will be horrified at the definition of his life dictated by his world-conception.

Let us take as an example a young man (among the young the energy of life is stronger and self-consciousness more hazy) of the wealthy classes of whatever tendency. Every decent young man considers it a shame not to help an old man, a child, or a woman; he considers that in a common undertaking it is a shame to expose another man's health or life to danger while avoiding it himself. Everyone considers it a shame and barbarous to do what Schuyler* tells us the Kirghiz do during a storm: they send out their wives

* *Eugene Schuyler (1840-90) was U.S.A. Secretary of Legation at Petersburg, 1873-6, and travelled in Central Asia in 1873.*

and old women to hold down the corners of the tent, while they themselves remain sitting in the tent drinking their kumys. Everybody considers it a shame to compel a feeble man to work for him, and an even greater shame at a moment of danger, on a burning ship for instance, for the stronger to shove aside the weaker and to climb first into the life-boat while leaving them in danger, and so forth. All this they consider shameful, and in certain exceptional conditions would on no account do it; but in ordinary life just such deeds, and much worse ones, are hidden from them by temptations and they constantly commit them.

They need only reflect, to see and be horrified.

A young man puts on a clean shirt every day. Who washes them at the river?* A woman, whatever condition she may be in, very often an old woman who might be the young man's grandmother or mother, and who sometimes is ill. What would that young man himself call anyone who for a whim changed his shirt which was still clean, and sent a woman old enough to be his mother to wash it for him?

A young man keeps horses to show off, and they are broken in at danger to life by a man old enough to be his father or grandfather, while the young man himself mounts the horse only when the danger is passed. What does that young man call one who, avoiding it himself, puts another in danger and avails himself of the danger for his own pleasure?

And the whole life of the wealthy classes is made up of a series of such actions. The excessive work of old men, of children, and of women, and things done by others at risk to their lives not that we may be able to work, but for our whims, fill our whole life. A fisherman is drowned catching fish for us; washerwomen catch cold and die; blacksmiths go blind; factory hands fall ill, and are mutilated by machines; wood-fellers are crushed by falling trees; workmen fall from a roof, and seamstresses become consumptive. All real work is done with loss and peril of life. To hide this and not to see it is impossible. The one salvation in this situation, the one exit from it—that a man of our time, shifting on to others the labour and peril of life, may not have, in accord with his own outlook on life, to call himself a scoundrel and a coward—is to take from others only

* It is usual in Russia for a washerwoman when washing linen to take it to a river, stream, or pond to rinse it.

what is essential for life, and himself to do real work at expense and risk to his own life.

A time will soon come, is already coming, when it will be a shame and a disgrace not only to eat a dinner of five courses served by footmen, but to eat a dinner that has not been cooked by the hosts themselves; it will be a shame not only to drive out with fast trotters but even in a common cab when one can use one's own legs; on work-days to wear clothes, boots, or gloves in which one cannot work, or to play on a piano costing £120 or even £5, while others, strangers, are having to work for one; or to feed a dog on milk and white bread while there are people who have no milk and bread; and to burn lights except to work by, or to heat a stove in which food is not cooked, while there are people who lack fire or light. To such a view we are inevitably and rapidly advancing. We already stand on the brink of that new life, and to establish that new view of life is the task of public opinion, and public opinion of that kind is rapidly forming itself. It is women who form public opinion, and in our day women are particularly powerful.

CHAPTER XL

AS IS SAID IN THE BIBLE, to man is given the law of labour, to woman the law of child-bearing. Although with our science *nous avons changé tout ca*, the law of the man as of the woman remains unaltered, as the liver remains in its place,—and the breach of it is still inevitably punished by death.

The only difference is that the general evasion of their duty by all men would be punished by death in such a near future as may be called the present, but the evasion of the law by all women would be punished in a more distant future. The general infringement of the law by all men destroys men at once, its infringement by all women destroys the next generation; but the evasion of the law by some men and some women does not destroy the human race, but deprives the offenders of their reasonable nature as human beings.

The neglect of the law by men began long ago in those classes which could coerce others and, ever widening, it has continued to the present time and has now reached to insanity—to an ideal of neglect of the law, to the ideal expressed by prince Blokhín and shared by Renan and the whole educated world: machines are to do the work, while people will become bundles of nerves enjoying themselves. Evasion of her duty by woman used to be almost unknown. It manifested itself only in prostitution and isolated crimes of abortion. Women of the wealthy classes continued to fulfil their law when the men had ceased to perform theirs, and consequently women's influence became stronger and they continue to govern, and ought to govern, men who have infringed the law and consequently lost their reason.

It is often said that women (Parisian women, especially those who are childless) have become so bewitching, utilizing all the arts of civilization, that they have mastered man by their fascinations. This is not only wrong, but is just the reverse of the case. It is not the childless woman who has mastered man, but the mother, the one who has fulfilled the law of her nature while man has neglected his.

The woman who artificially makes herself barren and bewitches man by her shoulders and curls, is not a woman mastering man but a woman who, depraved by man, has descended to his level, like him has abandoned her duty, and like him has lost every reasonable perception of life.

From this mistake has arisen that wonderful nonsense called 'women's rights'.

The formula of those rights is this: 'Ah! You, man,' says the woman, 'have violated your law of real work, and want us to bear the burden of ours. No! If that is so, then we, as well as you, can make a pretence of labour as you do, in banks, ministries, universities, academies, and studios; and like you we also wish to avail ourselves of other people's work and to live only to satisfy our lusts under pretext of a division of labour.'

They say this and show in practice that they can make a pretence of work not at all worse, but even better, than men.

The so-called feminist question arose, and could only arise, among men who had infringed the law of real labour.

One has only to return to that law and the feminist question cannot exist.

A woman having her special, unquestionable, and unavoidable labour, will never demand the right to share also in man's work in mines or in the ploughing field. She could demand only to share the sham labour of the wealthy classes.

The woman of our class was stronger than the man and still is stronger, not on account of her charms, not by her adroitness in making the same pharisaic pretence of work as man, but because she did not evade the law; because she bore that true labour at risk of life and with utmost effort—true labour from which the man of the wealthy classes had freed himself.

But within my own memory woman's fall—her infringement of her duty—has begun, and within my memory it has spread more and more widely.

Woman, having forgotten her law, has believed that her strength lies in the fascination of her allurements, or in her dexterity in the imitation of the sham work done by men.

But children are a hindrance to both of these. And so with the help of science (science is always ready to do anything nasty) within my memory it has come about that among the wealthy classes dozens of methods of preventing pregnancy have appeared, and appliances for preventing childbirth have become common accessories of the toilet; and so the women-mothers of the wealthy classes who held power in their hands are letting it slip in order to compete with street-women and not be outdone by them.

That evil has spread far and spreads farther every day, and soon it will have reached all the women of the wealthy classes; and then they will be on a level with the men and like them will lose every reasonable sense of life. And then for that class there will be no recovery: but there is yet time.

For all that, more women than men still fulfil their law, and so there are reasonable beings among them, and therefore some women of our class still hold in their hands the possibility of saving it.

Ah!—if those women understood their worth, their power, and used these in the work of saving their husbands, brothers, and children—saving mankind!

Women-mothers of the wealthy classes, in your hands alone is the salvation of the men of our world from the evils from which they suffer! Not those women who are occupied with their figures, bustles, coiffures, and their attractiveness for men, and who against their will, by inadvertence and in despair, bear children, and hand them over to wet-nurses;* nor yet those who attend various university lectures and talk about the psychomotor centres and differentials, and who also try to avoid child-bearing in order not to hinder the stupefaction they call their 'development',—but those women and mothers who, having the power to avoid child-birth, simply and consciously submit to that eternal, immutable law, knowing that the hardship and labour of that submission is their vocation. Those are the women and mothers of our wealthy classes in whose hands, more than in any others, lies the salvation of the men of our world from the evils that oppress them. You, women and mothers, who consciously submit to the law of God, you alone in our unhappy perverted circle which has lost the semblance of being human, you alone know the whole true meaning of life according to the law of God. And you alone can by your example show men that happiness of life in submission to God's will, of which they deprive themselves. You alone know those raptures and joys, seizing your whole being, and that bliss which is ordained for man when he does not evade God's law. You know the joy of love of your husband, a joy not ending, not broken-off like all others, but forming the beginning of a new joy of love for your child. You alone, when you are simple and submissive to God's will, know, not that farcical pretence of labour in uniforms and in illuminated halls which the men of our circle call labour, but the labour imposed on us by God, and you know the true rewards for it, the bliss it brings.

You know this when after the joys of love you await with agitation, terror, and hope, that torture of pregnancy which makes you ill for nine months, brings you to the verge of death and to unbearable sufferings and pains; you know the conditions of true labour when with joy you await the approach and increase of most dreadful sufferings, after which comes the bliss known to you alone.

You know it when, directly after these sufferings, without rest, without interruption, you undertake another series of labours and sufferings—those of nursing, in which you at once forgo, and subject to your duty and your feeling the strongest human demand—that of sleep (which the proverb says is 'dearer than father or mother'), and for months and years do not have an undisturbed night's sleep, but

* *The employment of wet-nurses was very much more usual in Russia than in England.*

sometimes, and often, do not sleep for whole nights together, but walk up and down with numbed arms rocking the sick child who is tearing your heart.

And when you do all this, not belauded by anyone, not noticed by anyone, not expecting praise or reward from anyone, when you do this not as an achievement but as the labourer in the Gospel parable who came from the field, considering that you are only doing your duty—then you know *what* is sham fictitious labour for the praise of men, and *what* is real labour to fulfil God's will—the indication of which you feel in your heart.

You know that if you are a real mother it is not enough that no one sees your labour or praises you for it—people merely consider that so it ought to be—but that even those for whom you have toiled will not only not thank you but will often torment and reproach you—and with the next child you will do the same: you will again suffer, again endure the unseen terrible labour, and again not expect reward from anyone, and will again feel the same satisfaction. In your hands, if you are such women, should be the influence over men, and in your hands lies their salvation. Every day your number diminishes: some occupy themselves with their fascination for men and become street-women, others are engaged in competing with men in their artificial, trifling occupations, others again who have not yet been false to their vocation, already repudiate it in their minds: they perform all the achievements of women and mothers, but accidentally, repiningly, with envy of the free, sterile women, and deprive themselves of their sole reward—the inner consciousness of the fulfilment of God's will—and instead of satisfaction, suffer from what should be their happiness.

We are so confused by our false way of life, we men of our circle have all so utterly lost the sense of life, that there is no longer any distinction between us. Having shifted the whole burden and danger of life on to the backs of others, we are unable to give ourselves the true name deserved by those who compel others to perish in providing life for them,—scoundrels and cowards.

But among women there is still a difference. There are women —human beings—women presenting the highest manifestation of a human being; and there are women—whores. And this distinction will be made by future generations, and we too cannot help making it.

Every woman, however she may dress herself and however she may call herself and however refined she may be, who refrains from child-birth without refraining from sexual relations, is a whore. And however fallen a woman may be, if she intentionally devotes herself to bearing children, she performs the best and highest service in life—fulfils the will of God—and no one ranks above her.

If you are such a woman, you will not, either after two or after twenty children, say that you have borne enough, any more than a fifty-year old workman will say he has worked enough, while he still eats and sleeps and has muscles demanding work. If you are such a woman you will not shift the nursing and tending of your children on to another mother any more than a workman will let another man finish the work he has begun and nearly completed, because you put your life in that work and therefore your life is fuller and happier the more of that work you have.

And if you are such a one—and happily for men there still are such women—then that law of the fulfilment of God's will by which you guide your own life, you will apply also to your husband's life and to that of your children and of those near to you.

If you are such a one and know by your own experience that only self-sacrificing, unseen, unrewarded labour done with danger of life and uttermost effort for the life of others, is the mission of man which gives satisfaction and strength, then you will apply those same demands to others, will incite your husband to such labour, and by such labour will value and estimate people's worth, and for such labour will prepare your children.

Only a mother who considers child-bearing an unpleasant accident and thinks that the meaning of life lies in the pleasures of love, the comforts of life, education, and sociability, will bring up her children so that they shall have as many pleasures and enjoy them as much as possible, will feed them daintily, dress them up, give them artificial amusements, and teach them not what will make them capable of self-sacrificing labour (male or female) done with risk to life and to the last extremity of effort, but what will secure them diplomas* and the opportunity not to labour. Only such a woman, having lost the significance of her life, will sympathize with that

* The diplomas of the higher educational establishments in Russia were essential for entry to various branches of Government service and to various professions.

deceptive, false, male work by which her husband, freeing himself from man's duty, finds it possible, together with her, to avail himself of other people's labour. Only a woman of that kind will choose such a husband for her daughter, and will esteem people not by what they themselves are, but for what is attached to them—position, money, and the power to take other people's labour. A real mother, who knows the will of God by experience, will prepare her children also to fulfil it. Such a mother will suffer if she sees her child overfed, effeminate, and dressed-up, for she knows that these things will make it difficult for it to fulfil the will of God which she recognizes.

Such a mother will teach not what will expose her son or daughter to the temptations presented by being able to escape labour, but whatever will enable them to bear the labour of life. She will not need to ask what she should teach her children or for what she should prepare them: she knows what man's vocation is, and what to teach and what to prepare them for. Such a woman will not only not incite her husband to sham, false work which aims only at making use of other people's labour, but will regard with aversion and horror an activity which serves as a double temptation to her children. Such a woman will not choose a husband for her daughter by the whiteness of his hands and the refinement of his manners, but knowing well what real labour is and what is deceit, she will always and everywhere, beginning with her own husband, respect and value in men and demand of them, real labour with expenditure and danger of life, and will despise that false, showy labour which aims at emancipating oneself from real work.

And let not those women who while renouncing woman's vocation wish to profit by its rights, say that such a view of life is impossible for a mother, she being too intimately bound by love to her children to refuse them dainties, amusements, and fine clothes, and not to fear to leave them unprovided for if her husband has no fortune or assured position, and not to fear for the future of her marrying daughters, and for her sons who have not received an 'education'.

All that is a lie, a most glaring lie!

A true mother will never say it. You cannot refrain from the desire to give them sweets and toys and to take them to the circus?

But you do not give them poisonous berries to eat, do not let them out alone in a boat, and do not take them to a café chantant! How is it you can refrain in the one case, but not in the other?

Because you are saying what is untrue.

You say you love your children so that you fear for their lives, fear hunger and cold, and therefore value the security given you by your husband's position which you admit to be unjustifiable.

You so fear those future possible misfortunes for your children—very distant and doubtful ones—that you encourage your husband in things you yourself regard as unjustifiable; but what are you doing now in the present conditions of your life to secure your children from the unfortunate occurrences of present-day life? Do you spend much of the day with your children? It is much if you spend one-tenth of it!

The rest of the time they are in the hands of strangers, hired people often taken from the street, or they are in institutions, exposed to physical and moral infection.

Your children eat, are nourished. Who prepares their dinner, and of what? For the most part you do not know. Who instils moral perceptions into them? You do not know that either. So do not say that you put up with evil for your children's good—it is not true. You do evil because you like it.

A true mother, one who sees in the bearing and bringing up of children her self-sacrificing vocation and the fulfilment of God's will, will not speak so.

She will not speak so, because she knows that her business lies not in making of her children what suits her or suits the prevailing tendency of the times. She knows that children—the coming generation—are the greatest and most sacred thing it is given to man actually to see, and that to serve this holy thing with her whole being is her life.

She herself knows, being constantly between life and death and safeguarding a barely dawning life, that life and death are not her business, her business is to serve life, and therefore she will not seek distant paths for that service but will only not neglect those near at hand.

Such a mother will bear children and will nurse them herself, will first of all feed another before herself, will prepare food for the children, will sew and wash for them, will teach them and will sleep and talk with them, because she sees therein her life-work. She knows that the security of every life lies in labour and the capacity to labour, and therefore she will not seek external security in her husband's money or in her children's diplomas, but will develop in them the same capacity for a self-sacrificing fulfilment of God's will which she has felt in herself, a capacity to endure toil with expenditure and danger of life. Such a mother will not ask others what she is to do, she will know it all and will fear nothing, and will always be at peace, for she will know that she has done what she had to do.

If there may be doubts for men and for a childless woman as to the way to fulfil the will of God, for a mother that path is firmly and clearly defined, and if she fulfils it humbly with a simple heart she stands on the highest point of perfection a human being can attain, and becomes for all a model of that complete performance of God's will which all desire.

Only a mother can before her death tranquilly say to Him who sent her into this world, and Whom she has served by bearing and bringing up children whom she has loved more than herself—only she having served Him in the way appointed to her can say with tranquillity, 'Now lettest Thou Thy servant depart in peace.' And that is the highest perfection to which, as to the highest good, men aspire.

Such women who fulfil their mission reign over men, and serve as a guiding star to mankind; such women form public opinion and prepare the coming generation; and therefore in their hands lies the highest power, the power to save men from the existing and threatening evils of our time.

Yes, women, mothers, in your hands more than in those of anyone else lies the salvation of the world.

February 14, 1886.

APPENDIX

[The following pages, omitted by Tolstoy from his final revision of the book, appear worth preserving at least as an appendix.

They were his first statement of the theme he eventually expanded into Chapters XVII-XX (dealing with money), and seemed to him unnecessary when he had made that fuller presentation of the case. Readers may nevertheless wish to have this brief and trenchant statement preserved. It begins with a reference to the incident narrated in Chapter XV, but in earlier editions it will be found printed as though it were the conclusion to Chapter XXI.

This is an instance of the need that has long existed for a proper editing of Tolstoy's works. —*Aylmer Maude*]

I was led into the error of supposing that I could help others, by the fact that I imagined that my money was the same as Semën's. But that was not so.

The general opinion is that money represents wealth and that wealth is the result of labour, and therefore that money represents labour. This opinion is as just as the opinion that every organization of the State is the result of an agreement (*contrat social*). Everybody wants to believe that money is merely a means of exchange of labour. I have made boots, you have grown grain, he has reared sheep; now, to exchange more conveniently, we introduce money, which represents a corresponding amount of labour, and by means of it we exchange leather soles for a brisket of lamb and ten pounds of flour. By means of money we exchange our products, and the money each of us has, represents our labour. This is quite true, but true only as long as no violence by one man towards another is perpetrated in the community where the exchange takes place—not merely no such violent seizure of a man's labour as occurs in war and in slavery, but not even violence to defend the products of one man's labour against another. It would be true only in a community whose members entirely fulfilled the Christian law—in a community in which people gave to him who asked and asked no return of what had been borrowed. But as soon as any violence is employed in the community, the significance of money for its possessor at once loses the meaning of something representing labour and acquires the meaning of a right based not on labour but on violence.

As soon as there is war and one man has taken something away from another, money can no longer always represent labour; the money a soldier or his commander has received for booty he has sold is by no means the produce of their labour, and has quite another significance from money received for making boots. Neither, when slave-owners and slaves exist as they always have done all over the world, can it be said that money represents labour. Women have woven linen, sold it and have received money; serfs have woven linen for their master and he has sold it and received money. This money and that are identical; but this was the product of labour and that was the product of violence. In the same way if a stranger, or my father, has given me money, and when giving it to me he knew, and I know, and everybody knows, that no one can take this money from me, and that if anyone tries to take it or even fails to repay it at a date he has promised, the authorities will act on my behalf and force him to return me the money, then again it is evident that this money cannot be said to represent labour, as the money did that Semën received for sawing up logs. So that in a community where anyone's money is taken by force or is even defended against others by force—there the money cannot always represent labour. In such a community it sometimes represents labour and sometimes violence.

So it would be if even a single act of violence by one man against another occurred amid perfectly free relations; but now, when accumulated money has passed through centuries of most varied forms of violence, when that violence—changing merely its form—continues to operate; when, as everyone admits, money itself by its accumulation occasions violence, when money which is the production of direct labour forms only a small part of the money that has been obtained by all sorts of violence—to say, now, that money represents the labour of him who possesses it, is an evident error or a deliberate lie. It may be said that it should be so, it may be said that it would be desirable, but certainly not that it is so.

Money represents labour. Yes. Money represents labour, but whose labour? In our society only in the very rarest cases does it represent the labour of its owner. Nearly always it represents the labour of other men—the past or future labour of others.

It represents a claim established by violence upon the labour of others.

Money, in its most exact and at the same time simplest definition, consists of conventional tokens which bestow a right, or more correctly a power, to use other people's labour. In its ideal meaning money should give this right or possibility only when it itself represents labour, and such money might exist in a society where no violence was used. But as soon as there is violence, that is to say, the possibility of employing other people's work without working oneself, then this possibility of taking the work of others without it being apparent what persons are subjected to this violence, is given solely by money.

An owner lays on his serfs a requisition in kind, making them bring a certain quantity of linen, grain, and cattle, or a corresponding sum of money. One household delivers the cattle, but pays money instead of bringing the linen. The owner accepts the money only because he knows that for it he can get the stipulated quantity of linen made (generally he takes rather more, so as to be quite sure of getting the full quantity of linen), and this money evidently represents for the owner a claim on other people's labour.

The peasant gives the money as a demand note drawn on persons unknown, but of whom there are many, who will weave so much linen for this money. Those who undertake to weave the linen will do so because they did not succeed in fattening the sheep, and must pay money for sheep; while the peasant who gets the money for the sheep takes it because he has to pay for grain, which failed this year. This same process goes on in this country and all over the world.

A man sells the produce of his past, present, or future toil, sometimes his food-stuff, not for the most part because money is for him a convenient means of exchange—he would exchange without money—but because money is forcibly demanded of him as a requisition on his labour.

When an Egyptian ruler demanded work of his slaves, the slaves gave it all, but only their past and present labour—they could not give their future work. But with the spread of money tokens and the credit system resulting from it, it has become possible to give also one's future work for money. Money, with the system of violence existing in society, makes possible a new form of impersonal slavery which replaces personal slavery. A slave-owner had a right to the work of Peter, Iván, and Sídor. But where money is demanded of everybody, its owner has a claim on the labour of all those unnamed people who need money. Money removes all that irksome side of slavery involved in an owner's knowledge of his claims on Iván, and at the same time it effaces all those human relations between the owner and the slave which softened the hardships of personal slavery.

I do not refer to the fact that such a state of things may have been necessary for humanity's development, for progress and so forth,—I will not dispute that. I only tried to clear up for myself the conception of money, and the common mistake, into which I had fallen, of accepting money as representing labour. I convinced myself by experience that money does not represent labour, but in most cases represents violence or specially complex artifices founded on violence.

Money in our time has quite lost its desirable significance as representing a man's own labour; it has that significance in exceptional cases, but as a general rule it has become a right, or possibility, of exploiting the labour of others.

The diffusion of money, of credit, and of all sorts of money tokens, confirms that significance of money more and more. Money is the possibility, or the right, to make use of other people's labour.

Money is a new form of slavery, differing from the old only in its impersonality, in the freedom it gives from any human relation with the slave.

Money is money, something valuable, always equal to itself and considered always quite correct and justifiable, and its use is not considered immoral, as slavery was.

In my young days the game of lotto was introduced into our clubs. Everybody played it eagerly, and it was said that many people were ruined and ruined their families, they lost money entrusted to them and government funds and they shot themselves, so the game was forbidden and remains forbidden till now.

I remember meeting old players, who were not sentimental but who told me that the game was particularly pleasant because one did not know who was losing, as one does in other games; the attendant did not even bring money, but counters: every one lost a small stake and his distress was not seen . . . . So it is with roulette, which is everywhere forbidden—not without cause.

And so it is with money. I have a magic inexhaustible purse; I cut coupons and have released myself from all the affairs of the world. Whom do I injure? I am the most inoffensive and kindly of men. But it is only a game of lotto or roulette in which I do not see the player who shoots himself on account of the losses he makes while furnishing me with the coupons which I carefully cut very straight off the bonds.

I have done nothing, do nothing, and shall do nothing, except cut off those little coupons, and firmly believe that money represents work. This is really amazing! Talk about lunatics! What degree of lunacy can be more terrible than that? A clever, learned, in all other respects rational, man lives irrationally and soothes himself by not speaking out fully the one thing essential to make sense of his ideas—and he considers himself justified. Coupons represent labour! Labour! Yes, but whose? Evidently not that of him who owns them, but of him who works.

Money is the same as slavery; its aim is the same, and so are its consequences. Its aim is to free oneself from the primal law (as it is truly called by a profound peasant writer,* from the natural law of life, as we call it—the law of personal labour for the satisfaction of one's needs. And the consequences of slavery are: for the owner degeneration, the interminable devising of ever fresh and fresh needs which are never satiated, effeminate wretchedness, and depravity; and for the slaves the oppression of a human being, and his debasement to the level of a beast.

Money is a new and terrible form of slavery, and like the old form of personal slavery it demoralizes both slave and slave-owner, only much more, for it frees the slave and the slave-owner from personal, human relations with one another.

* *Bóndarev, the author of 'Bread-labour'.*